Eritrea and Ethiopia
The Federal Experience

Tekeste Negash

Nordiska Afrikainstitutet, Uppsala 1997

Published in the United States by
Transaction Publishers
New Brunswick, NJ 08903

Indexing terms

National liberation movements
Political parties
Political power
State
War
Eritrea
Ethiopia

Language checking: Elaine Almén

ISBN 91-7106-406-0

Printed in Sweden by
Gotab, Stockholm 1997

To Lorenzo Taezaz, 1892–1947

Contents

ACRONYMS

ASMAE	Archivio Storico del Ministero degli Affari Esteri
ASMAI	Archivio Storico dell'Africa Italiana
ASMAI, AE	ASMAI Archivio Eritrea
BBCWB/ME	British Broadcasting Corporation, Middle East
BCA	British Consulate, Asmara, Eritrea
BCE	British Consulate, Cairo
BEAA	British Embassy, Addis Ababa
BMA	British Military Administration
CAS	Comitato azione segreta
CRIE	Comitato Rappresentativo degli italiani in Eritrea
EDF	Eritrean Democratic Front
EFLNA	Eritreans for Liberation in North America
ELA	Eritrean Liberation Army
ELF	Eritrean Liberation Front
EPDM	Ethiopian Peoples Democratic Movement
EPLF	Eritrea Peoples Liberation Forces
EPRDF	Ethiopian Peoples Revolutionary Democratic Front
EWN	Eritrean Weekly News
FO	Foreign Office (London, UK)
FPC	Four Power Commission
JAH	Journal of African History
JMAS	Journal of Modern African Studies
LPP	Liberal Progressive Party
MEF, HQ	Middle East Forces, Headqaurters
ML	Moslem League
MPR	Monthly Political Report
NEAS	Northeast African Studies
NTEN	New Times and Ethiopia News
PLF	Popular Liberation Forces
PLO	Palestinian Liberation Organization
PRO	Public Record Office
ROAPE	Review of African Political Economy
SDF	Sudan Defence Forces
SDO	Senior District Officer
UK	United Kingdom
UN	United Nations
UP	Unionist Party
WO	War Office (London, UK)
WWM	Woldeab Wolde Mariam

THE PROVINCES OF ERITREA IN 1950

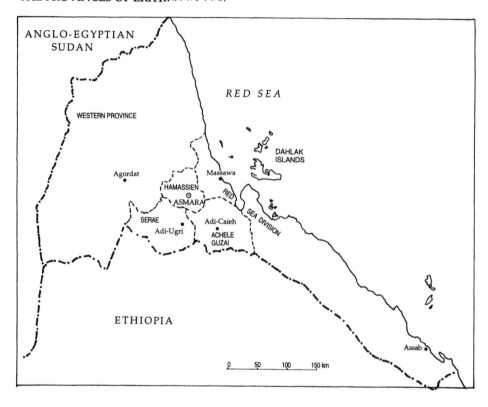

Source: Report of the United Nations Commission for Eritrea, New York 1950

Preface

On December 2, 1950, the United Nations passed resolution 390A (V) on the fate of the former Italian colony of Eritrea. The said resolution which came to be known as the Federal Act stipulated that "Eritrea shall constitute an autonomous unit federated with Ethiopia under the sovereignty of the Ethiopian crown". The resolution further stipulated that the Eritrean government would possess legislative, executive, and judicial powers in the field of domestic affairs. A United Nations Commissioner was simultaneously appointed to draft the Eritrean Constitution in consultation with the British Administering Authority, the Ethiopian government and the Eritrean people.

In pursuance of the UN resolution, the United Nations Commissioner supervised the election of a Constituent Assembly, drafted a Constitution, witnessed its coming into effect, and wound up his responsibility when the Union Jack was replaced by the Eritrean and Ethiopian flags on September 15, 1952. The federation between Eritrea and Ethiopia had only a ten year lease of life; it came to an end on November 15, 1962. A year earlier, Eritrean exiles in Cairo had formed an organization called the Eritrean Liberation Front.

This study was conceived in the summer of 1988 when the war between the Eritrean nationalist forces and the Ethiopian state appeared to have reached a stalemate. The victory that the Eritreans scored at Afabet in the early months of 1988 had brought to the attention of the leaders of Ethiopia that there was not going to be a military solution to the problem. The same view prevailed among the Eritrean camp even though this was camouflaged by the rhetoric of the Victory to the Masses. By 1988, the Eritrean war was entering its 28th year and was described as early as 1981 as Africa's longest war.

However, as late as 1988 the causes of Africa's longest war were very obscure indeed. There were few studies on the period preceding the era of conflict and these were either biased or were inadequately documented. There was a clear predominance of the interpretation of the conflict that had been handed down by the Eritrean Liberation movements. In the search for a peaceful solution, there was then a need for an exhaustive study on the period following Italian colonial rule, namely, 1941–62.

Why did the UN come to the decision to unite Eritrea with Ethiopia? Important as this question might be, it has been of marginal interest as far as this study is concerned. Apart from the fact that the resolution of the Eritrean case by the UN falls very much under International Law rather than Eritrean history, we have sufficient though slightly biased studies on the subject. The impact of the British period on Eritrean society, however, needs to be closely looked at because of its relevance towards a better understanding of the background to the conflict and also because it forms part of Eritrean political and social history.

The period where our knowledge remained least developed was, however, that covering the federation between Eritrea and Ethiopia, 1952–62. The Eritrean parties were quick enough to denounce the Ethiopian government for violating the federation thereby providing a precipitant condition for the conflict. In contrast the Ethiopian government remained with folded hands and watched the rewriting of an important part of the social and political history of the country by nationalist forces who by their nature were bound to twist and distort the past in order to suit their current objectives.

By 1988 prospects for a political solution did not look positive; there did not exist the preconditions for a negotiated settlement. There was also an awareness that a military solution was not within reach. At the level of research, our knowledge was extremely sketchy on far too many aspects of the conflict. The Eritrean nationalist forces and the Ethiopian government believed strongly in the justness of their cases. These strong beliefs, made visible by the pursuance of Africa's longest war, were no doubt based on subjective perceptions of the background, causes and nature of the conflict. Subjective perceptions about one's actions could, however, be altered through experience and above all through knowledge. The relevance of this study was, therefore predicated on the argument that a negotiated settlement could hardly be expected without the existence of a pool of knowledge on the subject available to both parties.

In May 1991 the Eritrean nationalist forces together with other nationalist cum regionalist forces defeated the Ethiopian government forces and thus brought the 30 year long war to an end. Contrary to what many observers, including this author, had earlier believed, the Eritrean war was resolved militarily.

What is presented here is very much the story of the slow but steady dissolution of the federation as seen and observed by the British diplomatic corps. Between 1952 and 1962, there were about 30 British nationals seconded to the Eritrean government. These expatriates kept in touch with the British Consulate-General whose responsibility was to protect the interests of British nationals as well as to report the developments to London. The conclusions and interpretations are, therefore, to a great extent based on that documentation with all the shortcomings inherent in such material.

Moreover, this study is a reconstruction of Eritrean history from 1952 to 1962. It is also a first attempt towards a synthesis. However, a more complete work of synthesis is several decades away due to the closeness of the period and the intensity with which some events and aspects are discussed. Furthermore, the ambiguities and ambivalences of the nationalist movement make it virtually impossible to even contemplate such a task. Yet the history of the federation has been told by a number of researchers; with very few exceptions these studies are either based on hearsay or on the ideologised interpretation of the Eritrean liberation organizations.

Finally this study is the first of its kind to follow the rise and decline of the federation. The dangers inherent in undue reliance on semi-colonial and entirely western documentation notwithstanding, it is my firm belief that this study can be seen as a challenge to young as well as veteran students of Eritrean affairs.

It is with pleasure that I acknowledge the institutions which contributed to the making of this book. First and foremost, I wish to extend my profound gratitude to the Swedish Agency for Research Cooperation with Developing Countries (SAREC) for generously financing the project. I am also grateful to SAREC for a substantial publication grant. My publishers, Nordic Africa Institute and Transaction Publishers have patiently guided me to take into account their readers' comments. At my department, the editors of *Acta Studia Historica Uppsaliensis*, professors Torstendahl, Lindgren and Jansson approved as well as encouraged me to publish this study outside the prestigious but not so well distributed *Acta*. At Addis Ababa University, the History Department and the Institute of Ethiopian Studies (IES) provided moral support as well as institutional affiliation. I am particularly indebted to professors Taddesse Tamrat, Taddesse Beyene, Bahru Zewde, and the librarian Ato Degfie Welde Tsadik.

After several years of haggling and a few weeks before the completion of this study, I was given the privilege of looking at the papers of the Ministero dell'Africa Italiana (ASMAI) for the 1947–50 period. It was too late to incorporate more fully this new Italian material; however, it ought to be mentioned that it is well organised and rich in variety and detail. Those who undertake to study the role of Italy in Eritrean political history will not be disappointed with it. I wish to thank Dr. Giovanni Cassis, superintendent of the historical archives at the Ministry of Foreign Affairs (where the MAI papers are deposited), and his colleagues Dr. Vicenzo Pellegrini, Dr. Stefania Ruggeri and Dr. Cinzia Aicardi for tolerating my persistent laments on the state of Italian archives and the arbitrariness of their archival rules.

Ato Assefa Habtu, Dr. Yeraswerk Admassie, Professor Sven Rubenson, Dr. Richard Pankhurst, Dr. Admassu Tassew, Dr. Merid Welde Aregay, Dr. Maria Leiva, Associate Professor Shiferaw Bekele, Dr. Svein Ege, Dr. Barbara Sorgoni and Professor Haggai Ehrlich have read drafts of the manuscript and made invaluable comments. I thank all of them for their support, criticism and encouragement. Yet the responsibility for all errors of fact and judgement is entirely mine.

I wish to acknowledge a special indebtedness to the unpretentious but knowledgeable Jan Petterson at the Nordic Africa Institute Library for invaluable assistance and companionship. My colleague Marie Clark Nelson has not only read an earlier draft with an editor's eye but she, as always, was generous with her time and discussed the organization and framework of each chapter. Of equal importance was the pleasant and stimulating environment provided by my colleagues at the Department of History, in particular, Linda Oja, Ylva Hasselberg, Niklas Stenlås, Örjan Simonsson, Anders Thoré, Åsa Lindeborg, Silke Neusinger, Cecilia Trenter, John Rogers, Hernan Horna, Bengt Schüllerqvist, Elizabeth Elgàn and Bengt Nilsson.

Finally I thank my daughters Miriam, Hannah and Ambesit for their indulgent love and Berit, my wife and friend, for everything.

Tekeste Negash
Department of History, Uppsala University
December, 1996

Chapter One

Introduction

THE LEGACY OF COLONIALISM: ITALIAN COLONIALISM

Although the creation of Eritrea as a colony is legally dated to the beginning of 1890, the process of colonization was set in motion the same year as the inauguration of the Suez Canal in 1869. Partly due to lack of interest and to the inherent weakness of the newly united state of Italy, interest in African colonies lay dormant until the beginning of the 1880s. The port of Assab, which had been purchased by a shipping company in a tacit agreement with the Savoy dynasty, was bought by the government in Rome in 1882. A few years later, the British, preferring Italy to France, encouraged and facilitated the Italian occupation of Massawa. Finding themselves owners of one of the hottest coastlines that stretched over one thousand kms., the Italians felt more or less compelled to push their way up into the highlands where the climate is temperate. This timid attempt at expansion was nipped in the bud in the early months of 1887 by the Ethiopian state of the period, which had its centre in the northern part of the country.

Unable to penetrate to the highlands, the Italians, pursuing the next best strategy, began to expand northwest, namely to the Semhar and Sahel regions. By the end of 1888, the Italians had established contacts with the Tigre, Habab and Beni Amer leaders. They were preparing the ground for eventual colonization by pushing protectorate treaties on the local leaders (Rubenson, 1976; Conti Rossini, 1935; Battaglia, 1958; Del Boca, 1976; Grassi & Goglia, 1981). By the end of 1888, Italian possessions in the Red Sea area stretched over a thousand sq.km. with, however, virtually no hinterland, and quite rightly, the Italians used the term possessions to denote the vast area which they had just colonized. The area from Massawa to Assab was different in every aspect from the area north of Massawa up to the vicinity of Port Said in the Sudan

The death of Emperor Yohannes (1889) and the shift of the centre of power from Tigrai to Shewa created favourable conditions for Italian colonial expansion. As early as 1887, Minilik, the King of Shoa, had expressed readiness to negotiate with the Italians for the supply of arms in exchange for a cession of territory, if this would ensure his speedy accession to power (Rubenson, 1976; Gebre Sellassie, 1975). Minilik seized the opportunity provided by the political vacuum created by the death of Yohannes and sealed an Italo-Ethiopian pact, i.e. the treaty of Wichale, in May 1889. A small area of northern Tigrai was thus ceded to Italy. In return the Italians agreed to supply him with arms and to support his bid for the emperorship. However, since the treaty of Wichale had to be ratified by the Italian government, the Italians in Eritrea used the period between the signing of the treaty and its formal ratification, which took place in October, to expand their possessions well beyond the areas designated in the document of May 1889. On January 1, 1890, these disparate possessions were consolidated into a single political entity henceforth to be known as Eritrea. For the first ten years of its life, the colony was administered by the Ministry of War from the port town of Massawa.

Eritrea contained ethnic and ecological diversity; a small part with Asmara at its centre was the homeland of the Tigreans.[1] Adherents of the Ethiopian Orthodox Church, the Tigreans together with the Amhara and the Oromo of Wello were the main pillars of the Ethiopian/Abyssinian polity (Markakis, 1987; Erlich, 1982). Most Italian economic activities and most of the colonial infrastructure were to be found in the highland plateau where the Tigreans were dominant. The western lowlands were inhabited by numerous ethnic groups with bitter memories of raid and plunder at the hands of Tigrean and Ethiopian leaders. For Tigrean leaders the western lowlands were either a buffer zone or no-man's land. The Beni Amer, Habab, Mensa, Marya, Baza, Kunama, and Bilen had suffered greatly under Tigrean/Abyssinian plunder. The arrival of Italian rule was highly welcomed (Negash, 1987). Islam was the dominant religion, followed by small pockets of Catholic and Protestant followers. (Arén, 1978; Da Nembro, 1953). The Saho and the Afar occupied the eastern escarpment and the long southern coastline. Largely because of hostile ecology, the Saho and Afar were for the most part left on their own. (See ethnic map on page 17.)

Once ensconced in the temperate zone, the Italians began to implement an ill-developed policy of settlement for landless peasants from southern Italy. This policy of state financed settlement aroused considerable resistance from the Eritrean peasantry which eventually led to a series of small scale wars with Ethiopia, culminating in the famous battle of Adwa in early March 1896 (Rubenson, 1976; Conti Rossini, 1935). The Italians lost over 4,600 of their co-nationals in that one day battle. In the aftermath of the debacle, Italy renounced the treaty which had given them a foothold in the highlands and the fate of their new colony hung in the balance.[2]

In the new treaty of October 1896 signed with the victorious emperor Minilik, the Italians were allowed to keep the territory which was delimited in 1890 in return for a modest financial compensation (Martini, 1946, vol. 2, p. 350; Batt-

---

[1] There is still no agreement as to the best designation. The present Eritrean government uses the term Tigrinya to describe the same ethnic group. I have also earlier used the term Tigrinya.

[2] The main cause of the battle of Adwa has hitherto been explained as a result of a controversy over article XVII of the treaty of Wichale whereby Italy claimed that Ethiopia had consented to be an Italian protectorate. Italian rejection of Ethiopian protests that the Amharic version of article XVII of the Treaty did not contain such a binding commitment led to war. The outcome of the war and the Addis Ababa Peace treaty signed in October of 1896 do indeed lend strong support to such argument. There is, however, another dimension of the conflict which has not been given due attention. According to this interpretation, the objective of the war was to expel Italian rule from Ethiopian territory (Negash, 1996a).

aglia, 1958; Rossetti, 1910). However, having learned a severe lesson, the post-Adwa Italian rulers of Eritrea as well as the leadership in Rome set out to keep what they had managed to negotiate with the Ethiopians. As evidence of good-will, the Italian government sent to Eritrea as civilian governor Senator Ferdinando Martini, one of the most competent statesmen of the period. Ferdinando Martini was empowered to rule if he could or otherwise liquidate the colony in the best possible manner. The sale or transfer of the colony to the King of the Belgians was under consideration (Rainero, 1971).

With his prior knowledge of Eritrea Ferdinando Martini was, however, determined to keep the colony for Italy, not so much for what the colony had to offer, but largely for prestige (Martini, 1913). As civilian governor, he toned down the military dimension and was intelligent enough to realize that a great deal of work had to be done before colonies could begin to be of some profit to the mother country. During his decade-long governorship, 1897–1907, Martini succeeded admirably well in laying down the foundations of a colonial government, more or less along the lines used by Britain and France.

By the time Ferdinando Martini left Eritrea (later to assume primary responsibility as the Minister of Colonies), the Italian position in Eritrea was very secure indeed. Through the recognition of their inalienable rights to the land, Eritrean peasants were pacified. The law and order which Martini established had already begun to pay dividends. The new colony of Eritrea became a haven for fugitives, job-seekers, and slaves from the northern part of Ethiopia.[1] As early as 1907 the policy of good neighbourliness and strict non-interference in the internal affairs of the areas adjoining Eritrea was beginning to distinguish the Italian colony from the adjoining areas administered by Ethiopian authorities.

As the power of Emperor Minilik, owing to prolonged sickness, continued to decline, the outlying territories were increasingly left to their own devices. In the meanwhile the Italian administered colony continued to gain from *Pax Italica*. This was reflected in the increase of trade. Moreover, a new venue for employment had begun to attract surplus manpower in the form of recruitment to the colonial army, a first contingent of which was sent to Somalia as early as 1906.

It did not take many years for Governor Martini to assess the potential of the colony. Short of conquering Ethiopia, the Italians perceived that the best they could do was to use Eritrea as an outlet for Ethiopian products (Martini, 1913). On the eve of their occupation of Ethiopia in 1935, up to 25 per cent of Ethiopian exports, as well as imports, were channelled through Eritrea (Santagata, 1935; Misghena, 1988; Negash, 1987).

The most important function of the colony remained as a supplier of colonial soldiers for Italian expansion elsewhere. It was, however, in Libya that Eritrea

---

[1] ASMAI, AE, 557 (1909–12). This file contains more than a dozen letters from the chiefs of Tigrai asking for the return of their serfs and slaves who fled to Eritrea and to liberty.

and its inhabitants compensated Italy for the lather's perseverance. Up to 4,000 Eritrean soldiers were permanently stationed in Libya between 1912 and 1932. The war in Libya, which dragged on until 1932, would have cost the Italian tax-payers much more had it not been for the presence of loyal and efficient Eritrean soldiers. It is not an exaggeration to state that the Libyan occupation was made possible by the continuous supply of fighting forces from the 'first-born colony' (la colonia primogenita) at a cost which the Italian tax-payers and the state could easily sustain.

The continued presence of Eritrean soldiers in Libya had meant a rather radical change in the relations between the colonial government and the Eritrean population. The wanton expropriation of land was completely discontinued. Moreover, more attention began to be paid to the reinstatement of customary laws. During the 1920s, Eritrea settled peacefully and, we may even add, comfortably into its dual function: first, as a source of manpower for the Italian wars of pacification in Libya, and second, as an outlet for a considerable portion of Ethiopian imports and exports. Meanwhile, the modern sector of the economy began to establish itself with the continued assistance and even guidance of the Eritrean (colonial) government.

In as far as employment, food supply and the availability of consumer goods were concerned, the 1920s and 1930s were indeed good years. The colonial army and the steadily growing modern sector may have provided employment for up to 15 per cent of the population. About five per cent of the labour force may have been employed both in the colonial bureaucracy (clerks, interpreters, native judges, etc) and in domestic service in Italian homes and establishments. The financial flow from employers (the colonial government and the Italian community) in turn created and stimulated the growth of the service sector which catered to the needs of the Eritrean community. Drought virtually ceased to be a catastrophic experience, since the colonial government could avert hunger crises through food imports (Negash, 1987:151–153; cf. Iliffe, 1983; O'Connor, 1991). There were no armed conflicts among the various ethnic groups, and no subversive activities were launched from the Ethiopian side of the border. By the end of the 1930s an entire generation of Eritreans had grown up under the peace established by the Italian colonial system.

From the mid-1930s a combination of three factors further contributed towards the evolution of what may rightly be called the Eritrean consciousness. The first was the growing racist ideology which began to draw a distinction between the Eritreans who were fortunate enough to be under the civilizing umbrella of Italy and the inhabitants of the Ethiopian empire (Pollera, 1935; Negash, 1987). This policy, though devised to bolster Italian imperial or colonial ego, appeared to have trickled down to the Eritrean literati. The language of many Eritrean politicians in the 1940s betrays the pervasiveness of the colonial racist ideology of the 1930s.[1]

---

[1] See Association of Eritrean Intellectuals, Asmara, 1949.

ETHNIC MAP OF ERITREA

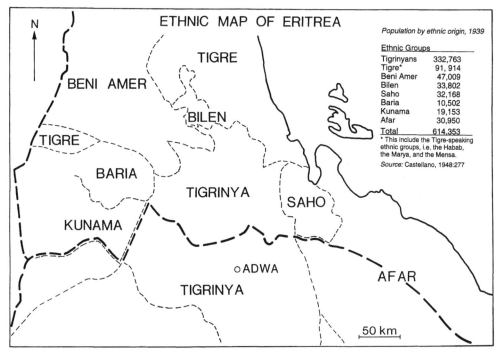

ETHNIC MAP OF ERITREA

Population by ethnic origin, 1939

Ethnic Groups	
Tigrinyans	332,763
Tigre*	91,914
Beni Amer	47,009
Bilen	33,802
Saho	32,168
Baria	10,502
Kunama	19,153
Afar	30,950
Total	614,353

* This include the Tigre-speaking ethnic groups, i.e. the Habab, the Marya, and the Mensa.

Source: Castellano, 1948:277

The second factor was the economic boom that Italy's war preparation against Ethiopia had created in Eritrea from 1932 onwards. The Italian population, which in 1934 accounted for not more than 4,600 souls (including infants) soon increased to exceed 50,000 by the end of 1935.[1] The amount of money and materials poured into the colony and the shortage of Eritrean labour which ensued with this second Italian invasion distinguished the Eritreans even further from the inhabitants of the Ethiopian Empire.

Finally, the third factor was the Italo-Ethiopian War itself and the role the Eritreans were made to play, first in the actual conquering of Ethiopia and later in its pacification. Unable to pacify an empire, at least ten times as large as Eritrea, the Italians resorted to exhorting the Eritreans to continue with the admirable job of pacification. The first colonial army in Ethiopia was made up of slightly more than 50,000 Eritrean soldiers whose role was considered very crucial. In recognition of both the past and future contribution, Rome passed a decree in 1937 distinguishing the Eritreans from other subjects of the newly founded empire. The Eritreans were to be addressed as Eritreans and not as natives, as was the case with the rest. Furthermore, priority was to be given to Eritreans in certain categories of jobs and professions.

The three factors mentioned above appear to have contributed greatly to the rather widely spread belief in what one might call separate and distinct Eritrean

---

[1] In 1938, the population in Asmara was made up of the following: 53,000 Italians and 43,000 Eritreans according to Guida Dell'Africa Italiana, Torino, 1938.

identity or consciousness. The main characteristic of this identity was based on the belief that the Eritreans and their country were more developed than the rest of the empire.

On the whole, Eritrean resistance to colonial rule was not of such a threatening nature. However, as attempts to either Catholicize the Christian Eritreans or to create a separate Orthodox Church for them proved futile, the Italians were worried about eventual resistance. On the other hand, Italian policy of wooing the loyalty of Moslem communities had more success. Italian colonialism protected and encouraged the revival and consolidation of Islam. Since most of the Moslem communities were earlier often raided and pillaged by Tigrean and Ethiopian rulers, the presence of Italian rule brought to an end such raiding and pillaging (Erlich, 1982; Negash, 1987:121–136). Throughout the colonial period, the Italians felt secure of the loyalty of their Moslem subjects while they continued to suspect that their Christian subjects might one day make common cause with their co-religionists in Ethiopia.

Italian colonialism came to an end in April 1941. The Italians were defeated by a joint Ethio-British force from the Anglo-Egyptian Sudan. Eritrea was the first enemy territory to be freed. The British were to stay in power until 1952 when Eritrea was federated to Ethiopia through a United Nations Resolution.

THE LEGACY OF COLONIALISM: THE BRITISH MILITARY
ADMINISTRATION

British policy on the future of Eritrea was put into effect soon after Italy declared war on the allies in June 1940. Working closely with Emperor Haile Sellassie, whom the British flew from London to the Sudan, the British made it known that, if the Eritrean people so wished, they could be united with Ethiopia. As early as 1940, the British and the Americans were discussing the possibility of handing to Ethiopia the Abyssinian (Tigrean) parts of Eritrea. During the war, however, the job of communicating with the Eritrean soldiers who were fighting beside the Italian army, was undertaken by a small intelligence group led by G.L. Steer. The prime motive was to encourage desertion and the disintegration of the Italian colonial army where the Eritrean contingents formed the main fighting forces. In practical terms, British policy was limited to the printing and distribution of leaflets to Eritrea, inciting its inhabitants to join the forces of either Emperor Haile Selassie or those of Great Britain. Although no great significance can be attached to such subversive material, the exercise seemed to have achieved its desired objective. According to the account of G.L. Steer, thousands of Eritreans deserted from the Italians between November 1940 and February 1941 (Steer, 1942).

From July 1940 until March 1941 about twenty numbers of a military bulletin known as Banderachin (Our Flag) were dropped by the Royal Air Force on Eritrea and other parts of Ethiopia. Out of all these pamphlets only two were directly aimed at Eritrea. The first was a poster dominated by the seal of

Emperor Haile Sellassie with the full title of the Emperor neatly and beautifully engraved. On the lower part was a slogan in Tigrinya that read "Fight for your king and your own flag". The second, which contained the first Ethiopian Imperial Decree, was issued in July 1940 and jointly written by the Emperor and his Minister of Foreign Affairs, the Eritrean Lorenzo Taezaz. In this decree, described by Steer as most impressive, the Emperor and his minister addressed the major ethnic groups in Eritrea, exhorting them to join in the struggle at the side of their Ethiopian brothers. Eritreans were further advised to refrain from being tools in the hands of the Italians "against your motherland of Ethiopia".[1]

The Ethio-British war against Italy that began in earnest in November 1940 came to an end, as far as Eritrea was concerned, in April 1941. The fifty year Italian colonial rule was over. On behalf of the Allies and until the end of the War, the British assumed responsibility over Eritrea with a bare skeleton of staff and with extremely tight financing. The subversive propaganda campaign carried out jointly by the British and Ethiopian authorities to undermine the morale of the Italian army, did indeed hasten the conclusion of the war in favour of the Allies. Once in power, the British immediately turned their attention to the future of Eritrea. Meanwhile, acting on the propaganda material showered over their heads, Eritrean leaders and elders formed Mahber Fikri Hager (Assocaition for the Love of Country) in May 1941. The objective of this organization was immediate and unconditional union with Ethiopia. This organization functioned as the spearhead of what the British described as the unionist or irredentist movement.

The idea of restructuring the colonial boundaries was widely discussed in the corridors of power even before the war against Italy was won. As early as 1942 two alternatives were discussed. These were: i) to hand over the Tigrean parts to Ethiopia; and ii) to establish a greater Somalia (Louis, 1977:68). However, it was only in 1943 that the question of the future of Eritrea was seriously confronted. In a despatch from Asmara, the military administrator Stephen Longrigg, who more than anyone else shaped British Eritrean policy, argued

---

[1] In view of the importance of the decree, reference to which was repeatedly made by the UP and the Emperor himself it is worthwhile to quote its relevant parts.

First decree of Emperor Haile Sellassie. "Ethiopia Stretches her Hands unto God. Haile Selassie the First, Elect of God, Emperor of Ethiopia.
Brave worriers of Ethiopia!

I know the merits of every one of you, and I speed to see your feat of arms. You the fighters, according to your bravery; you the old men and the men of God, according to the counsel that you have given to your people; you the farmers traders and artisans, according as your work has aided your Fatherland; you will all receive your recompense.

And you, the people of Hamassien, of Akelegousai (Akele Guzai), of Serae, of Beni Amer, of the Habab and of Mensah, whether you are on this side or the other side of Mareb, join in the struggle at the side of your Ethiopian brothers. Let none of you be a tool in the hands of the Italians against your motherland of Ethiopia, or against our friends the English.

I know the prayers of your heart, which are mine also, and the prayers besides of all the people of Ethiopia. Your destiny is strictly bound with that of the rest of Ethiopia".

For a complete translation of the decree see Steer, 1942:231–232.

passionately that Eritrea be partitioned between Ethiopia and the Anglo-Egyptian Sudan.[1]

Why did Longrigg argue consistently for the partition of Eritrea? Was he solely motivated by British imperial interests which he represented, or were his proposals based on his understanding of the history of the region, as well as on the unfolding political developments in Eritrea? British interests were no doubt in the forefront; however, in so far as these are documented, they were expressed in an extreme reluctance to use the taxpayers' money to administer an enemy-occupied territory whose future was unknown (Pankhurst, 1952). It appears to me fair to argue that for once Britain had no colonial ambition over Eritrea. However, as one of the Allies entrusted with the "disposal" of the colony, Britain had the obligation to make up her mind as how best to be relieved of her responsibilities after the end of the war.

Although detailed analysis of Longrigg's proposals would lead us into unwarranted digression, an outline of his views appears pertinent for clarifying the basis of British policy. His book (Longrigg, 1945), was written by the hand of a person who combined a solid knowledge of history and anthropology. In this book, by far the best introductory text on the history of the region, Longrigg argued that the Tigreans in Eritrea had always belonged to the Abyssinian political state system which in turn was made up of the Tigreans and the Amhara (Longrigg, 1945:169).

In March 1944, Longrigg once again returned to the subject in a long despatch on problems of the administration of Eritrea. After listing a series of problems related to security and administration, Longrigg attempted to justify his earlier position on partition on the grounds of the irredentist movement. In his capacity as administrator, he was in a good position to evaluate what he called "the problem of Ethiopian irredentism". Describing it as a major problem facing the BMA, Longrigg wrote that in addition to the anti-white and anti-foreign sentiment, the irredentist movement had certain specific elements of feeling or opinion that easily strengthened the pro-Ethiopian sentiment. "It goes without saying", reasoned Longrigg, "that the historical and cultural backgrounds of the Coptic Eritreans are identical with those in Tigrai. Linguistically, the Tigrinya of Eritrea is identical with that of the Tigrai and is first cousin to Amharic. The Tigrai, therefore, form a solid bridge connecting Eritrea with the main body of Ethiopia".[2]

After noting that the irredentist movement had thus far made little progress in the countryside, Longrigg proceeded, in an exemplary manner, to describe the features of the movement in Asmara—the movement's stronghold. In Asmara, a number of urban notables were favourable to it on the grounds of patriotic sentiment, of disappointment with the observed features of British rule, and of anticipated advancement under the Emperor. According to Long-

---

[1] WO 230/168. Longrigg to General Headquarters, Middle East Forces, Asmara, 12.10.43.
[2] WO 230/168. Longrigg to MEF, 12.7.44.

rigg, the younger intelligentsia, on the other hand, were all irredentists. Besides the Coptic Eritreans (who formed part of the Ethiopian Orthodox Church) the irredentist movement included Catholics and Protestants educated by the Swedish Mission. To this list of who's who in the irredentist movement might also be added a number of merchants.

That the irredentist movement was bound to create serious problems for the BMA as well as for the future of the colony appears to have been clearly perceived by Longrigg in the conclusion to his long despatch. He wrote:

> The Eritrean irredentist movement will almost certainly persist and grow—grow perhaps from town to country, and from intrigue to violence. Unless its demands or a main part of them are met at the peace conference, the movement will doubtless conform to the usual pattern of local nationalist movements and constantly embarrass the European occupier of the territory, if such remains.[1]

There could be little reason to doubt that the British were concerned about the anti-white and anti-foreign tones of the irredentist movement. Longrigg opposed strongly a private visit of the Ethiopian Crown Prince to Asmara on the grounds that such a visit would "give considerable strength to the present irredentist movement". In 1943, partly out of the classical imperial logic of divide and rule, and partly, I believe, due to his plausible notion about the viability of a Tigrai nation, Longrigg began suggesting to some Eritrean chiefs a new Eritrea different from that advocated by the irredentists. What exactly Longrigg intimated to those Eritreans whom he cultivated as counterforces to the irredentist movement cannot be known, since such intimation was presumably made verbally. However, from his own report on the impact of undercover work, it is apparent that Longrigg was engaged in spreading a political position that was essentially novel in Ethiopian political history. Longrigg reported that, one of the several solutions that a considerable section seemed to prefer was "the formation of a united Tigrai state under at least temporary foreign guidance".[2] Longrigg added that this view was increasingly held by leaders in Tigrai. The leaders of this view continued Longrigg, "would repudiate all connections with the Crown of Ethiopia, while pressing claims of the whole Tigrinya speaking block". It is in this despatch that Longrigg provides us with a glimpse of the workings of British colonial officers.

Longrigg left Eritrea at the end of 1944. A few months later, he published his *Short History of Eritrea*, a work most of which was presumably written in Eritrea and drawing heavily on the expertise of Kennedy Trevaskis and S.F. Nadel.[3] In a sweeping synthesis, that hitherto remains unrivalled, Longrigg argued on a historical basis that the most populous and homogenous part of Eritrea had been for many centuries an integral part of the Ethiopian state (Longrigg,

---

[1] FO 371/41531. Overseas Planning Committee: Plan for propaganda for Eritrea, 6.10.44.

[2] WO 230/168. Longrigg to General Headquarters, Middle East Forces, Asmara, 12.7.43.

[3] Kennedy Trevaskis was later to write *Eritrea. A Colony in Transition, 1941–1952*: 1960. S.F Nadel the Anthropologist wrote on the Land Tenure systems in the Eritrean highlands and on the history of the Beni Amer of western Eritrea before he left for West Africa.

1945:169). Putting forward his personal opinion as to the future of Eritrea, Long-rigg argued that the Moslem tribal areas adjoining the Anglo-Egyptian Sudan, be included with the Sudan, while the central Christian highlands of Eritrea, with the port of Massawa and the Samhar and the Saho tribes, should form part of a united Tigrai state or province, under the sovereignty of the Emperor (Long-rigg, 1945:174–175).

In London, the reports from Eritrea were primarily considered in the light of the administrative and security problems that might arise due to the growing irredentist movement. The British government was concerned with the avoid-ance of serious recurrent expenditure. On the basis of Longrigg's written and verbal accounts, the Interdepartmental Overseas Planning Committee laid down a strategy to counteract the challenge posed by the irredentist movement. This strategy called for "taking the initiative in our information services and searching for means to allow free discussion in the face of the propaganda in favour of union with Ethiopia".[1] In other words, London initiated a strategy for an open encouragement of opinion which could neutralise the irredentist move-ment.

The conclusion of the peace treaty with Italy in early 1947, triggered a renewed discussion on the future of the colony. According to the treaty, the Four Powers undertook to jointly determine how to finally dispose of Italy's ter-ritorial possessions after ascertaining the views and wishes of the population. The treaty also contained the provision that the Four Powers would send com-missions of enquiry in order to supply the Deputies of Foreign Ministers with the necessary data. Responding promptly to the stipulations of the treaty, the British in Eritrea proceeded to define their position as well as to assist the Eri-trean people on how to express their views on the future of their country. More-over, it was also incumbent on Britain as a caretaker power to provide the Four Power Commission of Enquiry with the necessary background material that could facilitate the task of the commission.

Between 1946 and November 1947, the BMA tried to put into practice the advice of Frank Stafford, based on his recent mission to Eritrea. A former finan-cial advisor to the Imperial Ethiopian Government, Stafford argued that people in Eritrea should be given every opportunity to learn of the alternatives that the Commission of Enquiry would raise: namely, a choice between incorporation into the Ethiopian Empire and administration under a trusteeship. "If the advantages of trusteeship were clearly explained", argued Stafford, "those uncertain of the benefit of becoming Ethiopian subjects would welcome the period of grace and the number of the Emperor's adherents would diminish".[2]

The salient points of this detailed memorandum dealt firstly with the method to be adopted to ascertain the wishes of the population, and, secondly, with the presentation of the alternatives, namely, incorporation into Ethiopia

---

[1] FO 371/41531. Overseas Planning Committee: Plan for propaganda for Eritrea, 6.10.44.
[2] FO 371/63175. F.E. Stafford to FO, Asmara, 2.12.46.

versus trusteeship. In so far as Britain's policy on the future of Eritrea was concerned, the most relevant section of the memorandum dealt with the definition of the alternatives.

Independence for Eritrea was entirely ruled out, partly due to the BMA's assessment of the viability of the colony and partly due to the resilience of the Unionist Party that campaigned for unconditional union with Ethiopia. It is worth noting here that the British wished that the majority of the Eritrean people would opt for a trusteeship, since "it would provide an attractive alternative to outright absorption into Ethiopia, whose present regime and status of development leave room for misgivings, particularly if the right to transfer to Ethiopia remains open during a period of trusteeship".[1] Britain would have liked to see Eritrea under British or Four Power trusteeship rather than be incorporated into Ethiopia.

In Eritrea, the chief administrator was laying the ground for the arrival of the Four Power Commission of Enquiry by supervising the formation of political organizations. The Unionist Party, reference to its existence had been made as early as 1943, was one of the first to be established in February 1947. The Unionist Party which campaigned for unconditional union with Ethiopia, remained the single largest party throughout the 1947–50 period. The Moslem League, next largest party, emerged after the chief administrator made it clear to the Moslem leaders that, "unless they are prepared to think for themselves, the plateau Christians will do the thinking for them". The Liberal Progressive Party that campaigned for the creation of a united Tigrai—an organization allegedly created by Stephen Longrigg—came into the open in early 1947. The New Eritrea Pro-Italy party was also formed in the early months of 1947 and advocated the return of Italy in one form or another. By the time of the arrival of the Four Power Commission of Enquiry in November 1947, four major political parties were ready to make their views known on the future of their country. From that time onwards, the future of the colony ceased to be a concern of Britain only. The outcome was dependent on both internal and external factors, where the role of Britain was by no means decisive.

The Four Power Commission of Enquiry visited Eritrea between November 1947 and January 1948. It then proceeded to analyze the data it had gathered. As was expected, in those early years of intensive cold war no agreement was reached on the future of Eritrea. Britain, contrary to the views elaborated by Stephen Longrigg and Stafford, proposed that Eritrea be given to Ethiopia. The United States, France and the Soviet Union put forward proposals which were unacceptable to Great Britain. In accordance with prior agreement, the question of the "disposal of Eritrea" was duly submitted to the newly formed United Nations Organization.

British policy on the future of Eritrea was based on three considerations: first, a consistent belief in the economic poverty of Eritrea; second, a recognition

---

[1] FO 371/63175. F.E. Stafford to FO, Asmara, 2.12.46.

of an irredentist movement that espoused union with Ethiopia; and third, an appreciation of the "legitimacy" of Ethiopian claims to all of Eritrea, parts of it, or at least an outlet to the sea. Although Britain, as the other three powers, accepted the "just claims" of Ethiopia to an outlet to the sea, she by no means felt bound to hand over all the ports in Eritrea to Ethiopia.

On the economic front, the decade of British administration was characterized by a severe restructuring of the Eritrean economy. Up to 1945, the British and the Americans used Italian equipment and skilled labour for war purposes, as well as to provide for the needs of the Allies in the Middle East. Such an economic boom created by the massive Italian participation continued up to the end of the war. Soon after the end of the war, however, the Eritrean economy experienced a combination of recession and depression which hit the local urban population hard. The war factories which had employed several thousand were closed down. The Italians began to be repatriated. Many of the small manufacturing plants which were established between 1936 and 1945 were forced out of business due to stiff competition from plants in Europe and the Middle East. Moreover, unlike the Italians, the British were determined to achieve a balanced budget. The cumbersome and sophisticated bureaucracy created by the Italians was soon dismantled with the inevitable consequences on employment and cash flow. The social strains created by the shortage of money, increasing cost of living and growing unemployment were made to bite even more by the lifting of the ban against political activities. For the first time in the history of Eritrea, the people were not only allowed but even encouraged to establish appropriate political organizations. The implications were far reaching. Although the Italian and British presence in Eritrea cannot be satisfactorily compared, such a comparison was, nonetheless, made by the common man in Asmara. In the late 1960s, the story was told in more or less the following manner. During the Italian period the rule was: eat but do not talk. The British changed the rule to: talk but do not eat. In the 1960s a third experience was added, namely the Ethiopian experience where the rule was: do not eat and do not talk.

STATE OF RESEARCH AND ORGANIZATION OF THE STUDY

State of research

Research on the 1941–62 period, by and large, is dominated by Kennedy Trevaskis and by those who by persuasion worked along the broad interpretative lines developed by the Eritrean nationalist forces. The war for the independence of Eritrea, first waged by the Eritrean Liberation Front (ELF) and later continued to victory by the Eritrean Peoples Liberation Front (EPLF), had to a great extent determined the priorities of research. In broad terms the Eritrean nationalist organizations argued that the majority of the Eritrean people wished for independence and that the federal arrangement was imposed upon them by the

United Nations. The dismantling of this federation by the Ethiopian government, continued the argument, was further evidence of the Eritrean desire for independence. The unilateral abolition of the federation by Ethiopia in effect turned Eritrea into a colony and therefore the relationship into that of a colonial one.

From the mid-1970s onward, the EPLF chose to concentrate on the illegality of the UN-decision uniting Eritrea with Ethiopia and on the right to self-determination, as a direct remedy to as well as a consequence of the mistake committed by the UN. The 1941–62 period was referred to, if at all, very selectively.

There is also another reason for the paucity of research on the 1941–62 period. Archival sources for the period, which were inaccessible in Ethiopia, were also inaccessible in Britain, due to the thirty year rule. Although the 1941–52 period could be studied from the mid-1980s, the entire coverage of the federation period, 1952–62 had to wait until the early 1990s. However, from the mid-1980s onwards, it was possible, and certainly profitable to study the first half of the life of the federation. Only few took the opportunity to check the archival records and many of them did so in a very haphazard manner.

The bulk of the literature on Eritrean history during the 1941–52 period is exclusively based on the pioneering study of G.K.N. Trevaskis whose privileged position as colonial officer from 1943–50 gave him exaggerated authority. His book with the modest title of *Eritrea: A Colony in Transition, 1941–52*, was published in 1960. Trevaskis' book is well-written and quite informative and will remain a good source, albeit apologetic and obviously pro-British, on the record of the British Military Administration (BMA) in Eritrea (Rubenson, 1962:520–530).

The major influence of Trevaskis' book lies, however, in its treatment of the Eritrean Unionist Party (UP). In the following paragraphs, I shall first outline the account of Trevaskis as regards the evolution of Ethiopian nationalism among the Eritreans during the decade of the 1940s. Then I shall briefly sketch the wide discrepancies between Trevaskis' account and that which can be reconstructed from the British colonial archival records.

In his chapter on the growth of political consciousness, Trevaskis outlines the evolution of the Eritrean political organization which advocated unconditional union with Ethiopia. By way of introduction he sketches Ethiopia's claim to Eritrea on historical, strategic and economic grounds. He even comments on the propaganda leaflets which were scattered from the air by the British Air Force, and promised the Eritreans freedom under the sovereignty of the Ethiopian emperor (Trevaskis, 1960:58).

He wrote that during the Italian colonial period the Tigreans in Eritrea had been surprisingly indifferent to their historical links with Ethiopia. When the Italians invaded Ethiopia in 1935, they had received the most loyal and wholehearted Eritrean cooperation (Trevaskis, 1960:59). The Ethiopians, Trevaskis continues his reconstruction, were profoundly shocked to find out that the British treated Eritrea as "legally Italian territory". Italian officials were allowed to retain their positions, and there was a widespread belief among the Italian community that Italian authority would return to Eritrea no matter what the outcome of the war (Trevaskis, 1960:59). With this background, Trevaskis approached the evolution of irredentism in Eritrea as a phenomenon that was wholly inspired from outside of Eritrea. He wrote:

> If they were not to lose their case by default, the Ethiopians had to arouse some Eritrean support. To this end they first turned to the Coptic Church. The Church had always been the custodian of Abyssinian tradition and could consequently be expected to exercise an exceptional influence amongst the Abyssinians in Eritrea and Ethiopia and, in its own interests, to work for their political union. .... By 1942 every priest had become a propagandist in the Ethiopian cause, every village had become a centre of Ethiopian nationalism, and popular religious feast days ... had become occasions for open displays of Ethiopian patriotism. (Trevaskis, 1960:59–60)

Such a description is, I maintain, far from correct. The Tigreans in Eritrea were far from indifferent to their historical links with Ethiopia. The Italians had failed to create loyal subjects of the Christian Eritreans. In fact one of the main factors which pushed Italy to invade Ethiopia was to preempt the growth of Ethiopian nationalism in Eritrea (Negash, 1987:127–131). Not even during the invasion of Ethiopia, 1935–36, did the Italians fully succeed in relying on their colonial army. Up to 20 per cent of the Italian colonial army had defected to the Ethiopian opposition forces and continued to engage Italian forces until Italy was finally defeated in 1941 (Negash, 1986:55–72).

Trevaskis' reconstruction of the Ethiopian situation is equally based on an inadequate understanding of Ethiopian history. Ethiopia was liberated from the brief but intensive Italian colonial rule in May 1941. During the following three years the Ethiopian government had other more important issues to deal with. The Second World War had not yet ended, and the Ethiopians had accepted the decision of the Allies that some parts of Ethiopia remain in British possession. Moreover, the British had a tight control over Ethiopian public finance. As regards Eritrea, the British had neither the mandate nor the juridical obligation to hand over Eritrea to Ethiopia. Italian occupation of Eritrea was of a long standing, whereas Rome's occupation of Ethiopia was part of the diplomacy of the 1930s which eventually led to the Second World War.

The government of Emperor Haile Selassie had neither the funds nor the human expertise to exercise such influence over the Church. Aware of the close links between the Church and Ethiopian nationalism, the Italians had made great efforts to weaken irredentist sentiments. Initially they tried to Catholicize the Coptic Christians with dismal results. Later on they attempted to separate the Ethiopian Orthodox Church in Eritrea from the Ethiopian Church by putting the former directly under the Patriarchate in Alexandria. From 1930 until the Italian occupation of Ethiopia, the Eritrean Orthodox Church was officially outside the spiritual jurisdiction of the Ethiopian Church. However, once the Italians gained control over Ethiopia, they undid their 1930 achievement by assimilating not only the church structure, but also the colony of Eritrea, into their Ethiopian Empire. Between 1936 and 1941, Eritrea constituted a province of the Italian East African Empire with its capital in Addis Ababa (Negash, 1987:127–129). The Italians affirmed the hegemony of the Ethiopian Church over all the orthodox churches of the empire (including Eritrea). Unwittingly the Italians did a memorable service to Ethiopia by declaring the Ethiopian Orthodox Church autocephalous thus breaking the sixteen hundred year long dependence of the Ethiopian church on Egypt (Negash, 129–130).

The Ethiopian Orthodox Church in Eritrea did not have to wait for mobilization by the Ethiopian state for its union with Ethiopia, since it had long been part of the Ethiopian establishment. Neither were the Eritreans as passive and docile as Trevaskis imagined them to be. Though not seriously bothered by Eritrean resistance, the Italians were, nevertheless, aware of the historical and cultural links between the Christian Eritreans and their co-religionists in the rest of Ethiopia. It appears that Trevaskis found it virtually impossible to understand how the Eritreans "who were loyal to the Italians" could at the earliest opportunity rise up against the dying Italian rule and challenge *Pax Britannica*.

The activities of the "Coptic Church", continues Trevaskis, prepared the way for the development of an organized political movement, which was brought about in 1942 by Ethiopian intervention. Ethiopia managed to achieve such a basis of support, presumably by a procession of young Ethiopian officials who were despatched to Asmara and made contact with the Eritrean intelligentsia. "In the event", Trevaskis concludes his account, "a society known as the Mahber Fikri Hager or Assocaition for love of country, and dedicated to uniting Eritrea with Ethiopia, came into being during 1942" (Trevaskis, 1960:60). The Mahber Fikri Hager (officially converted to a political party with the name of the Unionist Party in early 1947) was established in 1941 and not as Trevaskis stated in 1942.[1] It was formed the same day as the exiled Emperor Haile Sellassie made his triumphal entry into Addis Ababa on May 5, 1941. It has to be clearly stated that by 1942 the Ethiopian government hardly existed. It was run to a large extent by Great Britain (Marcus, 1983:8–20; Spencer, 1983). How was it that the Eritreans were so quick to get organized and demand immediate and unconditional union with Ethiopia? Perhaps unwittingly the British had greatly contributed to the articulation of Eritrean demands. Between July 1940 and April 1941, the British and the small Ethiopian contingent were busy encouraging Eritreans to betray their Italian rulers and fight for their emperor and country.

Most of the background to and the success of the joint British and Ethiopian intelligence operation have been recorded by one of its architects (Steer, 1942). The main thrust of the campaign was to entice Eritrean soldiers away from the Italians.

The British, as Trevaskis quite rightly pointed out, did not feel committed to assist either the Eritreans or the Ethiopian state in uniting Eritrea with Ethiopia.

---

[1] On the early history of the Mahber Fikri Hager, see EWN no. 227 (9.1.47) Ethiopia, no. 103 (17.4.49).

However, neither Trevaskis nor the British Military Administration were pre-
pared to consider the impact of their war propaganda on the Eritreans. Instead,
Trevaskis and his colleagues chose to interpret the existence of the Unionist
Party as a challenge to their rule.

The earliest mention of the Unionist movement, in the British archives, was
in 1943. By this time the irredentist movement was predominant in the urban
areas and was mainly made up of "young men of the educated class, supported
by the wealthy merchants and also by certain prominent religious leaders above
all the two bishops of the Coptic Christians and the Catholics of the Ethiopian
rite" (Negash, 1987).

The chiefs were reluctant to support the "nationalists", continued Trevaskis,
lest they displeased the British and they would have preferred to remain safely
on the fence until they knew on which side to alight had it not been for the
"sudden emergence" of an opposition movement to the nationalists during
1943.[1] The activists of the Mahber Fikri Hager, by now described as the nationalists, were suspicious of British support to the Separatist Movement and had
by the end of 1943, according to Trevaskis, begun to canvas for signatures to a
popular petition demanding immediate union with Ethiopia (Trevaskis,
1960:64). This opposition movement, which came to be known as the Separatist
Movement (and later as the Liberal Progressive Party), had no clear goal but was
known to be anti-Ethiopian and pro-British (Trevaskis, 1960:62). It was natural,
argued Trevaskis, that the British officers should feel better disposed towards
those who professed respect for them than towards those who were known to
abuse them. Such a provocative attitude was caused by the quite overt British
support of the Separatist movement and by a promise made by the British military administrator that Eritrean wishes would be taken into account when the
time came for the future of the country to be decided (Trevaskis, 1960:64).

The archival sources confirm the suspicions of the Unionist Movement. The
Separatist Movement did not as Trevaskis alleges suddenly emerge. The idea
for such a movement was suggested to some Eritrean chiefs by Stephen Longrigg, the chief administrator of Eritrea. Although the foundation of the Separatist Movement was instigated by the British and enjoyed their full support, it
remained confined to a few villages in the southern part of the highlands.

In an atmosphere of rumour and suspicion tension mounted, which made
the British flex their muscles. The Eritrean police strike in February 1944, where
the strikers demanded the removal of Italian police, the annulment of Italian
laws, and the dismissal of Italian judges, created an opportunity for the BMA to
dismiss a large number of active Nationalists in the police, thus breaking the
strike at once and giving a severe setback to the Nationalist Movement (Trevaskis, 1960:65). Suppressed in Eritrea, the Nationalist cause, continued Tre-

---

[1] The separatist movement did not emerge suddenly. It was instigated by Stephen Longrigg as part
of his plans to weaken the position of the Nationalists. For a more detailed discussion on the
origins of the Separatist Party, see Chapter Two.

vaskis, was taken up in Ethiopia by the Ethiopia-Hamasien Society, an organization of supposedly Eritrean residents in Ethiopia whose declared objective was the union of Eritrea with Ethiopia. According to Trevaskis, this organization was known to be financed and directed by the Ethiopian government. It is probable that the British may have caused the Unionist movement a severe setback, by showing favour to the Separatist movement and by the draconian measures taken against the police strike. But the UP was far from dead.

When the question of the disposal of Eritrea was first discussed in the autumn of 1945 at the London Conference, Ethiopian claims to Eritrea were not viewed with any sympathy. Not only were Ethiopian claims disregarded in the peace talks preceding the formation of the United Nations, such claims were also seen with great suspicion at the United Nations where the issue was finally resolved. The position of Ethiopia vis à vis Italy on Eritrea is a subject studied with great eloquence by Amare Tekle in a dissertation which unfortunately remains unpublished (Tekle, 1964). Virtual disregard of Ethiopian claims, wrote Trevaskis, "led to the dismay of the Nationalists and the jubilation of the Separatists who drew up a number of petitions addressed to the Foreign Ministers of the Allied Powers in which they demanded British trusteeship" (Trevaskis, 1960:66).

By the beginning of 1946, Trevaskis wrote that the Nationalists had to win international sympathy somehow if they were not to lose their case by default. The decisive step was, according to Trevaskis, taken by the Ethiopian government in appointing Colonel Negga Haile Selassie, as Ethiopian Liaison Officer with the evident intention of reviving the Nationalist Movement. While Colonel Negga presumably was settling into his job, Trevaskis wrote that the first part of 1946 witnessed an exceptionally bitter campaign against Arabs and Italians, carried out by the Nationalist Movement. These anti-Italian and anti-Arab campaigns were supported by a number of nationalist demonstrations and processions.

When appointed Colonel Negga Haile Selassie was a young man in his twenties. He was appointed as a consular liaison officer and had a junior rank in the Ethiopian service.[1] As an Ethiopian he was most probably looked up to by the Eritrean unionists. As an Ethiopian too, he supported, sympathised with and advocated the Unionist cause. Throughout the 1940s, the Ethiopian liaison office was staffed by two people, namely, Negga Haile Selassie and his secretary. How could two individuals revive a moribund movement, when the British with the entire power apparatus in their hands had only succeeded in creating a tiny Separatist Movement? How could Colonel Negga and his secretary breathe life into a severely crushed movement when the Italian community with full support from Rome was virtually[2] unable to soften the anti-Italian feel-

---

[1] In a conversation Negga Haile Selassie intimated to me that whatever he knew of Ethiopian history he learned it in Eritrea from the leaders of the Unionist Party.

[2] For further discussion and reconstruction of Italian political activities during the 1945–50 period, see Chapter Two.

ings in Eritrea? The archival sources do not provide any proof that the Ethiopian liaison officer was doing the job of the Unionist Movement.[1]

In the summer of 1946, Trevaskis continues, the British decided to put an end to the nationalist demonstrations. During one of the unauthorized demonstrations, the British colonial soldiers from the Sudan who had been stationed in Eritrea since 1941 intervened, thus breaking the demonstration and arresting a number of ringleaders. However, within an hour rioting broke out; a mob invaded the police station and freed the ringleaders. The British decision to re-arrest the ringleaders caused even more serious rioting. The Sudanese Defence Force was called into action and, according to Trevaskis "a few rounds were fired, four of the mob were killed, and order was immediately restored". The Sudanese Defence Force was made up of Sudanese soldiers who were brought to Eritrea during the Anglo-Italian campaign and were stationed in Eritrea to enable the British Military Administration to "keep law and order" (Trevaskis, 1960:67–68). Trevaskis did not deem it necessary to discuss whether the demonstrations were of a nature which called for provocative intervention. Both the Unionist Party and the Pro-Ethiopian weekly *New Times and Ethiopia News* argued strongly that the demonstration was a peaceful one. The British decision to break up the assembly and arrest the ringleaders in the middle of the procession was indeed a deliberate provocation (NTEN, August, 1946).

What Trevaskis generally described as "nationalist demonstrations" had in reality their origins in more concrete economic issues. The Eritrean Christians experienced daily the rising cost of living and dwindling job opportunities, while the Italians not only dominated the modern sector of the economy but were also heavily represented in the administration of the country. Moreover, Arab merchants and the Eritrean Moslem trading community known as *Jeberti* were seen as exploiting the little surplus that the peasantry and the urban workers managed to scrape together. In the rural areas, it was widely known that peasants sold their crops to Eritrean Moslem and Arab merchants many months before the crops were harvested. So, the demonstrations were not simply occasions for affirming the commitment of the Unionist Party to an unconditional and speedy union with Ethiopia; the demonstrations called for the Eritreanization of the administration and of the economy.

The incident of July 1946, where the Sudanese Defence Force killed four of the rioting mob revived deep-seated prejudices and ill-feeling between Sudanese and Abyssinians. Exactly a month later a Sudanese soldier was stoned to death by a mob, probably as revenge for the incident of the previous month. A few hours later about 70 soldiers from the Sudanese Defence Force surrounded the native part of the city killing 46 people and wounding more than 60. The British were held responsible for the murderous spree of their colonial

---

[1] The conspiratorial thesis of Trevaskis can be further disproved by citing what happened fifty years later. In the 1980s, the Ethiopian government had an army of ca. 100,000 stationed in Eritrea in an attempt to keep it within the Ethiopian state. By then the Ethiopian government had alienated the majority of the Eritrean people.

soldiers and they did not work very hard to dispel the wide spread suspicion and mistrust among the Christian Eritreans. The wave of indignation following the Asmara incident writes Trevaskis, swelled the Nationalist camp. After that incident the majority of the Christian Eritreans viewed alien European rule with bitter disillusionment and saw no other solution to their problems than Eritrea's union with Ethiopia (Trevaskis, 1960:68).

As can be seen from Trevaskis' own reconstruction, it was hardly the young Ethiopian liaison officer Negga Haile Selassie who revived and welded together the Unionist movement. By unleashing a reign of terror, it was the British themselves who provided the Unionist movement with the ammunition it required to consolidate its hold over the Christian population.

Trevaskis condemns the Mahber Fikri Hager (The Unionist Party) as an Ethiopian creation. Why was he not able to see it as, by and large, an Eritrean organization? Three factors appear to have influenced Trevaskis in shaping his points of departure. The first one was the reluctance of the BMA officers in Eritrea to come to terms with an anti-colonialist movement in the form of the UP. In the early 1940s it was commonly believed that British rule in Africa would endure for many decades, if not centuries. The winds of change that began to blow soon after the independence of India in 1947 were in the case of Africa grudgingly acknowledged only in the middle of the 1950s. Therefore, it was much easier for a number of BMA officers, including Trevaskis, to look upon these as Ethiopian subversive activities rather than as the autonomous action of the UP in Eritrea. The UP was far ahead of its time.

The British who were conducting a war and who were also beginning to evolve the restructuring of the map of Africa along ethnic lines were not pleased with this political cum cultural movement. The colonial ethos, after all, remained intact. So, no wonder that the British were not well disposed towards the Unionist Party. "Among some British", wrote Trevaskis, "there was undoubted resentment at the challenge to their authority (British power) implicit in Ethiopian pretensions and many British officers found it difficult to conceal their dislike of the bitter and touchy young men in the Mahber Fikri Hager" [Unionist Party] (Trevaskis, 1960:61).

The second factor was most likely related to the policies the BMA pursued in the formation of public opinion in Eritrea. It was, for instance, the British who provided the initial impetus in 1943 for the formation of the Separatist movement that later emerged as the Liberal Progressive Party (LPP). It was also the British who twisted the arms of the Moslem leaders in Eritrea to form the Moslem League (ML) towards the end of 1946. Trevaskis, who during this period was in Eritrea and who no doubt was deeply involved in the formation of British policy in Eritrea, must have found it rather natural to perceive the Ethiopian state as playing a game similar to that of the BMA. Even if we were to concede that the Ethiopian government did indeed play a similar game, it would have required much more manpower and funds at its disposal. These were in short supply. Moreover, the available research on Ethiopian foreign policy of the period suggests that Ethiopia's main expectation was an outlet to the sea (Spencer, 1983; Tekle, 1964; Marcus, 1983).

The third factor may well have been Trevaskis' profound knowledge of the role of the Ethiopian state in undermining the federal and autonomous status of Eritrea, facts widely known in the period when he was finalizing his book toward the end of 1958. There are strong reasons to believe that Trevaskis was reading history backwards, sometimes an irresistible temptation not only in the hands of amateurs but also among those trained in the historian's craft.

One of the most pervasive impacts of the Trevaskian treatment of the UP has been that later historians have continued to treat the UP in the same fashion. Even historians who ought to be aware of the biases of colonial writers appear to have fallen victim to the eloquent, albeit mistaken, reconstruction of Trevaskis. The most important of these authors are discussed in the chapter dealing with Eritrean political parties. However the greatest impact of Trevaskis has been on the Eritrean Liberation Fronts which were determined to re-write history. Like other nationalist movements elsewhere, the Eritrean organizations fighting for the establishment of an independent state continued to treat the Unionist Party as a movement which was hardly related to Eritrean history.[1] Trevaskis' description of the Unionist Party suited perfectly the objectives of those Eritreans who either rejected the federation or regretted it afterwards.

An examination of the British colonial sources, the local Eritrean sources, as well as the Ethiopian position on the future of Eritrea, will, I believe, enable us to redress the shortcomings of the Trevaskian account. It will also, I hope, do some justice to the Unionist Party, an organization which single-handedly played a crucial role in the history of Eritrea.

The academic literature on the federation period, 1952–62, though largely based on the political background sketched by Trevaskis shows, with few exceptions, glaring errors related to chronology and the unfolding of events. This is indeed unfortunate. Continuing a reconstruction of the history of the Eritrean armed insurrection against Ethiopia, Dr Tseggai wrote: "The new Eritrean government—a democratically elected government with a democratic constitution—would not coexist with Ethiopia's absolutist and archaic monarchy. With its labour unions and independent political parties, Eritrea was anathema to the Ethiopian entity" (Tseggai, 1988:74). With such a preamble, the 1952–62 period is treated with great ease as that of the dismantling of the Eritrean government apparatus by Ethiopia. The suppression of labour unions, and political parties, the introduction of the official language of Ethiopia, and the incursions into freedom of speech and assembly are all cited as the steps allegedly taken by the Ethiopian government between 1952 and 1962. These have all happened. But the question which writers like Tseggai appear keen to avoid was the role of the Eri-

---

[1] While Trevaskis' book was translated into Arabic by Othman Saleh Sabby, (leader of ELF), the essential points of the book have been used by the EPLF (1975) in its primers for political education.

trean government in the process of the dismantling of the federation. Tseggai further wrote: "A whole country was illegally reduced to a mere province of a neighbouring country, and the Eritreans were put under the rule of yet another occupier, this time a neighbouring black African power" (Tseggai, 1988:75). A simple reading of the Eritrean constitution and a cursory investigation of the functioning of the Eritrean government make it abundantly clear that the members of the Eritrean government were not as helpless as we are made to believe. This study shows that the Eritrean government on its own initiative dismantled the federation.

A far more flagrant example of the impact of Trevaskis as well as that of the knowledge derived from the Eritrean nationalist fronts is the study of Ogbazghi Yohannes (1991) which depicts the process of the termination of the federation as exclusively an act of the Ethiopian government. His account (described as the best documented) is so replete with factual and interpretative errors that it is virtually impossible within this context to point out its main weaknesses. Neither is the more recent study by Ruth Iyob different from this depiction of the Unionist Party as a supine instrument of the Ethiopian state (Ogbazghi, 1991; Iyob, 1995:82–107). This study shows that scholars like Tseggai, Iyob, and Yohannes would certainly have refrained from making such wild statements, if they had taken the trouble to look into the record of the Eritrean government.

Another author who has followed Trevaskis is John Markakis. In his major study (1987) Markakis attempted to steer a middle course, while at the same time restating the basic assumptions of Trevaskis. His wide knowledge and experience of Ethiopian society enabled him to explain satisfactorily the foundations of pro-Ethiopian ideology, as well as the politics of the most important Eritrean nationalist organization (The Eritrean Peoples Liberation Front). Yet his failure or reticence to consult the rich archival documentation on the 1941–62 period seriously weakened the value of his efforts. The same goes for David Pool, Richard Sherman, Haggai Erlich and many others as well. In an article entitled "Eritrean Nationalism", Pool takes for granted Trevaskis' interpretation as regards the 1940s and that of the liberation fronts for the 1950s, while Keller based his argument solely on biased pro-nationalist sources (Markakis, 1987; Pool, 1983:175–193; Keller, 1990:95–114; Erlich, 1981:171–182).

Another scholar who has studied the history of the federation is the prolific Bereket Habte Sellassie, not as a subject on its own but as part of a much wider field involving the United Nations. An Eritrean nationalist a priori, Habte Sellassie was neither interested in explaining the process nor in contextualising his bold statements. As a spokesman of the Eritrean Nationalist Movement, Habte Sellassie was too inclined to read history backwards. Fully satisfied by the biased statements of Trevaskis, he readily blamed the Ethiopian government for the dissolution of the federation. His main line of argument is that the marriage of democratic ideas and institutions (which presumably prevailed in Eritrea) to an imperial and feudal power was a fatal combination. Here Habte Sellassie took for granted that the Eritrean leaders (the executive and the legislative organs) were capable and willing to implement the constitution which was drafted for them by the United Nations. This study shows that long before the Eritrean constitution was approved by the Ethiopians, the Eritreans themselves had violated it. Further explaining the inevitable dissolution of the federation, Habte Selassie dwelt, firstly on the "inordinate ambition of Emperor Haile Sellassie to incorporate Eritrea as an integral part of his feudal empire". Secondly, he mentioned, "the fear and uncertainty of a feudal regime harnessed to a modern bourgeois democratic government" (Habte Selassie, 1989:42).

This study shows that Bereket Habte Sellassie had hardly any knowledge of the composition and functioning of the Eritrean government which came into existence in 1952. It was far from being modern, democratic or bourgeoise. Emperor Haile Sellassie did not have an inordinate ambition to incorporate Eritrea. Already in the mid 1960s Dr. Amare Tekle's study on the creation of the Ethio-Eritrean Federation showed clearly that Ethiopia's claims had few supporters and that it stood no chance against the Vatican-Mecca-Latin American Axis at the United Nations (Tekle, 1964).

Not all authors are such victims of the Trevaskian legacy as those cited above. Lloyd Ellingson's thesis on Eritrea substantially refutes the Trevaskian legacy by its recognition of the role of Eritrean actors during the 1941–52 period (Ellingson, 1986). In particular, Ellingson discussed the role played by the Italian community and the extent to which this provoked Eritrean organizations into action. Although Ellingson, as Trevaskis before him, exaggerated the role of the Ethiopian government, he, nonetheless, drew the conclusion that the Unionist Party had considerable autonomy and functioned with a clear objective (Ellingson, 1986:41–54). Ellingson completed his thesis in 1986 and was thus able to look into the archival material until the end of 1954 deposited at the Public Record Office (PRO).

An author who in my opinion has a clear grasp of the role of the Unionist Party is Thoma Killion. In his study, Killion had no problem in arguing that the federal state of Eritrea was run by the Unionist Party, working closely with the Ethiopian government. For Killion, the government in Eritrea was Unionist/Ethiopian. By this he meant that whereas the actual running of the business of the government was carried out by the former members of the Unionist Party, Ethiopian presence and power was felt in the areas which fell under its domain, namely, foreign and interstate trade, railways and communications, defence and foreign policy (Killion, 1985).

Organization of the study

This study is introduced by a long chapter on the Unionist Party and its relations with the other parties on the eve of the UN resolution of 1950. The Unionist Party (UP) campaigned for unconditional union between Eritrea and Ethiopia. Unfairly treated by Trevaskis, the Unionist Party was even more relegated to the sidelines by the Eritrean nationalist fronts as well as writers. In my opinion despite the archival documentation leaving a great deal to be desired, and the deplorable fact that very few memoirs have been left behind, the available sources are sufficient to undertake a reconstruction of the Unionist Party and its role in the destiny of Eritrea.

There is also another reason for paying particular attention to the political parties in general and the Unionist Party in particular. The events preceding the UN resolution, I believe, can be best understood when studied in the context of Eritrean political responses. Moreover, a study of the Eritrean political parties and their constantly shifting alliances provides a continuity as well as background to the main theme of the book, namely the rise and the fall of the federation between Eritrea and Ethiopia.

The story of how the federation came into existence and the first three years of the life of the federation are treated in the third chapter. The documentation is exclusively archival and given the nature of its collection (by consulates and embassies) the material is indeed satisfactory. Already in the first three years of the federation, we notice that the former members of the UP, now in government positions, were busy undermining the federation and calling for its dissolution. It is complete union that they were after and they were frustrated by the federal arrangement which they considered as foreign to their political conception and vocabulary. We also see clearly the transformation of some of the earlier political parties, namely the Moslem League, into champions of the federation.

Only three years after the launching of the federal arrangement Eritrea was for all intents and purposes a part of Ethiopia. In the process of dismantling the federation, the UP, now heavily dominating the Eritrean government, had a great role to play.

The protracted struggle of the ML against the Eritrean and Ethiopian governments is the main emphasis of the fourth chapter. Once again, the British archival documentation allows a satisfactory reconstruction. The continuity between the pre-federation agitation and post-federation protest can be clearly followed as well as established. The role of the Ethiopian government, firstly as a federal partner and secondly as the supreme authority over the country including Eritrea, is dealt with but perhaps not to the desired extent. It was more difficult for the British diplomatic corps to gather information inside Ethiopia since most of the decisions were taken by Emperor Haile Sellassie himself. Moreover, the Ethiopians did not have any serious worries as the federation was slowly but surely being dissolved, largely by Eritrean forces themselves. The chapter is concluded by a short discussion on the reasons for the dissolution of the federation and the role of the Ethiopian government in the process.

The unfolding of events after the incorporation of Eritrea into the Ethiopian empire (1962) is discussed in chapter five. The Eritreans initiated armed opposition against the dissolution of the federation but were divided as to the nature of the goals of the opposition as well as to who would assume power after the expulsion of Ethiopian rule. The issues which surfaced in the late 1940s continued to dominate the relations between the various Eritrean nationalist armed forces. By the 1970s all Eritrean armed opposition organizations had modified their political demands to that of complete independence. Yet as the chapter demonstrates, the Eritrean nationalist forces were divided into two irreconcilable camps which involved an articulation of the image of an independent Eritrea. Would Eritrea be part of the Arab and Moslem world, as the ELF argued or would Eritrea continue to be dominated by the Christian Eritreans with strong cultural and economic links with the central parts of Ethiopia? The latter position, argued by the EPLF was eventually to win.

The issue which had united the Eritrean nationalist forces since the 1970s was the independence of Eritrea. On this issue, there was a clear discontinuity of political objectives. Whereas there was a clear continuity between the ML and the ELF, there was no such continuity of objectives between the defunct UP and the EPLF. The EPLF cannot be described as a successor of the Unionist Party, although it promoted some of its programme, namely the hegemonic position of the Christian Eritreans (Tigreans) in the country.

The final short chapter attempts to sketch the challenges both internal and external which the newly independent state of Eritrea is likely to face in the foreseeable future.

Chapter Two

Eritrean Political Parties on the Eve of the UN Resolution of 1950

ESTABLISHMENT AND GROWTH OF THE UNIONIST PARTY

In this chapter the emphasis will be on the Unionist Party (Mahber Fikri Hager).[1] Available documentation has hitherto been derived mainly from Trevaskis. The Eritrean nationalist writers in their turn embellished the distorted description of Trevaskis since it suited them perfectly in their quest for the establishment of an independent Eritrea (Gebre-Medhin, 1989; Yohannes, 1991; Gayim, 1993).

The Unionist Party was established in Asmara on May 5, 1941, the same day as the victorious return of Emperor Haile Sellassie to his capital from five years of exile in Great Britain.[2] While the Emperor raised the Ethiopian flag in Addis Ababa, the people of Asmara held a demonstration calling for the unification of Eritrea with its motherland Ethiopia. On the same day, the leaders of the conference announced the formation of the Unionist Party—an organization that was to play a very important role in the fate of Eritrea.

Both the demonstration and the formation of the UP were probably of a very local nature, since their occurrence appears not to have been reported to London. The initial inspiration for the choice of the date for the demonstration and the formation of the UP has repeatedly been traced by the leaders of the UP to the messages of the propaganda war pamphlets that the British and Ethiopian authorities in the Sudan distributed widely among the Eritreans between October 1940 and April 1941.

Although evidence on the activities of the UP is scarce for the 1941–46 period, its leaders agree that the party functioned in a democratic manner and that there was a consensus on the objectives, namely, the unity of Eritrea with

---

[1] The Mahber Fikri Hager was described as a Unionist or irredentist movement until it was officially registered as the Unionist Party in 1947. It is important to note that the party kept its original name throughout the period. The name Unionist Party was given to it by the British Military Administration. For its members it remained Mahber Fikri Hager (Association for love of country).

[2] The UP was led by Abbuna Marcos, the head of the Ethiopian Orthodox Church in Eritrea. Its executive president was Gebremeskel Weldu until his replacement by Tedla Bairu in October 1946. In October 1948, the former president of UP, Gebremeskel Weldu wrote a short history of the UP where he dealt with the precise date for the formation of the UP and the unconditional union with Ethiopia as its objective. See Ethiopia, no. 79 (31.10.1948).

    The UP was, naturally, not recognised as a party by the British Military Administration (BMA) since political freedom was not allowed until the end of 1946.

Ethiopia.[1] During the first six years of its existence, the party was led by Gebremeskel Weldu who, to judge from his writings (1948–49), was competent as well
as sensitive to the subtle differences and contradictions between the Eritrean
adherents of the UP and the Ethiopian state. We know very little about the structure of the party during this early period, only that most of the prominent
people who were to advocate independence for Eritrea in the late 1940s, were
members of the UP. Some of those mentioned as previous members were
Ibrahim Sultan, Woldeab Wolde Mariam, and Abdulkadir Kebire, later all
staunch defenders of independence.[2]

From the accounts of the late 1940s, the UP managed its own ideology as well
as its affairs without Ethiopian intervention. A glance at the pro-unionist writings in the UP's Weekly and in the Tigrinya Weekly published by the BMA
lends support to Gebremeskel Weldu's account of the independence of action
enjoyed by the UP up to 1946. Moreover, Ethiopian intervention prior to 1946
was rather unlikely for a number of reasons. Firstly, the Ethiopian state was still
in the process of reconstructing itself within the greatly circumscribed climate
created by the demands of war in Africa and the Middle East. Secondly, the
newly reconstituted state at Addis Ababa had enough troubles on its hands with
the rebellion in eastern Tigrai where the centralizing policies of Emperor Haile
Selassie were challenged (Gebru, 1984; 1991).

The UP was imbued with religious values. Its leaders were deeply religious
people and came predominantly from Catholic and Evangelical backgrounds.[3]
The Ethiopian Orthodox Church was from the outset fully associated with the
objectives of the UP. The leaders of the Moslem religious and commercial community were also active members of the UP. Its leaders were convinced that the
ultimate goal of union with Ethiopia would find support in the eyes of God. At
the leadership level, the UP was indeed multi-religious. Out of the 44 members
of the Executive Committee, no less than 19 were Moslems (Hagos, 1963:80–1).
Although it was not surprising at all, as Trevaskis has commented, that by 1942
every village church had become a centre of Ethiopian nationalism, his argument that the Ethiopian state had to turn to the "Coptic Church" in search of Eritrean support for its cause can hardly be substantiated. The "Coptic Church"
did not have to wait for Ethiopian overtures. The declaration of intention made
widely known by the war-time pamphlets and the return of the Emperor to
power were in themselves sufficient grounds for setting the churches into
action.

---

[1]   Ethiopia, no. 79 (31.10.48).

[2]   Gebremeskel Weldu in Ethiopia, no. 79 31.10.48; Negga Haile Selassie's papers, A report on the
      reorganization of the UP, 1947.

[3]   The first president of the UP was a devout Catholic. His successor, Tedla Bairu, who also served
      as the first president of Eritrea, 1952–55, was a devout Evangelist. Gebremikael Girmu, the editor
      of the UP weekly newspaper, Ethiopia, was a devout Catholic. Most of the UP's written material
      was composed mainly by those who had extensive theological training at the Catholic Missions
      in Eritrea and Italy. The most notable were Dr. Abba Hailu Gebreyesus and Abba Yacob
      Gebreyesus.

Christian churches in general and the Ethiopian Church in particular had a long history of conflict with the policies of the Italian colonial state. While attempts at converting the Eritrean Orthodox to Catholicism were successfully challenged by the monks and priests in Eritrea, those few who were converted to Catholicism were so much imbued with Ethiopian liturgical tradition that they struggled successfully to get permission from the Holy See (the Vatican) to carry out mass according to Ethiopian Orthodox liturgical rites. The Catholic church of the Ethiopian rite (i.e. embracing Eritrean Catholics) was fully committed to the cause of unconditional union with Ethiopia (Negash, 1996b). Throughout the colonial period, many of the Eritrean adherents of the Swedish Evangelical Mission (active since 1866) had considered themselves as Ethiopians—a position that created problems between the Swedish Evangelical Mission and Italian authorities in Asmara (Negash, 1987:32–65).

During the first five years, the UP limited its activities to rallying people behind the slogan for union with Ethiopia. Partly due to restrictions on freedom of expression and partly due to lack of experience, the UP primarily used the opportunities created by the numerous religious feasts.

Although the UP held together up to 1946, it had begun to enconter problems which were to give it the character of an organization that did not take into consideration the interests of other social groups. The first leader, Gebremeskel Weldu, mentioned that the incident that contributed to the withdrawal of Moslems from the UP towards the end of 1946 took place as early as 1943 (*Eritrean Weekly News*, 17.8.47). Unfortunately, no details are provided. However as late as the end of 1946, some of the prominent Moslems who later were to lead the Moslem League were within the Unionist Movement. The most important of these, Ibrahim Sultan is twice mentioned as one of the Unionists. In the first document, dated 26.12.1946, the name of IbrahimSultan as a member is mentioned in connection with the resignation of the old leadership (IES, Negga Haile Sellasie papers). In the second document dated January 6, 1946, Ibrahim Sultan is one of the signatories protesting against BMA's support of the Separatist movement.[1] While the UP, led by educated Eritreans and fully supported by the Orthodox, Catholic and Evangelical denominations timidly pursued its mobilization campaigns in the city of Asmara, the British were deliberately poking the fire of cultural and political diversity in order to counterbalance the dominant position of the UP.

The BMA resented the presence of the UP. Moreover, the BMA's treatment of Eritrea and its subjects as belonging to Italy had complicated relations between the UP and the BMA. Very few British officers expected that they would be challenged by African colonial subjects. Besides, the BMA officers did not believe that Eritrea was culturally homogenous and already had vague notions as to how to dispose of the colony at the opportune moment. The move-

---

[1] IES, Negga Haile Sellasie papers. Gebremeskel Weldu to Senior Civil Affairs Officer, 4.1.46. Attached to the protest note is a list of signatories containing 64 names.

ment that the British assisted in its inception was the Separatist Movement, later
(1947) known as the Party of Eritrea for Eritreans or the Liberal Progressive
Party. This party held true to the parameters set out for it by the chief administrator Brigadier Stephen Longrigg.[1]

From the end of 1943 onwards, the UP shared the political underworld with
the Separatists who, though not completely against some form of union with
Ethiopia, insisted on the maintenance of the ethnic, cultural and political identity of the Tigreans inhabiting Eritrea and Tigrai. The Separatist movement, as
opposed to the UP, remained limited to a few districts in south central Eritrea.
The main challenge to the UP during the 1943–46 period, however, was not so
much the Separatist movement but the BMA, which at once favoured the Separatist Movement and resented the UP. The latter's demand for the dismissal of
Italian police personnel, Italian laws and Italian judges gave the BMA an opportunity to flex its muscles against the UP. Real and suspected ringleaders were
interned and eventually dismissed from their jobs. The UP, according to
Trevaskis' reflections on the events, received "a severe setback" (Trevaskis,
1960:65). The setback did not, however, appear as serious as Trevaskis has
assessed it to have been since the archival sources for the period report the continuous growth of the UP.

On September 14, 1945, at the same time as the Four Powers began their first
discussions on the disposal of Italian colonies, the UP formed a youth section.
Known as *Andinnet*, the youth section was most radical and uncompromising in
its demands for unconditional union. It was led by people who were elected to
serve only one year (Hagos, 1963:78). There was also a women's branch of the
UP, established, according to a later document, in 1948–49. Throughout the Federation period, this women's branch was led by a committee of three women.[2] Unfortunately, neither the EWN nor the colonial archives contain material on the
early history of the youth section. Knowledge on its formation is derived from
a short notice concerning the celebration of its second anniversary (EWN, 2.10.47).

THE UP AND THE BMA

Although the demands of the UP fitted very well into BMA's policy of restructuring the boundaries of former Italian colonies along ethnic lines (to be imple-

---

[1] Describing the attitude of the British to the separatist movement, Trevaskis limits himself to
stating that it was natural for the British to feel better disposed towards those who professed
respect for them, thereby dismissing the UP's belief that the separatist movement was sponsored
by the BMA. On October 12, 1944, the Chief Administrator Stephen Longrigg reporting to London
on the disposal of Eritrea advised on the formation of a United Tigrai state that would include
Eritrea and the Tigrai province of Ethiopia. After pointing out that this view appeared to be
increasingly held by the leaders in the Ethiopian Tigrai, Longrigg added that recently Eritreans
themselves were advocating it, "although it was suggested (naturally without their knowledge)
by myself fourteen months ago". (WO 230/168, Longrigg to Chief Civil Affairs Officer, Civil
Affairs Branch, Middle East Forces, Cairo, Asmara, 12.10.44.)

[2] These were according to Fesshaye Hagos, (1963:79), Askalemariam Yemane, Elsabet Tewelde-
medhin and Temrtsa Ogbazghi.

mented after the end of the war), the latter resented the confidence with which the UP campaigned for its objectives. Indeed, the UP recognized the role of the British in freeing Eritrea from Italian colonial rule. However, this recognition soon lost its value as the British continued to implement colonial legislation through the widespread use of Italian bureaucrats. In so far as the exercise of state power was concerned, the UP saw little difference between Italian colonial administration and that of the BMA. The latter's dogmatic insistence that the British were obliged to administer the colony in the same way as the Italians before them led to a collision course and to the growth of xenophobia among followers of the UP. Another factor that poisoned relations between the BMA and the UP was the uncertainty that shrouded the nature of the disposal of Eritrea after the war. Judging by the attitude of BMA towards Italians and Italian legislation, the UP feared Italy's return for a second round of colonial rule. The British, with their hands tied by their role as caretaker administrators, were in no position to mitigate the fears of the UP. Moreover, the British had neither a firm stand nor a possibility to dictate the outcome of the disposal of Eritrea.

By the summer of 1943, the British, it could be said, had worked out a plan for the disposal of Eritrea whereby the plateau region, a stronghold of the UP, was to revert to Ethiopia and the remaining part was to be amalgamated with the Anglo-Egyptian Sudan. This policy was kept secret, since implementation had to wait until the end of the war. Moreover, in deciding the fate of Eritrea, the British were aware that they were only one of the Four Powers. However, since only the UP campaigned for the unconditional union of the whole of Eritrea with Ethiopia, the BMA began, what might be called, the process of putting the UP in its proper place. This was done by making an informal proposal concerning the possibility of the emergence of a united and independent Tigrai (comprising of Hamassien, Akele Guzai and the rest of the northern Ethiopian province of Tigrai). At another level, the BMA proceeded to suppress strikes and demonstrations with a great show of force, thus making it clear to the UP who was in power in Eritrea.

The decision taken by the Allies (the Four Powers, i.e. UK, USA, France and the Soviet Union) to postpone the discussion on the fate of Eritrea until the signing of the peace treaty with Italy, the rapidly deteriorating economy of the great majority of Eritreans, the continued implementation of Italian colonial laws, and the dominant positions of Italians in the bureaucracy turned 1946 into a year with a series of confrontations between the BMA and the UP. The problem was complicated by the unenviable position that the British found themselves in—an administrating power without, however, the responsibility of disposing of Eritrea. Moreover, the British were irritated by the UP's continuous challenge to their wisdom as colonial rulers. Although the UP was agitating to bring about a favourable decision as well as a greater participation in the administration of the country, it refrained from violent methods. The only weapon that the UP resorted to was public demonstrations. However, the BMA considered such timid and peaceful challenges as going beyond the limits of toleration. The opportunity for a showdown occurred on July 28, 1946 during a demonstration organized by the UP. Quite naturally, the demonstrators found BMA's action provocative and, therefore, refused to accept the arrest of their ringleaders. On July 30, supporters of the arrested leaders gathered around the court to demand their release. They were fired at by the Sudanese Defence Force—a contingent of the forces from the Sudan that accompanied the British in 1940–41. Four Eritreans were killed.[1]

The UP accused the BMA of undue provocation; the Separatists, however, through their articulate spokesman Woldeab Wolde Mariam, interpreted the July incident as a matter of law and order, where the British officers were commended for their prompt action against looting that had accompanied the incident. The British themselves assessed the incident as a show of force where they were able to assert their position as an administering authority.

Relations between the BMA and the UP, already shaken by the incidents of July, deteriorated further. The close interaction between the Sudanese Defence Force (SDF), instruments of British power, and the adherents of the UP made some sort of conflict unavoidable. The SDF soldiers, although ethnically distinguishable, were dependent for food supplies and leisure on what was available in the native quarters of Asmara. A minor incident was sufficient to spark off a conflagration; and this occurred on August 28, 1946 when three Sudanese soldiers were assaulted and one of them was stoned to death. A few hours later, a fully armed company of about 70 SDF soldiers marched into the streets of the Eritrean quarters of the city and shot wantonly leaving behind 46 killed and 60 wounded.

The BMA was accused of giving the SDF a free hand in settling accounts with the Eritreans. The UP and the Separatists pointed out the BMA's negligence in the matter of Eritrean lives. Both Eritrean groups asked the chief military administrator why the British officers did not take prompt action to protect Eritrean lives in the same way they had done a month earlier when Arab lives and property were at stake (EWN, 5.9.46). Apart from a repeated statement that the BMA was deeply saddened by the August massacre, they made no satisfactory reply to the allegations.

The BMA's connivance or manifest negligence could hardly be denied. There has been, however, some speculation as to the motives (Gebre-Medhin, 1989; Tseggai, 1988). Fortunately for the BMA, barely a month after the August massacre, the Council of Ministers of the Four Powers came to an agreement that Italy would renounce its rights and that they would decide the future of the former colonies after ascertaining the wishes of their inhabitants. Meanwhile the immediate withdrawal of the SDF from Eritrea, which was a fulfilment of UP

---

[1] The demonstration was peaceful. The arrest of the leaders while the demonstration was in progress turned it into mob violence. For a detailed report see, FO371/53511, from the Middle East Forces to the War Office, August 1, 1946.

and Separatists demands, normalized the political climate, although the UP remained suspicious of British intentions up to the end of 1948.

Relations between the UP and the British were no doubt affected by the Anglo-Ethiopian Treaty of 1944 as well as the British commitment to carefully consider Ethiopian claims over Eritrea. Although the 1944 treaty gave Britain a dominant position in Ethiopia, the British did not consider themselves bound to defend Ethiopian claims. Their policy regarding the disposal of Eritrea was based primarily on their appreciation of the local realities, rather than on their commitment to Ethiopia. Nor did the Ethiopian government rely entirely on British support. From the Ethiopian side there was full awareness that the British might not provide key support and that consequently, Ethiopia might suffer rejection of its claims over Eritrea altogether.

On August 13, 1948 the British finally made known their views on the fate of Eritrea. They proposed that Ethiopia should be the administering authority in Eritrea for a period of ten years. At the end of ten years, the British proposed that the General Assembly of the United Nations should decide whether, and if so under what conditions, Ethiopian administration would continue indefinitely. The UK proposal was indeed a major modification of the series of reports despatched to London from the BMA in Eritrea. The British proposal ran counter to those put forward by the remaining three powers.[1] Therefore, as earlier agreed among the Four Powers, the matter was referred to the General Assembly of the United Nations for a final solution in the middle of September of 1948.

In Eritrea, the British position on the future of the country gave substantial support to the UP's campaign. As a look at the UP's weekly newspaper shows, the UP found an additional argument for the justness of its cause. Although the UP tried to improve its relations with the BMA, the latter continued to harass the UP. As late as July 1948, the BMA jailed the president of the UP and the

---

[1] FO371/69355, Council of Foreign Ministers (Deputies), Former Italian Colonies. Statement by the United States on the Disposition of Eritrea, Lancaster House, August 14, 1948.

"The United States favours the cession to Ethiopia of the southern section of Eritrea (including the Danakil Coast, and the districts of Acchele Guzai and Serae, the new frontier to start at the Gulf of Zula, following the northern borders of Acchele Guzai and Serae districts to the Ethiopian frontier). The United States also favours a postponement of the decision regarding the northern and predominantly Moslem portion of Eritrea, including Asmara and Massawa.

Due to the inherent difficulty of the problem and the divergence of views among the countries participating in the Commission of Investigation and among the governments which have presented views to the Deputies, the United States therefore proposes that the Foreign Ministers recommend to the General Assembly that it study the problem of Northern Eritrea for one year, before attempting to come to a definitive solution."

The French proposed: "With the exception of the territories situated between the Gulf of Zula and the Frech Coast of Somaliland, Eritrea will be placed under the trusteeship of Italy. The territories situated between the Gulf of Zula and the French Coast of Somaliland shall be assigned to Ethiopia with full sovereign powers."

The Soviet Union proposed that "Eritrea will be accorded the same treatment as in the case of Libya (independence) and the formation of a democratic administration composed of representatives of the local population will be guaranteed, the Advisory Committee in this case, however, to include two residents of Eritrea appointed by five governments. There will, however, be a territorial cession in favour of Ethiopia which will give Ethiopia access to the sea through the port of Assab".

editor of the Ethiopia Weekly and sentenced them to imprisonment conditional on good behaviour.[1] The reason was a speech delivered by the president of the UP on the occasion of the celebration of the birthday of the Emperor of Ethiopia. In spite of the BMA's contempt for the UP, relations between the UP and the BMA improved greatly; and later British policy declarations at the General Assembly were to further strengthen the bond.

THE UP AND OTHER POLITICAL PARTIES

Although the Paris Peace Treaty between Italy and the Four Powers was signed in February 1947, its general outline was known at least six months earlier. Italy was to renounce all its rights over its former colonies; the fate of the colonies was to be decided by the Council of Foreign Ministers of the Four Powers "in the light of the wishes and welfare of the inhabitants and the interests of peace and security". It was, therefore, agreed that the Deputies of the Foreign Ministers "send out a commission of investigation in order to supply the Deputies with the necessary data on this question and to ascertain the views of the local population".

During the month of October, Brigadier General Benoy, the military administrator, toured the country with the purpose of informing the Eritrean people that they should prepare themselves to make known their views to the Four Power Commission of Enquiry. Since, however, both the UP and the Separatists were already active, the brigadier's main task was to bring about a similar organization among Eritrean Moslems. According to the political intelligence reports, Brigadier General Benoy appeared to have made a strong impression and convinced Eritrean Moslems that "unless they are prepared to think for themselves, the Plateau Christians will do the thinking for them".[2]

During January and February 1947, the UP, the Separatists (henceforth known as the Liberal Progressive Party, LPP) and the Moslem League (ML) were duly registered. The Pro-Italy Party was formed towards the end of the year barely a few weeks before the arrival of the Commission of Enquiry. The Pro-Italy Party was dominated by the Italo-Eritrean Association, a group made up of Italians as well as half-castes who were well established in Eritrea.

With the exception of the UP, the political parties made little use of EWN (Eritrean Weekly News) to canvas political support, giving a strong impression that they were formed for the express purpose of making their views known to the Commission of Enquiry. Between February 1947 and February 1948, EWN contained a total of six articles advocating the views of LLP and ML, and 27 pro-unionist articles. This is in spite of the fact that the EWN was managed by one of the founders of the LPP. Among the many pro-UP contributors to the EWN,

---

[1] FO371/73841, BMA to FO, Asmara, 16.9.1948. The speech, a translated copy of which was sent to London, could hardly be said to have been provocative.

[2] FO371/63212. Eritrea: MPR, no.13 for January, 1947.

it should perhaps be noted that a considerable majority of the best reasoned articles were written by those who had a long training in the Catholic Theological Institutions. Two examples were Dr. Abba Hailu Gebreyesus and Abba Yacob Gebreyesus whose knowledge of the Tigrinya language and history was extensive.

The arrival of the FPC (The Four Powers Commission of Enquiry) in Eritrea in November 1947 signalled a climax to political agitation where the UP and the ML were the two main contestants. The LPP and the Pro-Italy party were of less significance, although the latter was to develop into a major threat to the UP toward the end of 1949. After a sojourn of about eight weeks, the FPC left Eritrea with detailed interviews and depositions of all political parties. The FPC also collected a huge amount of data (mostly provided by the BMA) on the social, economic and political conditions in the country.

Our knowledge concerning the political programmes of the parties and the extent of their support is derived firstly from the material compiled by the FPC, and secondly from the results of the first election for the Eritrean Constituent Assembly carried out in July 1952. According to the FPC, the UP was by far dominant over the others mobilising behind it about 48 per cent of the population.[1] The second largest party, the Moslem League was a highly fragmented organization whose programme varied from independence to union with the Sudan. The Liberal Progressive Party, campaigned for the establishment of a Tigrean state (encompassing all Tigrinya speaking peoples in Eritrea and Ethiopia) had the support of about 9 per cent of the population.[2] Finally, the Pro-Italy Party openly advocated the return of Italian rule and was, according to the assessment of the FPC, supported by about ten per cent of the population. With the exception of the UP, the other three major parties were to pass through a series of internal crises from which some of them hardly survived.

Whereas the UP continued to use the EWN and the Ethiopia Weekly to keep intact its base of support and for purposes of recruitment, the other parties, presumably satisfied by their performance, virtually ceased to make use of the EWN. It was not until mid-1949 when the partition of Eritrea had majority support at the United Nations that the other political parties began to be reactivated. During April, 1949, the UN agreed to vote on a disposal plan presented to it by the British and Italian Foreign Ministers. Known as the Bevin-Sforza deal, the plan had three components, i.e. Libya, Somalia and Eritrea. According to this deal, Eritrea was to be partitioned some of it going to Ethiopia and the western province to be incorporated in the Sudan. Voting on the components of

---

[1] The FPC Commission of enquiry followed two methods in ascertaining the wishes of the population. First, it interviewed political leaders and received petitions. Second, it interviewed traditionally elected representatives altogether 3,336 individuals. On such basis, the FPC stated that the Moslem League had the support of 30.9 percent, while the Pro-Italy and the Liberal Progressive Parties had 10.7 and 9.3 percent support respectively. Though these figures need to be taken literally, they are very useful as indicators of the political climate of the period.

[2] The name Liberal Progressive Party was given to it by the BMA. For its members it was known as the *Eritrea for Eritreans Party*.

the deal, the UN voted on May 15, 1949 in favour of the plan whereby Eritrea was to be partitioned: the Tigrean parts including Massawa and Assab to be united with Ethiopia. The Bevin-Sforza deal on the Western province was, however, rejected.[1] Partition would have taken place according to the map compiled by the BMA and the UN (see map on page 8). However, since the other component parts were voted down, the entire Bevin-Sforza package was rejected.

The question of how to dispose of Eritrea was postponed to the fourth regular session of the General Assembly due to meet towards the end of the year. Against strong protests from Great Britain and Ethiopia, the United Nations resolved to send yet another Commission of Enquiry to Eritrea before the final resolution of the Eritrean question. The United Nations Commission of Enquiry, made up of Burma, Pakistan, Guatemala, South Africa and Norway, was given wide latitude and six months to submit its reports.[2]

The party that the UP considered most threatening was first the LPP (up to June 1949) and later the Independence Bloc from summer 1949 to June 1950. The Liberal Progressive Party (LPP) traces its origin to the Separatist Movement that was formed with the connivance of the BMA. The LPP advocated a ten year United Kingdom trusteeship to be followed by independence of a united Tigrai.

---

[1] Year Book of the United Nations for 1948–49, p. 260. The Bevin-Sforza proposal was voted upon in three parts. The first paragraph, which provided that the territory, except for the western province, be incorporated into Ethiopia with appropriate municipal charters for the cities of Asmara and Massawa, was adopted by 36 votes to 6, with 15 abstentions. The second paragraph, which called for the incorporation of the western province in the adjacent Sudan, was rejected by 19 votes to 16, with 21 abstentions.

[2] The United Nations resolution (289(IVA) was passed on 21 November 1949. The relevant parts dealing with Eritrea:
"1. That a commission consisting of representatives of not more than five member states, as follows, Burma, Guatemala, Norway, Pakistan and the Union of South Africa, shall be established to ascertain more fully the wishes and the best means of promoting the welfare of the inhabitants of Eritrea, to examine the question of the disposal of Eritrea and to prepare a report for the General Assembly, together with such proposal or proposals as it may deem appropriate for the solution of the problem of Eritrea;
2. That in carrying out its responsibilities the Commission shall ascertain all the relevant facts, including written or oral information from the present administering Power, from representatives of the population of the territory, including minorities, from Governments and such organizations and individuals as it may deem necessary. In particular, the Commission shall take into account :
(a) The wishes and welfare of the inhabitants of Eritrea, including the views of the various racial, religious and political groups of the provinces of the territory and the capacity of the people for self-government;
(b) The interests of peace and security in East Africa;
(c) The rights and claims of Ethiopia based on geographical, historical, ethnic or economic reasons, including in particular Ethiopia's legitimate need for adequate access to the sea;
3. That in considering its proposals the Commission shall take into account the various suggestions for the disposal of Eritrea submitted during the fourth regular session of the General Assembly;
4. That the Commission shall assemble at the Headquarters of the United Nations as soon as possible. It shall travel to Eritrea and may visit such other places as in its judgement may be necessary in carrying out its responsibilities. The Commission shall adopt its own rules of procedure. Its report and proposal or proposals shall be communicated to the Secretary-General not later than 15 June 1950 for distribution to member states so as to enable final consideration during the fifth regular session of the General Assembly".

The LPP's sphere of influence remained limited to a very small area in Akele Guzai and to some individuals in Asmara, the most prominent of whom was Woldeab Wolde Mariam, the chief editor of the EWN. The LPP was the party most favoured both by the British and the FPC for its explicit recognition of the British contributions in Eritrea and for its willingness to entertain a long period of Western trusteeship.

Although the Separatists, (known as LPP or as the Party of Eritrea for Eritreans) were not, as late as October 1946, against conditional union with Ethiopia, their later attempts to justify their platform for the independence of Eritrea elicited strong reactions from the UP. Most of the articles that were submitted to the EWN and those published in the UP's weekly up to mid-1949 were against the explicit or implicit assumptions of the LPP. The UP evolved two strategies to contain the LPP threat. Firstly, it identified its own cause with religious fundamentalism, thus making full use of the Ethiopian Orthodox Church and its networks. Here it is not being argued that the UP consciously evolved a more fundamentalist line. The close connection between church and state can be traced both to the Italian colonial state in Eritrea, as well as to the newly reconstituted state in Ethiopia. What is being argued here is that the leadership of the UP was permeated with deeply religious people belonging to different denominations.

Unconditional union with Ethiopia was presented as a fulfilment of the enduring desire of the Eritrean people—an objective in the process of being realized through "the Will, the Mercy and the Compassion of the Almighty". The UP appealed to its supporters to strengthen their religious commitment as a guarantee. Virtually every other week, the Ethiopia Weekly contained a new supplicatory prayer (for recital by each one of the faithful) asking for the intercession of the Almighty in the fulfilment of their desire, namely, the reunion of Eritrea with Ethiopia. For the UP, the fate of Eritrea in general and that of the highlands in particular, lay in the hands of God. The Almighty had several names: the Holy Trinity, the God of Israel, the God of Ethiopia etc. The coming to power of Tefferi Mekonnen who assumed the throne name of Haile Selassie (by the power of the Holy Trinity), was referred to as additional evidence of the proximity of liberation and independence.

The UP's crowning success against the LPP lay, however, in its ability to create common ground with the Catholic and Evangelical Churches in Eritrea. The UP, it can be said, functioned as an executive committee carrying out the wishes of the Eritrean religious denominations. While the UP's close affiliation with the churches greatly circumscribed LPP's room for manoeuvre, the Ethiopian Orthodox Church provided additional assistance to UP by threatening active LPP followers with excommunication. Apart from the account of Trevaskis, there is little information in the archives on the extent to which the Orthodox Church in Eritrea resorted to such threats, which was indeed a very strong measure. Although there is no reason to doubt the account of Trevaskis, it needs to be mentioned that this threat applied only to the few supporters of the LPP who adhered to the Orthodox faith. To the extent that the Orthodox Church actually resorted to such measure, it demonstrated the close links between state and church in Abyssinian (Ethiopian) society (cf. Tamrat, 1972).

The UP also extensively utilized a Youth League with the task of ensuring that members toed the party line. The members of the Youth League, who were the most uncompromising in their position of unconditional union, were engaged in persuading members to leave the LPP and at times may have even resorted to harassment. The main target of the Youth League was, however, the continued presence of Italians whose economic and political power was securely protected by the BMA.

Soon after the departure of the FPC, the LPP declined due to internal splits. Its articulate leader Woldeab Wolde Mariam left it to join a new group called the Association of Eritrean Intellectuals, presumably after repeated criticism from UP circles questioning his Eritrean background.[1] A new splinter group that advocated conditional union and known as the Eritrean Independent Democratic Party came into existence. The name LPP and its founding president, however, remained in current use. The Independence Bloc that was established in June 1949 was to include the LPP (as it had existed in 1947) among the organizations in the coalition.

Another party that tended to challenge UP's dominant position was the New Eritrea Pro-Italy Party which was established a few weeks before the arrival of FPC in November 1947. The Pro-Italy Party had first come into existence in early 1947 as an interest organization known by the name of the Eritrean War Veterans Association. The formation of the Association could, in turn, be directly linked to a declaration that Italy would settle claims due to its ex-colonial soldiers. The Pro-Italy Party was not a major threat, partly because there was little interest among the core members of the UP for the Italian proposal and partly due to the fact that the overwhelming majority of the members were Moslems.

Surprisingly enough the UP did not consider as a threat the Moslem League which during the presence of the FPC (November 1947–January 1948) may have embraced up to 30 per cent of the entire population. For the UP, the ML was an organization with several internal divisions and contradictions. Whereas the ML was exclusively Moslem, the UP had many Moslems in its leadership as well as in its rank and file. Since neither the Church nor the Youth League of the UP could be mobilized to bring pressure on the ML, it was left virtually free to pursue its political activities. Moreover, there was a belief that was made known by mid-1949 that the predominantly Moslem inhabited regions of Eritrea could opt either for separation, independence or incorporation into the Sudan.[2] In

---

[1] WWM was not a native Eritrean.

[2] In May 1949 soon after the Bevin-Sforza proposals were made known, both the UP and the Ethiopian government accepted the partition of Eritrea, thereby recognizing as well as respecting a separate solution to the Western Province—the region inhabited by predominantly Moslem communities. See Year Book of the United Nations for 1949, p. 270.

contrast to the ML which throughout the 1947–48 period advocated the independence of Eritrea under its hegemonic leadership, the UP recognized implicitly the right of the Moslem inhabitants of the lowland regions to either accept union together with the UP or opt for another solution. During this formative period what the UP found unimaginable was the concept of a free and independent Eritrea. However, the UP was sufficiently confident that the independence option was completely ruled out. For the UP independence meant the union of Eritrea with Ethiopia (EWN, 9.1.47; Ethiopia Weekly, 28.8.49).

The real threat to the UP was the Independence Bloc that surfaced in July 1949 a few weeks after the demise of the Bevin-Sforza plan. Fully supported by Italy, the Bevin-Sforza plan had the intention of partitioning Eritrea into two. According to the draft proposal presented to the United Nations, "Eritrea, except for the Western Province, is to be incorporated into Ethiopia under terms and conditions which would include the provision of appropriate guarantees for the protection of minorities and, without prejudice to the sovereignty of Ethiopia, appropriate municipal charters for the cities of Asmara and Massawa".[1] The Western Province was to be incorporated into the adjacent Sudan. As pointed out earlier, the United Nations voted in favour of a part of the Bevin-Sforza proposal, but it was later rejected. A point which is often forgotten is that Ethiopia voted for the Bevin-Sforza plan.[2] Although the May 15, 1949 resolution set the tone for future discussion on the question of disposal of the territory, the formation of the Independence Bloc was considered as a serious challenge. The reasons for the UP's concern were several and clear. For the first time, the ML, LPP, and the Pro-Italy Party formed a coalition and claimed the independence of Eritrea. There appeared to be a qualitative development in the process. The demand of the new Bloc, formed in New York and fully supported by Italy, which after the demise of the Bevin-Sforza plan immediately began to campaign for the independence of Eritrea, created considerable discussion at the United Nations.

The Independence Bloc had a brief but intensive existence (between June and November 1949), until it disintegrated through the UP's successful exposure of the bloc's internal contradictions. It was known that the Independence Bloc was managed by Italian residents and generously financed from Italian quarters including the Italian government. It was also known that the Pro-Italy Party as well as the Italo-Eritrean Association had a long history of wanting the return of Italy. Another additional factor in the evolution of UP's anti-bloc strategy was the underlying frustration created by the long drawn out process of the disposal of the fate of Eritrea. Consequently the UP evolved and implemented three strategies. The first was to show that independence meant the return of Italy and colonial rule. The pro-Italian sympathies of the leaders of the Indepen-

---

[1] Year Book of the United Nations for 1948–49, p. 260.

[2] Spencer, 1983:, 211. This was consistent with earlier and later policy orientation. The foundation of Ethiopian foreign policy at the period was the acquisition of an outlet to the sea. The most preferable solution was through Massawa and Assab thus controlling the Eritrean highlands.

dence Bloc, Signior Luigi Casciani and Signior Alberto Pollera were repeatedly mentioned as evidence. The second strategy was the tightening of the loyalty of the UP members through the increased activities of the Youth League and the introduction of the oath of loyalty.[1] The third and quite crucial strategy was the demonstration of UP's readiness to resist any form of independence by force. According to the UP, the goal of the Bloc would either lead to Italian recolonization or to total chaos (*Ethiopia Weekly*, nos. 125–27, September 1949).

It was clear for the BMA that the intensification of banditry and political terrorism (generally known as *shifta*) was provoked by the heavy backing of the Italian government and the Italian community in Eritrea. The Italians had two organizations. The first organization embraced all the Italians under an organizational umbrella known as *Comitato rappresentativo degli italiani dell'Eritrea* (CRIE). Established in the first months of 1947 CRIE set out to make use of the freedom of association which the BMA initiated in order to allow the Eritreans a say in their future. CRIE was led officially by Vincenzo Di Meglio. Its prominent members were quite well known businessmen such as Luigi Casciani, Guido De Rossi and Alberto Pollera. CRIE claimed that they represented the ca. 20,000 Italian residents in Eritrea. A few weeks after it was formed CRIE managed to mobilise the ca. 15,000 half-castes and those native Eritreans who were connected with Italy into a semi-political organization which came to be known as the Italo-Eritrean Association. At the same time as CRIE and the Italo-Eritrean Association were agitating openly, the Italian community created in July 1947 a secret committee known as *Comitato di azione segreta* (CAS) with the explicit purpose of secretly financing and coordinating the activities of CRIE and the Italo-Eritrean Association.[2]

According to the BMA, funds originating from Italy were given "to the ordinary man in the street or peasant taking in exchange that person's Unionist Party card".[3] Until the formal establishment of an Italian diplomatic mission in

---

[1]   Ethiopia Weekly, no. 148 (4.12.49). The oath of loyalty was produced by the leaders and elders of Hammasien (the most central region encompassing Asmara). The oath forbade its members from entering into any kind of contact with the adherents of the Bloc. Specifically, UP members were forbidden to intermarry with the Bloc people and the members of UP were to abstain from taking part in any burial or funeral arrangements. As stated in the preamble the oath of loyalty was taken on the eve of the visit of the UN Commission of Enquiry.

[2]   The Italian Ministry of Colonies believed that it had the majority of the Eritrean people behind it. In May 1947, the Minister of Colonies wrote a long memo to the Ministers of Foreign Affairs, Finance, and External Commerce stressing one point. The Minister asked his colleagues to provide him with the required funds to assist Italian organizations and to encourage those indigenous movements favourable to Italy. The movements he referred to were the Moslem League and the Liberal Progressive Party. See ASMAI, Affari Politici, Direzione Generale, pacco 65, fascicolo 97, May 29, 1947. For information on on the Italian community in Eritrea, I am grateful to Del Boca (1984:126–7).

[3]   FO371/73789, Chief Administrator Drew to the Foreign Office, Asmara, November 17, 1949. Drew further wrote that the Italians distributed food and clothing under the guise of charitable assistance for which every recipient signed. A list containing such signatures was to be produced to a visiting Commission to prove supporters. Noting that there was no lack of recipients for any money that was offered, owing to the difficult economic situation, Drew concluded that the Unionists resented the Italian campaign fiercely.

Eritrea in 1949, Rome channelled its funds to pro-Italian organizations through CRIE and CAS. The Italian government in Rome and the Italian community in Eritrea were pumping in something in the range of 100,000 East African shillings monthly in order to keep the pro-Italian organizations afloat (Del Boca, 1984:134). Addressing a delegation from the Italian community, the chief administrator wrote:

> We have to realise that large numbers of the Coptic population on the plateau consider they want union with Ethiopia and there is also no doubt that they view with great suspicion the Italian government openly backing the Independence Bloc, both in this country and in the international field. They resent it and that leads undoubtedly to the anti-Italian activities and acts of terrorism. You must realise that large numbers of Eritreans do not appreciate the benefits bestowed on them by the Italian government even though this means many of them might actually not have been born. They resent the Italian presence here and that attitude is not confined to Copts; similar views are widely held by other communities, Moslems for instance, they are resentful of any return of an Italian regime in the territory. I believe both Copts and a proportion of the Moslems regard the independence movement as a manoeuvre on the part of the Italians to retain their hold on the country. It is obvious that in the event of independence the Italians would necessarily have the main say in the running of the country. For this reason the Coptic communities and some of the Moslems view postponement and the coming Commission as an attempt to restore the Italian regime. As I see it that is the political background and in these circumstances you must expect trouble.... I appreciate your difficulties but the fact of distributing money for propaganda purposes is viewed as something to provoke and bring trouble.[1]

Rome relied heavily on the Italian community in Eritrea to pursue its changing policies there. Between September 1947 when the Italian government began financing the activities of CRIE and CAS and the formal dissolution of CRIE in 1951, Rome pursued three widely divergent policies on Eritrea. Between 1947 and May 1949, Italy attempted to persuade the Allies that Eritrea should remain under Italian trusteeship. This policy was developed in early September of 1947. A couple of months later, the Italian community in Eritrea (CRIE and CAS), moving at a remarkable speed, were able to transform a voluntary ex-Italian colonial soldiers' association into a fully fledged political party known as New Eritrea Pro-Italy Party with the explicit programme of the return of Italy as a trustee (Del Boca, 1984:129). Not fully convinced about the capacity of CRIE and CAS to perform the job, the Italian Ministry of Colonies despatched a one man mission. Luigi Talamonti, a respected district officer in Eritrea since the beginning of the century, was despatched to win over Eritreans who had fallen victim to the machinations of either the UP or the British Administration. According to the records consulted by Angelo Del Boca, Talamonti had no shortage of funds; his mission is reputed to have cost over three million shillings (Del Boca, 1984:135). This was indeed a lot of money in relation to the total revenue of Eritrea for 1947 which was in the range of 30 million shillings.[2]

---

[1] FO371/73790, Asmara, December 6, 1949, Drew to the Foreign Office, London. The Italian community did not challenge the presentation of the facts by Drew.

[2] WO230/260. Memo on municipal taxation, 25.2.1946.

In the first half of 1949, the Italian government, virtually sacrificing Eritrea for the more strategic colony of Libya, agreed with the old British plan of partitioning the colony into two halves where the western half inhabited by Moslems would go the Anglo-Egyptian Sudan and the remaining part would go to Ethiopia. Fortunately for the Italian community, this "treasonable" policy did not last long.[1] Hatched in April the plan to divide Eritrea (also known as the Bevin-Sforza package) was dead by the end of May. The third policy and that which led to the intensification of terrorist (*shifta*) activity was the one developed in early June of 1949 in the aftermath of the rejection of the Bevin-Sforza package.

Soon after it became known that the UN had rejected the plan for the partition of Eritrea, the Italian government, set immediately into action the policy of campaigning for the complete and immediate independence of Eritrea. The representatives of the Eritrean Political Parties, namely, the ML, the LPP, the Pro-Italy, the Italo-Eritrean were brought together by Italian diplomats in New York where the idea of a coalition bloc was discussed.

The Independence Bloc—made up of eight political cum professional organizations— appeared impressive both on paper and in front of the United Nations owing to the considerable influence that Italy enjoyed there.[2] In Eritrea, however, the basis of the Bloc was indeed shallow. The Independence Bloc was formally established on July 25, 1949. By the end of October 1949, the chief administrator, reporting to London, wrote that in contrast to the Unionist Party the Independence Bloc appeared lifeless and artificial. He believed that the Independent Bloc deputies were "obviously got together by the Italians and half-castes and a noticeable thing was that Italian was the language used by the delegates".[3]

Unlike the Pro-Italy Party, the ML and LPP had greatly changed from what they were in 1947–48. The ML was in the midst of an organizational and ideological crisis when the religious leader of all Moslem Communities in Eritrea, Said Baker el Morgani abandoned it and joined the UP.[4] Although Said Baker el Morgani's ditching of the ML caught the BMA by surprise, the latter attempted to belittle the damage to its assessment of Eritrea and the ML. The UP, fully appreciating the rift within the ML, conducted its campaign accordingly. In the early months of 1949, the ML was reduced to about half of the size it was during the presence of the FPC. Soon after the official British view on the fate of Eritrea

---

[1] The Bevin-Sforza package was worked out by the anti-fascist minister of Foreign Affairs, while the Ministry of Colonies which was not dissolved until 1953, remained convinced about winning back Eritrea. For further details see, Del Boca (1984:136).

[2] The Independence Bloc was made up of the following parties and organizations: i) Moslem League, ii) Liberal Progressive, iii) New Eritrea Pro-Italy, iv) Italo-Eritrean Association, v) War Veterans Assocation, vi) Association of Intellectuals, vii) National Party, and viii) Independent Eritrea Party. Report of the UN Commission for Eritrea, 1950: 29.

[3] FO371/73788, Drew to the Foreign Office, telegram no. 184, Asmara, 27.10.1949.

[4] FO371/73841, BMA to the Foreign Office, Asmara, 6.11.1948. Informing the Secretary for Foreign Affairs, the Civil Affairs Officer Mr. R.W.Mason concentrated on Said Baker el Morgani as a man of straw whose political views were valueless. Mason was either not interested in or not capableof seeing the rejection of the goals of the ML by its president as profoundly serious.

became known, the LPP split into two, one splinter group campaigning for a conditional union with Ethiopia.

By the time the United Nations resolved (November 21, 1949) to send its own Commission of Enquiry to Eritrea, the ML had not only lost its religious leader but also lost about half of its membership to a splinter group known as the ML of the Western Province which demanded the incorporation of the Western Province into the Sudan. The ML as it had existed in 1947–48 had become history. Trevaskis has argued that the ML's troubles were due to the mistaken policies of its leader, Mr. Ibrahim Sultan, who pushed the party into a coalition with other parties and organizations known to favour either the return of Italy or close cooperation with it. What Trevaskis was not keen to add was the role of the UP's organ in pointing out the real or imagined consequences of an independent Eritrea led by Italy and the Italians in Eritrea. The articles that appeared in the UP's weekly from June to September 1949 appealed to the rank and file ML members who appeared likely to lose more in an Eritrea led by the Independence Bloc. The UP articles showed the contradictions between the pro-Italian position of its leader Mr. Ibrahim Sultan and the majority of the members whose memory of Italy was not that positive. Nor did Trevaskis assess fully the impact of the withdrawal of the support of Said Baker el Morgani.

By February 1950 when the United Nations Commission of Enquiry arrived in Eritrea, they were met by an even more consolidated UP and several other opposition parties with varying objectives. There were three types of political parties. There were those who favoured independence, campaigning under the greatly weakened Independence Bloc. There was the ML of the Western Province which was established towards the end of 1949. And finally, there were the parties which favoured union with Ethiopia.[1] On paper the parties favouring independence were twice as many as those campaigning for union. The Independence Bloc was made up of the following organizations. The first was the remaining faction of the ML after the defection of Said Baker el Morgani and the breaking away of the faction representing the Western Province. If we assume that the ML had in 1947 a support of ca. 30 per cent of the entire population, this support was reduced at least by half by early 1950.[2] The second organization favouring independence was the Liberal Progressive Party, which also experienced internal crises and splits between 1947 and 1949. In 1947 the Liberal Progressive Party was estimated to gain support of about 9 per cent of the votes.[3] The third organization which barely survived the arrival of the UN Commission of Enquiry was the New Eritrea Party. Formerly, known as the New Eritrea Pro-

---

[1] Report of the United Nations Commission for Eritrea, 1950, p. 29.

[2] The first elections to the Constituent Assembly confirmed the weakened position of the Independence Bloc and the ML. The election results showed that the Independence Bloc and ML got 18 seats out of 68.

[3] In the elections of 1952, the LPP won one seat only.

Italy Party, it was reputed to be supported by about ten per cent of the population.[1] The fourth organization, more an instrument of Italian policies than a political party, was the Italo-Eritrean Association. Composed of prominent Italians, half-castes and their relatives, the Association was most vocal and influential; it was the inspiring body behind the Independence Bloc as well as the main source of finance (Del Boca, 1984).

The fifth organization was the War Veterans Association whose main interest lay in safeguarding the financial interests of the former colonial soldiers. Organized and funded by the Italo-Eritrean Association, the usefulness of the Veterans Association was to impress the UN Commission of Enquiry of the width and depth of the Independence Bloc. Another interest group which very much resembled the Veterans Association was the Intellectual Party, also known as the Association of Eritrean Intellectuals.[2] Finally, there were two very small parties known as the National Party with its headquarters at Massawa and the Independent Eritrea Party.

Enriched by earlier experience, and strengthened by additional membership from the Moslem communities, the UP showed more confidence in 1950 than during the earlier period. According to John Spencer, the main motive behind the UN Commission of Enquiry was to diminish the impact of the Report of the Four Power Commission where the UP came out as the largest and best organised party in the country. The four members of the UN Commission of Enquiry, with the exception of Norway, had opposed the return of Eritrea to Ethiopia (Spencer, 1983:217). Writing in the early 1980s, long after he had left service as Imperial Ethiopian legal advisor, John Spencer, wrote that it was remarkable that the majority of the UN Commission could come out with proposals for federation or union rather than for independence, as had been intended (Spencer, 1983:232; Amar, 1992:87; Araya, 1990). Moreover, according to the study of Amare Tekle Ethiopian intervention at the UN was clumsy, poorly coordinated and without effect (Tekle, 1964:173–180).

THE UP AND ITS ETHIOPIAN CONNECTIONS

As early as 1940, Emperor Haile Selassie had made known his commitment to the reunification of Eritrea with Ethiopia. His messages resulted in the formation of the UP in the spring of 1941. It would, however, be wrong to accuse either the Emperor or his country of "expansionist ambitions". In 1940–41, it could be said that the Emperor was virtually surrounded by Eritrean loyalists. About half of the first Imperial Army of 1,500 men, organized from the Ethiopian refugees in Kenya and the Sudan, was made up of Eritreans (Steer, 1942:26; Pankhurst, 1969:102). His Secretary for Foreign Affairs during the era of exile and the

---

[1] The New Eritrea Party failed to win a seat at the 1952 elections for the Eritrean Assembly.

[2] By 1950 there was no Eritrean with a university degree. The exceptions were those Eritreans who joined the Catholic religious orders; these were without exception pro-Union.

person who laid down the foundation of Ethiopian policy on Eritrea was the versatile Eritrean Lorenzo Taezaz. The Eritreans in Ethiopia, who by 1944 numbered as many as 100,000, treated themselves as Ethiopian subjects. It would have been highly irresponsible, if not outright treason, had the Emperor not claimed Eritrea as part of Ethiopia.

From 1941 up to the end of the Second World War in 1945, Ethiopian initiative was limited to the formation of the Eritrean-Ethiopian Association for the purpose of the reunification of Eritrea with Ethiopia. This occurred in 1944. The Association began its activities by issuing a weekly newspaper, first called The Voice of Hamassien and later changed to The Voice of Eritrea. In Eritrea, the UP continued to pray as well as agitate for a speedy reunion of Eritrea with the motherland.

The Ethiopian position on Eritrea was first seriously put forward in connection with the Foreign Ministers Conference (of the Allied Powers and seventeen other countries who fought against the Axis Powers) in Paris in the summer of 1945. In a series of memoranda, the Ethiopian government presented historical claims to Eritrea. Apart from a vague recognition of Ethiopian legitimate claims to access to a sea port, the foreign ministers wrangled among themselves as to who ought to administer the former Italian colonies (Perham, 1948:439). In the international climate of the period, Ethiopian claims appeared to have little chance of even being considered, let alone met. The situation improved in the following spring (1946) when Great Britain proposed, through its Minister of Foreign Affairs the honourable Mr. Bevin, that "a greater part of Eritrea be awarded to Ethiopia" (Perham, 1948:439). In Eritrea, since the end of the war meant the winding down of the BMA, the Ethiopian government managed to negotiate the opening of a consular office in March 1946. The office was headed by Colonel Negga Haile Selassie.

The Peace Treaty Conference came to a conclusion in October 1946, although it was not signed until February of the following year. Italy renounced all rights to her former colonies whose futures were to be decided within a year after a Four Power Commission of Enquiry had ascertained the wishes of the inhabitants. Supported by France, the Italian government's claim to trusteeship remained a strong possibility. The only note of hope that remained available for the Ethiopian government was Great Britain's concurrence on the "impressive desire of Ethiopia to incorporate in her territory at any rate a large part of Eritrea" on historical and ethnic grounds (Perham, 1948:441).

The odds against Ethiopian claims at the peace conference were much greater than those against the Italian government's claim to Eritrea under the newly popularized form of trusteeship. The Soviet Union, France and the United States had rejected Ethiopian claims. The cautious support that the British put forward was part of a linkage strategy where in exchange Ethiopia would be asked to renounce its sovereignty over Ogaden (Spencer, 1983:176). Leaving aside the rhetoric of the Ethiopian government in favour of its claims, there was full awareness among Ethiopian officials that the Four Powers as well as the United Nations might fail to satisfy Ethiopian demands. Ethiopian leaders may have also judged that the British support might either shift or prove unsuccessful. The British, as we are able to learn, did not feel at all committed to assist Ethiopia regarding Eritrea.[1]

Notwithstanding the presence of the ca. 100,000 Eritrean subjects in Ethiopia and the sustained agitation of the UP for reunion, the Ethiopian government looked for an alternative strategy. During the 1945–50 period we discern three main priorities which we shall at present outline in the order of their importance. The first priority was access to the sea. The second was the incorporation of Eritrea on historical, economic and cultural grounds. The third priority, predicated on the failure of the second alternative, was the partition of Eritrea along the lines delineated by the British Administration.

Of utmost concern to Ethiopia was access to the sea. Although the future of Eritrea had finally come up for decision, and Ethiopia was one of the claimants, the Ethiopian government felt by no means sure of the outcome. As far as the archival sources shed some light on the foreign policy of Ethiopia, there was very little ambition to either grab, or swallow Eritrea. Ethiopia had survived without Eritrea for over half a century. In so far as one can speak of Ethiopian policy through the last few centuries, the occupation of the sea coast had not been an important strategy. What Ethiopia needed was an access for its trade needs and it had managed to negotiate such access with France and Italy. Suspicious of British support and uncertain of the outcome of the disposal of Eritrea, the Ethiopian government initiated secret negotiations with Great Britain to obtain a corridor to Zeila in exchange for a territorial concession in Ogaden (Spencer, 1983:177). Negotiations on the Ethiopian initiative were first started in January 1946 and kept floating until the end of 1948 when the international climate had suddenly changed considerably. In August 1948, on the basis of their fact finding mission, the Deputies of the Four Powers all agreed that some of the Eritrean highlands (with the exception of Massawa and Asmara) and the entire Danakil coastlands be incorporated into Ethiopia.

The decision of the Four Powers was undoubtedly encouraging news for Ethiopia whose claims on historical, ethnic and economic grounds were fully accepted. In view of the fact that France, the United States and the Soviet Union had earlier (1946) rejected Ethiopian claims, their change of policy after their fact

---

[1] In a reply to a letter from the Chiefs of Staff, the Secretary for Foreign Affairs Mr. Ernest Bevin wrote:
"The actual position is that we are waiting for the results of the Italian elections to decide whether we can fix on a future line of action. If the Popular Front wins or the result is nearly even I think we shall have to revise our whole policy. If, as we hope, the Communists are defeated, we shall take up the question again with the United States and try to obtain their help in persuading the French and the Italians that it is in all our interests that Great Britain should have the trusteeship of the whole of Libya. If we can do that we are (in accordance with the Cabinet decision) prepared to back a recommendation that Italy should be given her old colony in Somaliland in trusteeship, as well as that part of Eritrea that she developed and where an appreciable percentage of the population seem to welcome their return". FO371/69330, FO to the Right Honourable General A.V. Alexander, London, April 13, 1948, para. 6.

finding mission was noteworthy. The credit for bringing about such a substantial change must go to the UP's convincing political agitation.

Nonetheless, just at the period when the UP had succeeded in convincing the Four Powers of its irredentist position, some circles in the Ethiopian leadership were beginning to question the long term desirability of the incorporation of Eritrea into Ethiopia. The evidence available to prove the reluctance of the Ethiopian government in pushing its claims on Eritrea is derived through interviews and informal conversations. Although this type of source can be highly misleading, there is strong reason to believe that the intelligence gathered by the British diplomatic mission and the BMA on the attitudes of the Ethiopian government on Eritrea were indeed realistic. The intelligence report compiled by the BMA was derived essentially from the British Chargé d'Affaires Lassales Farquhar, the British Member of Parliament Tom McPherson who had business interests in Eritrea, and from a former Swedish minister in London Björn Prytz.[1] In view of the overwhelming, though unsubstantiated allegations of Ethiopian involvement in Eritrean affairs, a full reproduction of the intelligence report would be of benefit to readers.

> Intelligence. Ethiopian Claims to Eritrea and Somaliland. Asmara, March 30, 1948. Secret.[2]
>
> 1. When passing through here in December last, [1947] Mr. Farquhar told me that he thought that, whereas the Emperor [Haile Selassie] was still fanatical in pressing his claims to Eritrea, his responsible advisers and the more intelligent Ethiopians were beginning to realise that Eritrea would be a financial liability and that they were at least not more than lukewarm in pressing the claims of Ethiopia thereto.
>
> 2. In Addis Ababa on 22nd March, H.M. Chargé d'Affaires confirmed that the above was his impression with the important modification that he thought that even the Emperor was now resigned to not getting Eritrea. He was however determined to get a port: he would like Massawa but would probably be content with Assab.
>
> 3. It is significant that during my visit to Ato Aklilu [Ato Aklilu, the Ethiopian deputy foreign minister] on 22nd March, Mr. Weld Forester spoke openly of the possibility of a trusteeship for Eritrea. Contrary to my expectations there was no "come-back" of any kind from the Deputy Foreign Minister.
>
> 4. At Asmara on 28th March I met Mr. Pritz (sic) who was returning from a visit to African territories and has spent several days in Addis. Mr. Pritz was Swedish Minister in London from 1938 to 1947. He volunteered to me his very definite impression that the Ethiopian government did not want to press their claim to Eritrea, for two good reasons: first, because they realised that it would be an added financial liability to an already empty treasury; secondly, because it would make Ethiopia too big, would increase the existing centripetal tendencies, and would produce a real danger that Eritrea might make common cause with Tigre [the Ethiopian province of Tigrai] and split off from Ethiopia (from an impartial and experienced observer I regard this as significant).
>
> 5. At Asmara on 28th March, Mr. Tom McPherson, M.P., informed me that the

---

[1] Björn Prytz' knowledge of Ethiopia dates back to 1934 when he accompanied the Swedish Crown Prince on his visit to Ethiopia. Prytz was a businessman as well as a senior diplomat.

[2] FO371/69353, Chief Administrator Brigadier F.G. Drew to Chief Civil Affairs Officer, Middle East Forces, Asmara, March 30, 1948.

Emperor in a personal interview on 24th March had specifically informed him (Mr. McPherson) that if only he could obtain a port for Ethiopia he thought his work for his country would be complete: he very clearly implied that he did not expect to get either Eritrea or Somalia, and that he would probably be content with Assab.

A similar conclusion was reached by the Italians as early as July 1947. According to their intelligence report, Haile Sellassie was secretly against the campaign for acquiring Eritrea. His principal fear was that the incorporation of Eritrea would strengthen the Tigrean element in Ethiopia. He was afraid that a united Tigrai would rebel and eventually claim independence.[1] Other incidental evidence also substantiates the Ethiopian government's acceptance of a different fate for Eritrea. Emperor Haile Sellassie made a remark on the occasion of an audience given to a group of Ethiopian students on their way to Europe for further studies. Three of the eight students were of Eritrean origin one of whom was Dr. Bereket Habte Sellassie. Confirming his firm belief that sooner or later Eritrea would be reunited with its motherland, the Emperor further said that "whether Eritrea is united or not, there is nothing that separates it from Ethiopia" (Ethiopia Weekly, no.79, 31.10.48).

It needs to be remembered that Ethiopia had survived without her Red Sea ports since 1865. Moreover, throughout the colonial period Italian attempts to redirect Ethiopia's import and export routes from Djibouti could hardly be said to have been successful. Up to 80 per cent of Ethiopia's trade with the outside world was conducted via Djibouti. Another factor of considerable importance was the political and military crisis that the Ethiopian government faced throughout 1943 in the province of Tigrai, where Ethiopia felt compelled to ask for British Air Force intervention. The memory of the Tigrai insurrection remained too fresh.

However, by the end of 1947, the wishes of the Eritrean people where the UP and its supporters figured most, were to be given more consideration than Ethiopian claims. The decisive period occurred when the United Nations under the great influence of Italy resolved to send its own Commission of Enquiry to Eritrea. According to an eye witness report, members of the United Nations Commission of Enquiry, with the exception of Norway, were known for their pro-Italian positions (Spencer, 1983:217).

The United Nations Commission of Enquiry arrived in Eritrea in early 1950 and after a sojourn of about six weeks returned to New York to submit its reports. Two reports were presented. The majority report compiled by Burma, Norway and the Union of South Africa recommended that Eritrea be incorporated into Ethiopia. The minority report presented by Pakistan and Guatemala proposed that Eritrea be independent after a period of trusteeship. The UP was once again articulate enough to convince the majority of the members of the United Nations Commission of its commitment to reunion with Ethiopia (UN, 1950).

---

[1] ASMAE, Affari Politici, 1946–50, Ethiopia, busta 2, *Attegiamento del Negus nei confronti dell'Eritrea e della Somalia*, July, 12, 1947.

Under these circumstances, the United Nations adopted the most logical solution, i.e., to federate Eritrea as an autonomous entity under the Ethiopian Crown. Ethiopia ended up by incorporating all of Eritrea, when it would have been satisfied with the Eritrean highlands and the Danakil coast. Credit for the incorporation of Eritrea into the Ethiopian Empire, needs to be given to the UP—one of the most articulate and persistent anti-colonialist movements in Africa of the period. Since, however, this interpretation is in sharp contrast with the prevailing state of research it would be worthwhile, by way of conclusion, to put it into context.

THE UP AND ITS CRITICS

Critics of the UP resort to three sets of arguments, two of which may be directly traced to Trevaskis. The first set of arguments states that it was Ethiopian intrigues in Eritrea, through the notorious liaison officer Colonel Negga Haile Selassie, that influenced the opinion of the Commission of Enquiry in favour of the goals of the UP. The political armed violence that was widespread in Eritrea from 1947 to 1950, according to this view was directed and financed from Ethiopia. The second set of arguments questions the patriotism of the UP adherents and sweepingly condemns most of the UP members as a confused lot of people or as those who vacillated between Eritrean nationalism and the criminal position of adhering to the Greater Ethiopia tradition (Gebre-Medhin, 1989:80–81). Finally, the third set of arguments attempts to show that the UP was not as strong as it was in 1947 and that the Independence Bloc had the following of the majority of the Eritrean population.

There are at least two reasons for the prevalence of the Trevaskian legacy. The first one is the common understanding that Trevaskis had covered the period comprehensively, and, therefore, there was no need to go back to the colonial and other sources and re-examine the political climate of the 1940s. This is apparent too even among those who claim to re-evaluate the 1941–50 period such as Bereket Habte Sellassie, Jordan Gebre-Medhin, John Markakis and Lloyd Ellingson. The second reason, by far the most important, is that virtually all those who wrote on the period see a connection between the political climate of the 1940s and the war for independence led by the Eritrean liberation fronts in general and by the Eritrean Peoples Liberation Front (EPLF) in particular. The underlying logic of their research can be briefly outlined as follows. Since the Eritrean people led by the EPLF were waging an anti-colonial war, they could not have really belonged to the UP in the 1940s. The main structure of the writings of Jordan Gebre-Medhin and Bereket Habte Sellassie is built around this fallacious argumentation. Even if the first part of the argumentation i.e. that many Eritreans either willingly or under duress fought for the EPLF, may be accepted, the second part, i.e. that many Eritreans did not fully subscribe to the objectives of the UP, need not follow from the first. The reasons for the Eritreo-Ethiopian conflict (1961–1991) have to be sought in the changes that took place both in Eritrea and Ethiopia from the late 1950s onwards, rather than merely in the political climate of the 1940s.

Examined in the light of British and Eritrean sources, the evidence produced to substantiate the three sets of arguments is highly inadequate. Let us begin with the most persistent set of arguments, namely the role of Ethiopia in Eritrean affairs. The position of Ethiopia, repeatedly stated, was simple and clear. The Ethiopian government claimed Eritrea on historical, cultural, strategic and economic grounds. There was a considerable awareness of the strategic value of Eritrea as the gateway for the launching of foreign aggression. Ethiopian fear of foreign aggression, using Eritrea as a platform, was coupled with the claim for an outlet to the sea as a guaranteeing factor for the survival of the country. In 1948 the Four Powers accepted Ethiopian claims for an outlet to the sea as legitimate.

The economic reason for the incorporation of Eritrea into Ethiopia was grounded in the widespread appraisal of the period that the former would not survive economically if granted independence. Its dependence on Ethiopia for vital food imports was repeatedly stressed. This argument, by far the weakest, was first put forward by the BMA and only later picked up by the Ethiopian government.

The strongest argument remained that of the historical and cultural ties between the Eritrean highland regions and Ethiopia. The prominent position of Eritreans within the Ethiopian Ministry of Foreign Affairs, the ca. 2,000 Eritrean civil servants employed in other departments and ca. 100,000 Eritreans gainfully employed in all parts of Ethiopia were continual reminders of this connection. In Eritrea, the UP, as we can discern from the EWN, Ethiopia Weekly and British sources, pursued its own politics of irredentism in the unswerving faith of the support of Emperor Haile Sellassie.

However, Ethiopian policy on Eritrea showed wider flexibility as well as some strands of uncertainty. Ethiopia was responding to a series of external and internal changes, as she acquired new allies (the United States) outside of Europe thus reducing her dependence on Britain and France. The FPC and the Bevin-Sforza pact and the conflicting reports of the United Nations Commission of Enquiry appeared to have caused a reassessment of Ethiopian policies towards Eritrea. The acceptance by Ethiopia of the Bevin-Sforza deal which called for the partition of Eritrea and disposal of the Moslem lowlands by referendum is a strong indication of the flexibility of Ethiopian claims, while her acceptance of a general plebiscite lends further support to the confidence that prevailed both in Eritrea and Ethiopia on the issue.

An author who has pushed the Trevaskian legacy to the extreme is Jordan Gebre-Medhin. On the basis of interviews, the veracity of which cannot be checked, Jordan has argued that the shifta activity (armed violence) against the Italians and other anti-unionists was directed and financed by Ethiopia. His arguments are skilfully woven around a few documents confiscated by the British in 1949 during a raid on the headquarters of the Youth League of the UP, and information provided to him in 1986 on the use of the town of Aksum by the Ethiopian government as the rear base for financing shifta activities in Eritrea (Gebre-Medhin, 1989:127). There would have been serious reason to consider such allegations if Jordan had been able to support his story of Aksum as the rear base for financing shifta activity by referring to testimonies provided by the Ethiopian Liaison Officer, Colonel Negga Haile Selassie and Ato Woldeab Wolde Mariam, the editor of EWN and one of the leaders of LPP.[1] The information was not derived from people who were in a position to know. As things now stand, Gebre-Medhin's statements about Aksum need to be treated, at best, as an allegation that has yet to be substantiated. At worst, it is an example of research devoid of seriousness and commitment to the study of the past as it was.

The couple of letters from the headquarters of the Youth League did indeed establish a link between the secretary of the Ethiopian Liaison Office and the Youth League. On the basis of this evidence the Youth League was banned. In Addis Ababa, reacting to British official complaints, the Ethiopian authorities recalled Colonel Negga and instructed him to adhere strictly to his consular activities. From the evidence, the BMA was not able to establish whether the secretary of the Liaison Office worked on his own initiative or on instructions from Addis Ababa. Reporting on the impact of the British complaints, the British Embassy in Addis Ababa reported that the Ethiopian government had little control over what took place in Eritrea.

My readings of the BMA and other Eritrean sources lead me to maintain that the shifta activity that dominated the Eritrean scene from 1947–50 was exclusively an Eritrean affair with little or insignificant involvement from the side of the Ethiopian government.[2] I maintain that Trevaskis in the late 1950s and Gebre-Medhin in the late 1980s have for several reasons found it convenient to hold the Ethiopian government responsible for shifta activity in Eritrea. In the case of Trevaskis, we discern a deliberate intent of underestimating the political and patriotic consciousness of the adherents of the UP. In this, as he admitted himself, Trevaskis shared a common BMA contempt for a movement that challenged British rule Gebre-Medhin's efforts to locate Ethiopian involvement behind every shifta activity appear to be based on his ideological position, namely that of establishing a connection between the political reality of the 1940s and the EPLF led "war of independence".

SHIFTA (BANDITRY) AND ETHIOPIAN INVOLVEMENT

The word shifta included all those who for political or other reasons fled to the bush and were sufficiently armed to defend themselves. Throughout the 1942–

---

[1] These knowledgeable people either denied the fact or dismissed it as false.

[2] It is important to note that what Trevaskis wrote in 1952 on the origins of the shifta was different from what he wrote in general terms later in his book. See his contribution to NTEN, nos. 837–9, June, 1952.

52 period, three types of shifta are discernible. The first type of shifta included those who ran away for personal or clan reasons. They were mostly engaged in clan feuds. The second type were shifta originating from the northern province of Tigrai and were purely motivated by the ease by which people in Eritrea were robbed and their livestock stolen. The third type of shifta were those who openly declared their motive, firstly, to free Eritrea from both Italian rule and the possibility of its return; secondly, to unite Eritrea with Ethiopia. They harassed Italians and other enemies of the UP. All of these shifta lived by stealing from the population.

Before we begin a reconstruction of the landscape of the shifta phenomenon, it is worthwhile to cite an example of a tendency towards manifest distortion consistently pursued by Dr. Jordan Gebre-Medhin. A few days after the massacre of innocent Eritreans by the SDF soldiers, the BMA printed in the EWN that three SDF soldiers were killed and thirteen others wounded on the night of August 28, 1946. Solely on the basis of what the British had chosen to put into their censored newspaper, Gebre-Medhin argued that "the bullets that shot the SDF soldiers might have come from hired guns of the Ethiopian state" (Gebre-Medhin, 1989:85). If the interest of the author had been other than to show Ethiopian involvement, he would have attempted to corroborate the evidence put into the EWN by looking into the despatches from Asmara to London. The series of telegrams sent to London and the Monthly Political Intelligence Report for August 1946 make no mention of either three SDF soldiers killed or thirteen wounded. There was no way that the telegrams accounting for the night of August 28 hour by hour would have failed to mention the death of British colonial soldiers. They did not because there were no SDF soldiers killed or wounded.[1] The item in the EWN was deliberate misinformation planted by the BMA in order to appease critical voices from the Eritrean population.[2]

The shifta activity that outlived the BMA was the first type, i.e., those who ran away for personal or clan reasons. The most notorious among these shifta was Hamid Idris Awate of Beni Amer origin. Idris Awate began his career in early 1942 and by 1948 his army may have numbered about 50. His main activity was to raid the Kunama and Baria people. In the middle of 1950, he participated in the clan feud between the Beni Amer and the adjoining districts of Hamassien, namely Liben and Anseba. Idris Awate was one of the three shifta leaders about whom the British were most concerned. In 1949 the BMA offered a considerable

---

[1] For an account of the evening of August 28, see FO371/53511, From the Commander in Chief of Middle East Foreces to the War Office, September 4, 1946. Trevaskis, who was most probably in Asmara and who described the incident in some details in p. 68 did not mention any SDF killed or wounded.

[2] This was not the only time that the BMA used its newspaper for such a purpose. A few days after the rejection of the Bevin-Sforza pact by the United Nations Assembly, the BMA wrote in the EWN that the Ethiopian vote against the entire Bevin-Sforza package was decisive, and that Ethiopia acted against its own interest. This was of course not true. The Ethiopian government voted for the Bevin-Sforza proposal on Eritrea where the Eritrean highlands were to be incorporated into Ethiopia and the fate of the remaining part to be decided by referendum.

sum as a reward for the capture of Idris Awate, dead or alive (EWN, 17.12.49). Idris Awate was not the only one. Many of the pastoral and semi-pastoral communities in Eritrea had their own shifta men in the territory. The Assaworta had Ramadan Suleman (EWN, 8.4.48); the Afar had Ahmed Ali Mohamed;[1] the Kunama had Humed Hufan (EWN, 27.1.49); and the Marya had Mohamed Omer (EWN, 10.2.49). Together these shifta leaders may have had an army comprised of between 400 and 500 men.

Idris Awate surrendered in 1951 at the time when the British, after muddling around for nearly a decade, devised the efficient decree 104 of 1951 where entire villages were held responsible for shifta crimes committed by their members.[2] Dr. Gebre-Medhin is singularly silent about this type of shifta activity. Since the sources are derived from those he has allegedly studied, we argue that he refrained from taking this information into account because of the complications these sources create for his main thesis, namely, all shifta activity was financed and directed from Ethiopia.

The second type of shifta activity that also continued well after the British departure in 1952 was that carried out mainly by people from the Ethiopian province of Tigrai (Tigre). Disparate information on shifta from Tigrai operating in Eritrea appeared in EWN but there were no attempts to explain them until 1953. In a leading article entitled "Do not do unto others what you do not want done unto you", the editor of the official newspaper of the Eritrean government wrote that for the past several years the people of the province of Tigrai had treated Eritrea as a haven for the accumulation of instant wealth (Zemen, 11.8.53). The young people of Tigrai were encouraged and challenged to go to Eritrea as shifta and become wealthy rather than lounge around in poverty at home.

Although we are far from being able to ascertain in percentage terms the strength and extent of the various types of shifta activity, there can really be no doubt that such activity was prominent after the mid-1940s. It may also be argued that the Ethiopian state could not have been involved with the formation and persistence of the two types of shifta activities.

The third type of shifta activity was that carried out by people who gave political motives for their actions, and these actions were mainly directed against Italians and their property. The goal of these shifta was the termination of Italian rule and the reunification of Eritrea with Ethiopia. Since the main objective of the politically motivated shifta was shared by the UP and the Ethiopian government, it was convenient for the British to point an accusing finger at the Ethiopian state. Whereas, however, the British were cautious (due to their

---

[1] Active since the early 1940s, Ahmed Ali was still active in the beginning of 1953. A reward was announced for his capture, dead or alive in the Eritrean Weekly News and Zemen Biweekly of 6.2.1953.

[2] EWN, 16.8.1951. It is in this article that we learn that Hamid Idris Awate had been a shifta since 1942.

daily exposure and knowledge of the reality)[1] later writers such as Gebre-Medhin were to draw conclusions striking for their lack of seriousness in the collection and interpretation of the sources.

The politically motivated shifta started initially as a reaction against Italian funding of political organizations. By 1948 there may have been up to ten groups that could be identified as political shifta. Besides living by plunder and highway banditry, the political shifta concentrated on ambushing Italians and destroying their property. Between 1947 and 1950, the political shifta bands had killed 25 Italians.

The BMA gave three reasons for the origins and spread of the shifta phenomenon. The first, they argued, was the widespread uncertainty that prevailed in the country as to its future. Throughout 1949 and 1950, the fate of Eritrea remained an open question. Several conflicting solutions were continuously discussed. The country might be partitioned, thus threatening Italian economic stability. Eritrea might be given back to Italy in the form of trusteeship, an eventuality very much feared by the UP.

The second reason for the spread of shifta activity, the British argued, was to a large measure due to the campaign carried out by the Italian community in Eritrea. Although shocked by the Bevin-Sforza deal advocating the partition of Eritrea, the Italian community remained confident in the take-over of the country. Through the daily newspaper *Il Corriere Eritreo*, the Italians exuded confidence as to how they were going to rule Eritrea after the withdrawal of the British. The Italian community provoked the UP and its sympathisers to resort to political terrorism.

The third reason that the British with some justification argued was the assistance that the shifta received from the Ethiopian state. The British saw that many shifta crossed the border to the Tigrai province of Ethiopia with their loot and that the Ethiopian government took no action to either apprehend the shifta or return stolen property. The British were aware that the Ethiopian government had very little control over Tigrai province. The fact that in 1943 the Ethiopian government was compelled to accept the assistance of the British Air Force to suppress the Weyane rebellion in eastern Tigrai was too fresh in the memory of Ethiopian officials. The Ethiopians, according to British archival sources, appear to have had even less control over the shifta activity in Eritrea. The British were, however, not aware that for many a Tigrean, Eritrea was considered a no man's land where, through a brief shifta career considerable wealth could be acquired. So those shifta who crossed the Ethiopian frontier were not necessarily political shifta but others who after accumulating some instant wealth had decided to return home.

Apart from the incident of April 1949 where the secretary of the Ethiopian Liaison Office was implicated in the terrorist activities of the Youth League of

---

[1] FO371/73789. 8.12.49 "...ardent unionists insist on regarding themselves as Ethiopians and not Eritreans".

the UP, the British were, in spite of a remarkable intelligence network, unable to come up with convincing evidence on Ethiopian involvement with the shifta activity. The Ethiopian state, it appears, was implicated in the eyes of the British with the shifta phenomenon not so much for its active assistance, but because it upheld the same objective as that of the political shifta, namely, the union of Eritrea with Ethiopia. The politically motivated shifta activity came to an end soon after the UN resolution federating Eritrea became known at the end of 1950, while the other two types of shifta, though on a much reduced scale, continued well into the 1950s.

The BMA were well aware of the fact that political shiftaism was carried out by Eritreans alone without the involvement of either the Ethiopian Liaison Officer or his government. This was clearly stressed by the Eritrean administrator Brigadier Drew in his reply to Italian complaints on the issue. Owing to its precise relevance regarding the role of Ethiopia, Drew's reply to the Foreign Office deserves to be quoted in full:

> 1. The administration has made no secret of its view that terrorist activities are politically inspired. I have also repeatedly stated that Italian interference in local politics has been the fundamental cause of these most regrettable murders which however cannot be condoned on this account.
>
> 2. It is untrue that terroristic action is conducted by Ethiopian Agents from over the border. These activities are [undeciphered] local Eritrean shifta leaders, with perhaps some Ethiopians in their gangs, who have sympathetic instigation from the local Unionist Party. It is part of Italian policy to make out that local Italians are popular with Eritreans and that these attacks against Italians are the work of Ethiopians who have been specifically infiltrated across the border for this purpose.
>
> 3. Following are my comments on individual cases mentioned in the Italian note:
>
> (1) Documents seized from the offices of the Andinet Party [Youth League of the UP] did not implicate Colonel Negga [Liaison Officer of the Ethiopian government] in any terroristic plan.
>
> (2) Colonel Negga is not the head of the Ethiopian Military Mission to Eritrea which does not exist.
>
> (3) The two men mentioned were convicted not of murder but of incitement, resistance to orders and engagement in activities likely to cause a breach of the peace.[1]

To the incessant claims by the Italian community that the UP was behind the political shifta, the BMA replied that they could not take any action against leaders of the UP without proof. That the British were all too willing to send the leaders of the UP to prison was evidenced when the Italian Liaison Officer Count di Gropello informed the former (on November 15, 1949) that a quantity of arms was concealed in the house of the head of the Ethiopian Orthodox Church at the Monastery of Bizen. The Monastery was stormed in the early hours of November 18 and nothing whatsoever was found.[2]

---

[1] FO371/73791, Chief Administrator Drew to the Foreign Office, London, telegram no.238, December 15, 1949.

[2] FO371/73789, Drew to the Foreign Office, telegram no.5, Asmara 22.11.1949.

Political shiftaism has a long antecedent in Ethiopian and Eritrean history. Virtually all political leaders had, prior to the era of colonialism, shifta careers behind them before their acquisition of legal power. During the colonial period resistance to colonialism was carried out by shifta. Thousands of Eritreans were in the forefront as political shifta (known also as patriots) fighting against Italy during the latter's brief occupation of the country, 1936–41.

Political shiftaism was given additional impetus by the supply of readily accessible weaponry. There was no shortage of weapons since the sudden collapse of Italian colonial rule had meant the dispersal of ca. 50,000 Eritrean soldiers with their armaments. And the British, perennially understaffed and unwilling to spend more than what was available through local revenue, were in no position to exercise effective control. When the UP and its adherents felt threatened by the rich and powerful Italian community in the late 1940s, they resorted to political shiftaism—a course of action with which they were fully acquainted. Indeed Dr Gebre-Medhin underestimates the commitment of the adherents of the UP when he attempts to put forward the argument that the Ethiopian Liaison Office manned by two people, financed and directed the shifta activity.

Even Trevaskis, biased as he was, did not implicate Ethiopia of either financing the shifta or infiltrating the Eritrean countryside with Ethiopian shifta disguised as Eritreans. In a long article he published in the summer of 1952 he argued that the main problem for the shifta was the shortage of land and the manner by which the Italian and British rulers had taken away land from the inhabitants. Of the three types of shifta activities identified by Trevaskis, I shall here discuss political shiftaism which he described as the anti-Italian shifta activity.[1] He wrote that although there were occasional attacks on Italian life it was only after 1947 that certain shifta leaders assumed a definite anti-Italian role. The reason for this, continued Trevaskis, had been Italian intervention in local politics. Up to 1949, anti-Italian shifta activity was directly and exclusively against the Italian residents in the district of Keren as these had been principally responsible for the formation of the Pro-Italy Party. An indiscriminate campaign directed against Italians only developed during 1949 after the formation of the Independence Bloc under Italian patronage.

The underlying causes of the shifta phenomenon need to be sought in the nature of the British administration in Eritrea rather than in Ethiopian policy. Two causes can be identified. The first and quite important cause was the international juridical restrictions imposed by the Hague Convention of 1907 on the British Military Administration. The British as caretakers felt bound to administer Eritrea on behalf of Italy. With minor exceptions, they implemented colonial

---

[1] NTEN, nos. 837–9, June, 1952. The other two types were i) communal feuds, the most important of which were those between the Beni Amer against the Baria, Marya and Kunama. Of less intensity were the feuds between the Kunama against the Marya, Baria and Hamassien. ii) The second type of shifta activity was motivated by dynastic feuds in virtually all districts of Eritrea caused by the continuous dismissals from and appointments to chieftaincies.

legislation and kept virtually intact the Italian colonial bureaucracy. The treatment of Eritrea as belonging to Italy (up to the signing of the Paris Peace Treaty of 1947) was in sharp contrast to the promises the British made to the Eritrean people. It was only towards the end of 1948 that the Eritreans were informed about British intentions on Eritrea. However, even after this date, the BMA attempts to preserve a special role for the Italian community had caused the UP to raise questions as to whether it was the British or the Italians who ruled over their country.

The second cause was the failure on the part of the BMA to maintain an adequate police force. In contrast to the Italian colonial state, which had an indigenous army of ca. 6,000, the British tried to administer Eritrea with a total force of ca. 2,000 made up of newly recruited soldiers. This force was absolutely inadequate to maintain law and order in a country that was undergoing serious social, economic and political upheaval. The BMA was fully aware of the inadequacy of its police force but felt restrained from expanding it due to its strictly implemented policy of balancing expenditures with revenue. The British, we argue, could have managed to control the shifta phenomenon, including the political shifta, in the same manner as the Italians did if they had given priority to law and order rather than to fiscal concerns.

Out of the other three authors who dealt with Eritrean political history, Lloyd Ellingson deserves special attention. In sharp contrast to Jordan Gebre-Medhin, Ellingson explained in sufficient detail the role of the Italian community in Eritrean politics. The author argued that the involvement of the Italian community in local political affairs, firstly in favour of the return of Italian colonial rule and later in favour of independence, created serious conflicts within the Moslem League—conflicts which eventually led to its disintegration (Ellingson, 1986:75). The great majority of the adherents of the Moslem League feared the politically dominant position that Italians would have in an independent Eritrea. The underlying motive for the Italian community to support independence was, according to Ellingson, "in order to create a nominally independent Eritrea under Italian economic and political domination". Interpreting his sources, mainly those of the BMA, correctly, Ellingson also noted that the Italian community led by its government's liaison officer generously financed the Independence Bloc, thus causing a serious threat to the UP whose financial support from Ethiopia was in no way comparable (Ellingson, 1986:59, 75).

Ellingson pointed out, albeit in a footnote, that there were three types of shifta activities and that the spread of politically motivated shifta was a response to the Italian community's attempts to regain state power by manipulating the Independence Bloc. Notwithstanding some exemplary interpretations from the often biased colonial archival sources, Ellingson's study on the Eritrean political parties in general and the UP in particular is highly inadequate and follows the biases first put forward by Trevaskis.

CONCLUSION

The incorporation of Eritrea into the Ethiopian Empire through the UN resolution of 1950 cannot be explained without taking into account the successful politics of irredentism carried out by the UP. To the extent that the UN resolution
was imposed on Eritrea, one can naturally question the wisdom of the decision.
The UN resolution was, however, based on the conclusions reached firstly, by
the Four Power Commission of Enquiry, and secondly, by the UN's own Commission of Enquiry. In the reports of both of these commissions, the wishes of
the Eritrean people were given clear precedence over the claims of the Ethiopian
government. It is worth remembering that Ethiopian claims were rejected by
France, the Soviet Union and the United States in 1946.

It was indeed greatly due to the effective presence of the Unionist Party that
the Four Powers began to seriously entertain Ethiopian claims. The UP produced the evidence that the Ethiopian government needed to convince the
world of the rightness of its claims. Ethiopian diplomacy, however, was no
match for that of Italy.

The UN had sufficient basis to decide Eritrea's fate in the spring of 1949, and
it did so in May of the same year when it approved the Bevin-Sforza proposal
on partition. The failure of the Bevin-Sforza package gave rise to a new realign-
ment, where the Soviet Union and Italy, with the support of several Latin
American and Arab states, began to campaign for the immediate independence
of Eritrea. Italy's radical change of policy, from partition of Eritrea to immediate
independence introduced an element of uncertainty which, in turn, necessitated
the sending of a UN Commission of Enquiry. Although Ethiopia managed to
establish its need for adequate access to the sea as legitimate, the latter's demand
that the UN decide the issue either on the findings of the Four Power Commission of Enquiry or along the Bevin-Sforza line was to no avail. Here it needs to
be clearly stressed that in so far as Haile Sellassie's Ethiopia had territorial ambitions these were put forward within the realm of the possible. Ethiopia and its
leaders were fully aware that their claims to all or parts of Eritrea might not at
all be fulfilled.

If there were some doubts among the member states of the United Nations
as to the wishes of the Eritrean people, these were dispelled by the findings of
the UN Commission of Enquiry where the majority report recommended the
incorporation of Eritrea into Ethiopia. In an early statement from 1968, even the
Eritrean Liberation Front did justice to the UN resolution as a compromise one.[1]
Ethiopian claims and its legitimate right to access to the sea were indeed consid-

---

[1] The Eritrean Liberation Front, "Eritrean Tragedy". A memorandum sent to the World Council of
Churches, assembled in Uppsala Sweden, July, 1968. The full phrase runs as follows: "The
General Assembly on the basis of the proposals and draft Resolution submitted by the UN Commission, adopted a compromise federal solution by 46 to 10 votes with 4 abstentions. This was in
December 1950, during the fifth session. The solution adopted could not be other than a compromise. The solution recommended by the population themselves ranged from union with Ethiopia
to independence", p. 5.

ered; however, what persuaded the majority of the members of the UN Commission of Enquiry in favour of the reunion of Eritrea with Ethiopia was no doubt the coherent position of the UP. If it were not for the resilience of the UP, the question of Ethiopian legitimate rights to the sea would have been resolved differently. It is indeed possible to speculate that Ethiopia would either have managed to negotiate a corridor to the sea through Zeila or continued with its earlier policy and negotiated access through Assab, Djibouti and other outlets.

The UP and the crucial role it played, force us to look afresh into the causes of the Eritrean conflict where, among others, the relations between an autonomous Eritrea and an imperial Ethiopia would occupy a prominent position. So far no attempt has been made to study the decade of the 1950s—a decade that witnessed the rise and decline of the federal experiment. It is only when this issue has been studied that we can begin to search for explanations different from the mechanical and highly distorted ones currently available.

Finally it is appropriate to conclude this chapter by raising the question once again as to whether the Unionist Party was an instrument of the Ethiopian State. A reconstruction of the history of the Unionist Party has I believe shown that it was not an instrument of Ethiopia at all. The UP knew what it wanted, fought for it and won. To the extent that Ethiopia also showed interest in reunification, then there was a common objective. It has to be remembered that, throughout the 1946–52 period, the Ethiopian government was represented by only two people in Eritrea. The Ethiopian Liaison Officer, young and inexperienced, was indeed a lonely man.[1] Although the last word has yet to be spoken, one can emphatically state that if it were not for the UP's determined political activity Eritrea would not have been united with Ethiopia. This statement can be supported by citing the problems that the Ethiopian state had in the late 1980s in its attempt to keep Eritrea under its umbrella. Throughout the 1980s, there were up to 100,000 Ethiopian soldiers permanently stationed in Eritrea. By this time, however, there were sufficient numbers of Eritreans who were prepared to withstand the pressure of such a huge and powerful presence. The Ethiopians were defeated before it dawned on them that they could not keep Eritrea without the consent and active support of the majority of its inhabitants.

---

[1] Colonel Negga Haile Selassie was in the 1940s a young man in his twenties. When I met him in London, in 1991, he told me that he was more of a student than a leader of the pro-Ethiopian community in Eritrea.

Chapter Three

The Eritreo–Ethiopian Federation 1952–1955

THE ESTABLISHMENT OF THE FEDERATION

The UN resolution 390(V) A of December 2, 1950 contained 15 articles. The first seven articles regulating the relations between Eritrea and Ethiopia are known as the Federal Act. According to the first article of this UN legal document, Eritrea was to constitute "an autonomous unit federated with Ethiopia under the sovereignty of the Ethiopian Crown". According to article three of the Federal Act, the jurisdiction of the Federal Government covered defence, foreign affairs, currency and finance, foreign and interstate commerce and external and interstate communications, including ports. In addition, the Federal Government had the legal powers to maintain the integrity of the Federation (appendix 1). The same article further stipulated that the jurisdiction of the Eritrean government should extend to all matters not vested in the Federal Government, including the power to maintain the internal police, to levy taxes to meet the expenses of domestic functions and services, and to adopt its own budget.

What made the UN resolution appear like a federal instrument in form rather than content was the provision made in article five stipulating the establishment of an Imperial Federal Council composed of an equal number of Ethiopian and Eritrean representatives whose function was to advise the Emperor upon the common affairs of the Federation. The said article also stated that the Eritreans should participate in the executive and judicial branches of the Ethiopian (federal) government and be represented in the legislative branch in accordance with the law and in the proportion that the population of Eritrea bore to the population of Ethiopia.

Article six of the UN resolution established that a single nationality should prevail throughout the Federation. The following article enjoined the Federal Government as well as that of Eritrea to ensure the residents of Eritrea the enjoyment of human rights and fundamental liberties.

Articles eight to fifteen of the UN resolution outlined the transitional process during which time the Eritrean government would be organised and the Eritrean Constitution prepared and put into effect.

A few days after UN resolution 390 A (V), the UN elected Mr. Eduardo Anze Matienzo as the UN Commissioner for Eritrea and entrusted him to implement its resolution (UN, 1952:2).

In a speech delivered on the occasion of UN Resolution 390, the Ethiopian Emperor reiterated the view that in uniting Eritrea with Ethiopia, the UN and the powerful states had finally recognised the interests of Ethiopia and the decision of the majority of the Eritrean people about union with Ethiopia (Hagos, 1963:26–28).

In so far as it was the newly organised United Nations which resolved to federate Eritrea with Ethiopia, there can be no escaping the fact that such a solution was externally imposed both on Eritrea and Ethiopia. However, the UN resolution was based, first, on the voluminous material collected by the Four Power Commission and second, on the reports commissioned by itself. However, there are three questions which still remain unresolved. Firstly, did the UN resolution reflect sufficiently the political realities in Eritrea? Secondly, was the resolution solely a result of international diplomacy? Thirdly, did Ethiopian claims play any significant role in the making of the resolution? As regards the first question the early writings of the Eritrean Liberation Front (ELF) give a clear indication that the UN resolution federating Eritrea to Ethiopia was indeed based on the political realities of Eritrea (ELF, 1967; 1968; 1971; Trevaskis, 1960; Markakis, 1987:68). It is only after the establishment of the Eritrean Peoples Liberation Front (EPLF), a rival of ELF, that the entire operation of the UN, the role of international diplomatic rivalries and that of Ethiopia became issues of controversy.[1]

In my opinion a look at the findings of the FPC and the reports of the UN Commission of Enquiry makes it clear that the solution of the United Nations was the most feasible alternative. According to the findings of FPC, carried out in 1948, nearly 48 per cent of the Eritrean people, the overwhelming majority of them Christians, had expressed a desire for an unconditional union with Ethiopia. Nearly thirty per cent of the Eritrean population, all Moslems, had opposed the unification of Eritrea with Ethiopia. These were organised within the Moslem League, whose political objectives remained vague, ranging from independence to trusteeship and the amalgamation of the western parts of Eritrea with the Anglo-Egyptian Sudan. Far more important for this study is the fact that once the resolution was made known it was accepted by all political parties in Eritrea.

The process of federating Eritrea to Ethiopia has been thoroughly studied by several authors. Mention has earlier been made of the hitherto unrivalled study by Dr. Amare Tekle (1964). More recently the process has also been studied by Eyassu Gayim. His main conclusion was that the federation was designed to

---

[1] The group which later formed the EPLF (Eritrean Peoples Liberation Front) was first established in 1969. Known as the Essayas Group, its membership was exclusively Christian. It was formed by those who broke away from the (ELF) Eritrean Liberation Front which, at this period, identified itself as an integral part of the Arab and Moslem world. The Christian Eritrean had very little role to play in such an organization. Moreover, the ELF considered Christian Eritreans as potential spies of the Christian Ethiopian state. In such circumstances, the Essayas Group and later the EPLF had to pursue a political objective which would protect them from ELF suspicions. One such strategy, I believe, was a total rejection of the UN resolution. For the views of EPLF on ELF, see the English translation of its maiden publication of 1971 in EFLNA, 1973: 5–23.

protect the interests of mainly, Great Britain, the United Sates and Ethiopia (Gayim, 1993: chapter 4). Although Eyassu Gayim accepted the FPC's finding that nearly 48 per cent of the Eritrean population voted through their delegates for unconditional union with Ethiopia, he argued against the UN resolution on the simple and naive ground that the rest of the population were against union (Gayim, 1993:319–320). Great Britain pushed first for the partition of Eritrea and later argued for federation in order to protect its interests in the adjoining colonies. The United States supported the federal solution because they would in return increase their presence in Ethiopia and moreover continue to avail themselves of the satellite communication base in Eritrea which was established in 1942 (Gayim 1993:320–321). The Unionist Party, which on the eve of the FPC visit to Eritrea had emerged stronger vis à vis the opposition parties is treated in a Trevaskian manner, i.e. as an instrument of Ethiopian foreign policy. As regards Ethiopian claims Eyassu Gayim would have learned a great deal if he had either properly consulted the available literature or read carefully the study of Amare Tekle.[1]

In my opinion Eyassu Gayim has pushed the conspiratorial theory ad absurdum. Neither of the culprit states condemned by Eyassu Gayim had attached so much importance to the disposal of Eritrea. The idea of colonial restructuring in Africa had among British policy makers already begun in 1940 long before the outcome of the war. The United States of America, whose main interest was in a satellite communications base at Asmara (established in 1942) had no need of Ethiopian assistance. If the Americans had wanted to keep their base in Eritrea, all they had to do was negotiate access with whoever had power.[2] The disposal of Eritrea became a long drawn out affair because it formed part of a total solution to all former Italian colonies. As regards Ethiopia's claim to all or parts of Eritrea, these claims were not taken seriously. However, virtually every member of the United Nations recognised Ethiopia's moral right for some sort of compensation as a victim of Italian aggression (Tekle, 1964:268). An outlet to the sea was considered a realistic claim. Eyassu Gayim's handling of the policies of Britain, Ethiopia, the United States and the Unionist Party are, therefore, inadequate and unconvincing.[3]

The federal government, which was the same as the Ethiopian government, had wide powers in Eritrea. The federal government was also bestowed with powers of maintaining the integrity of the Federation, and the right to impose uniform taxes throughout the Federation (UN, 1950:368–370). Other powers not

---

[1] It is remarkable that Eyassu Gayim has neither commented nor discussed the issues raised by Tekle. The only place where Tekle is mentioned is in the bibliography.

[2] The pro-Eritrean argument that the US supported the federal solution in order to retain the communication base in Asmara is convincingly refuted by Tiruneh (1981:114). This relevant study is significantly absent from Eyassu Gayim's bibliography.

[3] The policies of Great Britain and the United States on Ethiopia are thoroughly treated in Harold Marcus, 1983; while the Ethiopian position at the United Nations during the period is dealt with by John Spencer, 1983. Neither in the text nor even in the bibliography are these standard and essential works mentioned.

vested in the federal government came under the jurisdiction of the Eritrean government. The Federal Act also stipulated that the Federation should constitute a single area for customs purposes, and there should be no barriers to the free movement of goods and persons within the area. However, custom duties on goods entering or leaving the Federation which had their final destination or origin in Eritrea should be assigned to Eritrea.

The Federal Act, moreover, contained a long list of human rights and fundamental liberties that the Ethiopian and Eritrean governments were to extend to nationals as well as to resident foreign nationals. These were: i) the right to life, liberty and the security of person; ii) the right to own and dispose of property; iii) the right to freedom of opinion and expression; iv) the right to education; v) the right to freedom of peaceful assembly and association; vi) the right to inviolability of correspondence and domicile; vii) the right to an equitable and fair trial. These rights were further strengthened by provisions which deterred the authorities from arresting or detaining any person without an order of a competent authority.

The responsibility for incorporating the provisions of the Federal Act (UN Resolution 390 A) into the Eritrean constitution was entrusted to the Bolivian diplomat Eduardo Anze Matienzo. According to the praxis of the period, the UN Commissioner was provided with a team of international legal experts. The Commissioner soon established himself in the Eritrean capital and began drafting a constitution on the basis of consultations with the Eritrean political leaders and the Ethiopian authorities.

The task of the UN Commissioner was made complex by the UN resolution itself, where Eritrea is treated both as an autonomous entity within the Ethiopian empire and as an entity federated to Ethiopia. As far as the Ethiopian government was concerned Eritrea had become united with Ethiopia and had as a consequence to be treated as the other provinces of the empire. The powers which fell to the Ethiopian authorities were of such a nature as to lend support to such an opinion. Therefore, as far as the Ethiopians were concerned, the UN Resolution 390(V) was conceived as a compensation for the effects of "pre-war fascism"; something which, at all costs, had to be repudiated (Spencer, 1983:240; Redda, 1954).

In early 1952 Anze Matienzo, the United Nations Commissioner for Eritrea, and the British Administration set out to conclude their work by the end of the year. There were several issues to be dealt with; the most important of which were the election of a Constituent Assembly, the drafting of the constitution, its adoption by an Eritrean constituent assembly and the Ethiopian government; the creation of a government, the definition of the division of powers between the government and the Imperial Federal Government, and the budget.

The elections to the Constituent Assembly were held on 25 and 26 March without any "genuine inconsistency discovered".[1] With the exception of free

---

[1] FO371/96720. MPR 75 for the period 23.2 up to 22.3, 1952.

and direct elections in the towns of Asmara and Massawa, the practice followed
in the rest of the country was that of indirect election. The country was divided
into constituencies where the chiefs (administrative officers) constituted the ex-
officio members of an electoral college with the power to elect a representative
to the assembly. Put out by the British Administration, it was made clear that
this electoral law was only for the specific purpose of electing a representative
to the assembly. It was understood that the Eritrean government would in due
course promulgate a more permanent electoral law.

The elections for the Constituent Assembly were contested by the Unionist
Party, the Moslem League of the Western Province and the Eritrean Democratic
Front (a leftover of the ML after the breakaway of the ML of the Western Province) and the Liberal Progressive Party. The Eritrean Democratic Front was led
by Ibrahim Sultan. An organization which did not do so well in the elections
was the Eritrean Liberal Progressive Party which reputedly had the support of
about nine per cent of the population. Its leaders Woldeab Wolde Mariam and
Tesema Asberom campaigned as independents. While the latter, who safely sat
as a district chief, was returned unopposed, Woldeab Wolde Mariam, the indefatigable campaigner, failed to win a seat in a direct election contest in Asmara.

Asmara was divided into seven electoral districts, Massawa into two. In
Asmara, altogether eleven thousand votes were cast for seventeen candidates
contesting seven seats. Among the five candidates from the market area of
Asmara was Woldeab Wolde Mariam. In spite of his popularity as the most
articulate champion of independence and prolific writer on the subject, he had
very little chance to win a seat. Out of the 2,511 votes cast, 1,471 went to the
winner while Woldeab Wolde Mariam had the confidence of only 135 voters. In
view of the claims made in the late 1940s about the support that the Liberal Progressive Party led by Woldeab Wolde Mariam had among the population, the
election result calls for a cautious reinterpretation of the strength of the political
parties.

The outcome of the election reflected to a great extent the impact of culture
and religion: there was no candidate who secured a seat in a constituency inhabited by people who professed a religion different from his own. The Unionist
Party won 31 seats out of 34 in its constituencies where Christians were the
majority of the population. The ML and the EDP divided among themselves the
constituencies in the predominantly Moslem areas.

From April to July the newly elected Constituent Assembly worked with Mr.
Anze Matienzo, the United Nations Commissioner, in finalising the details of a
Constitution for Eritrea along the lines of United Nations Resolution 390 (V) of
December 2, 1950. The United Nations resolution had to a great extent met the
demands of the political parties. For the Unionists, the UN resolution was tantamount to union with Ethiopia; that this union was called a Federation was in
early 1952 seen as a minor problem. For the ML of the Western Province, the UN
resolution guaranteed its cultural and political autonomy established by the
Italians and respected by the British. Their equal representation in the assembly

made them cooperative in the drafting of the constitution. The only group that vacillated between cooperation and noisy criticism was the Eritrean Democratic Front led by Ibrahim Sultan.[1] The constitution that the Eritrean Assembly was to approve had by March 1952 already reached a final stage. The UN commissioner had together with the representatives of the Ethiopian government been working on it since the beginning of 1951.

The UN document (The Federal Act) was a faulty document indeed. The Imperial Ethiopian government was expected to function at the same time as the Federal Government. The UN document entertained a vision whereby the issues arising between the Eritrean and Ethiopian governments would be harmoniously solved by the Ethiopian government. With hindsight, one can argue that the United Nations ought not to have passed resolution 390(V), because it had no authority to enforce a federal constitution on the Ethiopian Government. And one wonders how the United Nations organization could federate a territory to another sovereign territory without first confirming the consent and willingness of the sovereign partner to introduce the required restructuring of power. This problem was pointed out by the Ethiopian delegation very clearly. The Federal Act, binding Ethiopia to a United Nations Resolution, was seen as a disguised form of UN trusteeship (Spencer, 1983:226). The Ethiopian delegation made it clear that once the Federation between them had come into being, its future fate would solely depend on Eritrea and Ethiopia. As far as Ethiopia was concerned, the role of the United Nations would come to an end, and for good, with the submission of the final report of the UN Commissioner for Eritrea to the UN. It has been argued that the Ethiopian position was implicitly accepted as there was no revision clause in the Federal Act (Meron and Pappas, 1981:210).

A draft constitution was debated and discussed by the Eritrean Constituent Assembly between April and July of 1952. Those Eritreans who opposed union with Ethiopia understood the constitution literally as a federal document where the powers of the representative of the Ethiopian government were subject to routine control as well as to continuous negotiation. The Eritrean Constituent Assembly, at least the members of the ML and EDF, were led to believe, by the UN Commissioner, that the representative of the Imperial Federal Government would limit his activities to those specified in article three of the Federal Act. However, the only instance where the Eritrean government could explain its views in cases of disagreement was the Imperial Federal Council where the head of the Ethiopian State was also the head of the Federation.

The Constitution was approved by the Eritrean Constituent Assembly on July 15, 1952. The deliberations of the assembly were duly reported in the Eritrean Weekly News. As long as the British were still in control, there was very

---

[1]　The Independence Bloc was officially dissolved soon after the UN Resolution 390 (V) federating Eritrea to Ethiopia. A new umbrella organization known as the Eritrean Democratic Front was established. This Front was to a large extent made up of the remnants of the Moslem League after the split which led to the formation of the ML of the Western Province.

little danger of censure or threats of it. Therefore, Eritreans of many political colours expressed their views on the nature of relations they wished to see with Ethiopia. However, while the Unionist Party looked forward to the end of British rule, the ML "continued to fulminate against the Ethiopian-British plot to sell the full autonomy of Eritrea".[1]

The Federal Act was approved by the Emperor on August 11, 1952. The Eritrean Constitution and the Eritrean government were approved by the same Emperor on September 12. Three days later the British handed over their power to the Ethiopian representative and the Chief Executive of the Eritrean government. From then onwards, Britain had a small consular representation headed by Wardle-Smith. Furthermore, there were about thirty British advisors seconded to the Eritrean government.[2] The Eritrean government where power was shared between the UP and the various factions of the ML was formed during July and August. The post of the Chief Executive went to Tedla Bairu, the president of the Unionist Party. The post of the president of the Eritrean Assembly went to Sheik Ali Redai, a leader of the ML from the Western Province. A couple of years previously, Sheik Ali Redai had campaigned for the independence of the western province.

As far as the Ethiopian government was concerned, once the Federation had come into existence the UN General Assembly could no longer be involved in the relations between Eritrea and Ethiopia. The Federal Act was indeed a product of the United Nations which in turn gave rise to the federal agreement between Eritrea and Ethiopia. As John Spencer, the American advisor to the Ethiopian government put it, "if at some time the Eritrean Assembly and Ethiopia should agree to terminate that agreement, the federation itself would be automatically dissolved without any possible recourse or objection by the United Nations" (Spencer, 1983:236–237). Such a view was, however, not shared by the UN Commissioner for Eritrea and the panel of international law experts whom he consulted. Eduardo Anze Matienzo expressed another opinion. In his final report he wrote:

> [If] it were either to amend or interpret the Federal Act, only the General Assembly as the author of that instrument would be competent to take a decision. Similarly if the Federal Act were violated, the General Assembly could be seized(sic!) of the matter. (UN, 1952:para 202.)

The question, therefore, as to whether the UN with the submission of the Commissioner's report had completely and finally disposed of Eritrea remained juridically unresolved. From the 1960s onwards, Eritrean nationalists were to

---

[1]   FO371/96720. MPR no. 80 for 23.7.52 – 22.8.52, para.88. The British believed that the activities of the ML were financed by the Italians. The conclusion of the MPR on the ML is noteworthy. "They thus make a great deal of noise but to little local effect".

[2]   FO371/102652. Post in Eritrean government departments filled by British staff, October 1953.

attach a great deal of importance to the opinion of the UN Commissioner. In practice, however, the UN agreed with the Ethiopian interpretation.[1]

Since the establishment of political parties in 1947, the Eritrean political elite had learned to articulate its views on Eritrea and its links with Ethiopia. The 1947–52 period was indeed a period when the Eritrean political class could express its opinions on Ethiopia with impunity. The consistent anti-Ethiopian position of the ML which during the drafting of the constitution maintained a strict and rigid federalist position further strengthened the climate of political criticism that was to harass the government of Eritrea. The ML's anti-Ethiopian position was contested with equal vigour by the Unionist Party whose members had no sympathy for the detailed rules and regulations of the Federation and Constitution. They campaigned for the complete union of Eritrea with Ethiopia—a country many of them knew by tradition and from the earlier generation. What many members of the UP did not realize was the extent to which they were influenced by the politics of the ML in favour of either independence or strict federal relations with Ethiopia.

On September 15, 1952, the Union Jack was replaced by the Eritrean and Ethiopian flags. The Federation was born. The Eritrean government had three branches of government. The Executive responsibility remained with the Chief Executive and his cabinet, made up of six heads of departments (Constitution of Eritrea, articles 67–73). The legislative function lay with the Eritrean Assembly. During the first five years of its life the Eritrean Assembly had the British Fergus McCleary as its clerk. The judicial function was entrusted to the Chief Justice of the Supreme Court. Until 1959, the office of the Chief Justice was occupied by Sir James Shearer.

It is worthwhile to describe in some detail the understanding of the Ethiopian government as to what was expected of it. On September 11, 1952 on the eve of the proclamation of the federation between Eritrea and Ethiopia, the Emperor gave a speech where he began by saying that "Ethiopia stretches her hands unto God in thanksgiving for the wondrous (sic) of justice which God has vouchsafed to His people of Ethiopia and Eritrea" (NTEN, no. 854, 27.9.52). The Emperor continued and said that the exact words of the message which he transmitted to the Eritrean people twelve years ago had been fulfilled. He noted the crucial support rendered to Ethiopia by the United States and France supporting the basic settlement put forward by Britain seven years previously, which I consider a point worth reflecting on. It has to be recalled that between 1940 and 1949 the British policy on Eritrea weighed heavily towards partition, whereas, the UN resolution of 1950 had virtually handed the whole of Eritrea to Ethiopia.[2] So as far as this speech is concerned, it appeared that the emperor did

---

[1] When the federation between Eritrea and Ethiopia was abolished ten years later, the UN was not seized of the matter. It accepted the incorporation of Eritrea into the Ethiopian empire.

[2] It is possible to argue, on the basis of the imperial speech, that certainly the emperor was either not aware of the implications of the Federal Act or did not care about the western part of Eritrea.

not think of the fact that the UN resolution had given him and his country much more in terms of territory than he had hoped.

Soon after the establishment of the federation, the emperor paying his first visit to Eritrea made another speech on the Mareb river which had hitherto divided Eritrea and Ethiopia. As was his custom, he began his speech by thanking the Almighty God for the justice that was achieved. "...The Mareb no longer as from today has the role of separating brothers" (NTEN, no. 859, 1.11.52). The emperor concluded that his visit signified to the entire world the "sacred, inviolable and eternal character of the relations which we have established between the brother peoples". The same evening (October 4, 1952) the Emperor made another much longer speech at Asmara; he talked of the thousand year long historical links stressing that Eritrea had always been an integral part of the Ethiopian empire. He further talked of his efforts to regain Eritrea even before the Second World War. He mentioned that Eritreans, in their thousands, had come to set up home in Ethiopia during the colonial period and that he had personally taken care of their education not only in Ethiopia but also abroad. In his efforts to give the new reality a new lease of life, the emperor conceded that during the long struggle (1941–52) "certain alien political elements and some belonging to the population itself, had sought other solutions for the question". He continued and explained that now all of this had become past history and that he retained no bitterness towards those elements which most probably "pursued their aims in all sincerity". Affirming that henceforth only common and mutual interest should inspire the actions of all the inhabitants of the empire, the Emperor concluded his speech by thanking once again the Almighty God for "having watched over our life, for having sustained us throughout the long struggle to obtain justice for our beloved subjects of Eritrea re-united with their brothers of Ethiopia".

Since most of the real power in Eritrea lay in the hands of Ethiopian authorities, the Emperor's Representative had clear precedence over the Chief Executive of the Eritrean Government. Ethiopia was a state where all political power was concentrated in the hands of His Imperial Majesty, Haile Selassie the First. By virtue of the annointment received from the Ethiopian Orthodox Church, the body of the Emperor was inviolable and his power indisputable. His first Representative in Eritrea, Andargatchew Messai, was no less than his son-in-law.[1] Since September 12, 1952, the Emperor's Representative had his private and official residence at the Palace of the Governor, formerly built by the Italians. In addition to his function as the official communicator between the Eritrean population and the extremely popular Emperor, the Emperor's Representative was also the head of the institutions which were assigned to the Ethiopian/Federal authorities, such as telecommunications, railways, defence, and customs.

---

[1] The Emperor's decision to send his son-in-law as his representative to Eritrea was a strong indication of the importance attached to the newly incorporated land.

While the Eritrean constitution was being examined by the August Emperor Haile Sellassie, the British, the new semi-official Eritrean government, and the Ethiopian authorities were engaged in laying down the basis of the Eritrean budget—a problem the solution of which defied the ingenuity of many experts. There were two issues involved. The first was the attempt by the British to make the Ethiopians realize the deficit in the Eritrean budget and their obligation to deal with it within the federal framework. The Ethiopians were aware that they would have to shoulder the responsibility but preferred to deal with it later. There was no way of making them see the urgency of the matter. The British who were winding down their involvement wanted to leave behind them administrative mechanisms for identifying the magnitude of the deficit as well as for balancing it. For the Ethiopians, the problem of the deficit of the Eritrean budget was more hypothetical rather than urgent since the Ethiopian government would, as a matter of course, take full responsibility over the Eritrean economy.

The second issue was the establishing of Eritrea's share of the revenue from customs. As an important gateway for Ethiopian import and export trade, Eritrea had been the recipient of considerable revenue from customs.[1] In fact during the British period revenue from customs provided up to 45 per cent of the total income of the territory. Now that revenue from customs was to be collected by the Imperial Federal Government, the British engaged the Ethiopians in the need for ascertaining Eritrea's share. Once again, the Ethiopians felt that the British were making a big fuss of a small problem given the fact that they were going to bear the entire responsibility for Eritrea as a whole. The issue was finally resolved to the satisfaction of the British when the Imperial Ethiopian government accepted the sum of 681,000 pounds as the Eritrean share of the revenue from customs. This figure was, however, soon reduced by 20,000 pounds thus introducing a new element of uncertainty as well as further grounds for the members of the ML to accuse the Federal government of keeping for themselves revenue from customs due to Eritrea.

The British left behind them a very precarious budget. The Eritrean share of the customs revenue did amount to nearly 45 per cent of total revenue but the collection of the remaining portion was understood to depend on policies adopted by the Eritrean and Federal governments as well as on "the opportunities given and taken for further development of industry in Eritrea".[2]

Relations between the Eritrean government and the Imperial Ethiopian government were to be regulated by resorting to the sphere of activities mentioned in the Federal Act. In cases of dispute, the Eritrean government had no other power to resort to other than the Imperial Ethiopian government. There was no federal structure in Ethiopia entrusted with regulating the relations of

---

[1] During the Italian period up to 25 per cent of Ethiopian export and import trade was through the Eritrean ports of Massawa and Assab. This trend continued during the British period as well (Negash, 1987).

[2] FO371/96761. FO to F.E. Stafford, United Kingdom Delegation, New York, 22.10.1952.

members of the federation. Although leaders of the ML had accepted the Federal Act and extended their cooperation to the UN Commissioner for Eritrea, they did not believe in the viability of the UN resolution. Just a few days after the establishment of the federation Ibrahim Sultan, "the leader of the only party representing Moslems" wrote to a Pakistani political organization informing the latter that "Moslems in Eritrea would struggle to establish another Pakistan".[1]

The achievement of the United Nations was that it smoothed the process of the integration of Eritrea into Ethiopia by devising a model of autonomy which it, quite mistakenly, designated as a federal one. Neither did the British as they admitted later believe in the success of the federation.[2] To the extent that the Ethiopian government incorporated Eritrea as its fourteenth province in 1962 without a word of censure from any member of the United Nations, it is most likely that the incorporation was seen as a logical consequence of the UN sponsored Constitution. However, the incorporation of Eritrea, smooth as it might have appeared, was a process that had been both contested as well as hastened by Eritrean social forces.

THE FIRST YEAR OF THE FEDERATION

No sooner had the ink dried on the constitution, than the Constituent Assembly undermined its democratic basis when its members voted to sit for four years. The Constituent Assembly had been elected for the specific purpose of approving the constitution. The decision of the assembly to extend its term of office created, according to the compiler of the MPR, "a widespread criticism" and the assembly was regarded as "having blundered".[3] It was by no means a good start.

The first dispute concerning the division of power was raised in the Eritrean Assembly in its session on the morning of December 29, 1952. In an outspoken and unequivocal criticism, a member of the assembly, Abba Habte-Mariam Nugurru wrote a motion asking the assembly to resolve that "the Notice issued by the Representative of his Imperial Majesty the Emperor concerning the registration of foreigners is an interference in the internal affairs of Eritrea".[4] Arguing that the task of registering foreign nationals and issuing identity cards and the payment of documentation fees were domestic affairs, Abba Habte-Mariam asked the government to take the necessary steps. The motion was

---

[1] NTEN, no. 854. 27.9.1952. The item of news was not commented.

[2] WO97/2817. FO to BEAA, 31.3.53. Allen Roger at the Foreign Office writing to the British Ambassador, D.L.Busk on the serious breakdown of the political situation in Eritrea, "I think I can say that we never really in our hearts expected the exact United Nations solution to last in the long run. The important thing was to have a solution with some chance of success which would release us from the task of administering indefinitely a territory whose inhabitants did not want us to rule them indefinitely. Such a solution having being reached, our concern was that there should not be an immediate breakdown for which we could be blamed".

[3] FO371/96720. MPR, No. 71 for the period 23.6.52–22.7.52, para. 74.

[4] FO371/102671. BCA, to BEAA, 3.1.1953.

based on rather weak grounds. The federal government had the responsibility over foreigners, the issue being whether registration fees belonged to Eritrea or to the federal government. However, the government of Tedla Bairu was either unable or unwilling to deal with the motion properly. We are told that the chief executive, Tedla Bairu "summarily rejected the appeal on the remarkable ground that, in invoking the name of the Emperor's Representative, the Assembly was guilty of irreverence".[1] This occurred after Tedla Bairu had a pungent interview with the emperor's representative. Abba Habte-Mariam, a young Catholic priest and a graduate of the Ethiopian College in the Vatican, was hardly a person to be bought off or co-opted to the Unionist line as represented by Tedla Bairu.[2]

From outside the assembly, Woldeab Wolde Mariam, the former leader of the Eritrean Liberal Progressive Party, now a founding member of the Association of Eritrean Workers, continued to write widely on the Shoan and Amhara plans to absorb Eritrea. Attempts to murder him a few weeks after the suppressed motion of Abba Habte-Mariam inflamed the political climate. It was widely believed that the chief executive, Tedla Bairu, was behind the attempted murder.[3]

For the majority of the people federation marked a deterioration of their economic conditions rather than an improvement. According to an anonymous letter addressed to the Emperor in January 1953, the authors reminded the Emperor that taxes had increased three times, that customs duties had risen and that they had been subjected to carrying identity cards that cost the "wages of three days work".[4] According to the assessment of the British Consulate, much could be attributed to the arrogant attitude of the government towards the British advisors. Only five months after the establishment of the Eritrean government, Wardle-Smith reported that the British advisors did not hold the executive positions to which they were appointed and that almost all of them complained that "their advice is seldom asked for and when it is, is seldom taken". In plain words, the leader of the Eritrean government ignored his British advisors whom he himself recruited. Further elaborating on the total disregard of the Eritrean government to heed advice, Wardle-Smith informed the Foreign Office that the British financial advisor to the Eritrean government had in the past two months seen Tedla Bairu only once and for approximately five minutes. His nine memoranda on financial and economic affairs to Tedla Bairu had neither been acknowledged nor commented upon.[5] On March 30, 1953, Wilson

---

[1] FO371/102671. BCA, to BEAA, 3.1.1953.

[2] Abba Habte-Mariam was born in Keren in 1922, studied theology in Eritrea and Italy and was received into the Catholic priesthood in 1946. See, Puglisi (1952:158),

[3] WO97/2817. BCA, to FO, 17.1.53. The attempt on WWM's life took place on 13.1.53. The report further stated that prior to federation WWM "was an ardent separatist, closely identified with the Tigrai secession movement and known to be in the pay of the Italians".

[4] WO97/2817. The letter is not dated. In the preamble it refers to the Emperor's first visit to Asmara which was in October 1952.

[5] FO371/102632. BCA, to FO, 4.2.53.

Heathcote, the financial advisor, resigned from his post on the grounds that he did not want to share the blame for the impending financial collapse.

While Eritrea was being quickly transformed from an efficiently administered colony into an Ethiopian region run by the Unionist Party-dominated Eritrean government, the federal authorities were also contributing their share to speeding up the process. Although the Ethiopian authorities committed themselves to release quarterly 1,400,000 Ethiopian dollars as Eritrea's share from the federal import taxes, it does not seem to have occurred to them that this amount should have been paid regularly.[1] The Eritrean government was put in a situation where they had to wait upon the mercy of federal authorities in Addis Ababa to receive what they were entitled to.[2]

The greatest cause of irritation was, however, the inefficiency of the federal authorities in the areas of their jurisdiction, i.e. customs, post and telecommunications, railways, defence and justice. The Eritreans were further irritated by the fact that the federal offices were more Ethiopian than federal, since they were filled by Ethiopian officials. The Eritreans saw very little that was federal in these offices since they were excluded from what they considered fair representation. The cause of such misunderstanding was, however, a misreading of the Federal Act rather than the reluctance of the Ethiopian authorities to share power with their Eritrean co-nationals. According to article five of the Federal Act, the Eritreans were to participate in the executive, judicial and legislative branches of the federal government in accordance with the law and in proportion to the relative size of the Eritrean population.

By the end of March 1953, the federation was facing serious problems, and the opinion that it was not working was quite widespread. Moreover, the Eritrean government's inefficient allocation of the budget created a spiralling economic recession which resulted in an increased tax burden on the population.[3] Explanations as to why the federation was not working, however, depended on who was talking and with whom. According to the president of the Eritrean Assembly Sheik Ali Redai, the problems of the federation lay in the fact that the

---

[1] FO371/102655. BCA to FO,19.2.53. In this despatch, Wardle-Smith was informed by Wilson-Heathcote, the financial advisor, that between 50 and 60 per cent of Eritrean revenue was derived from federal import taxes. Furthermore, Wardle-Smith was informed that "of the estimated 13 million Ethiopian dollars per annum, nearly 50 per cent is paid to salaries for the administration staff of the Eritrean government". Wilson-Heathcote was informed by Tedla Bairu that for political reasons it was impossible to reduce that figure at any rate for the moment.

[2] Government of Eritrea: Office of the Auditor General, Audit Report and General Account for the year ending on the 10th of September 1961. The Contribution from the Ethiopian Government was entered under Customs. This contribution remained fixed throughout the period at Ethiopian dollars 4,627,581. This was equivalent to 2.3 million US dollars to which the Ethiopian currency was related.

[3] Government of Eritrea: Office of the Auditor General, Audit Report and General Account for the year ending on the 10th of September 1961. The Auditor General, K.N.Pagdivala noted that 70 per cent of state expenditure was spent on salaries, thus leaving little for investments.

"Ethiopians never answered letters, never gave answers to specific queries, and in fact ignored the Eritrean government".[1]

As far as the president of the assembly was concerned, the federation had been a bad arrangement and, resorting to a more traditional form of expression, he said that "a hyena had been put with a goat and the result was obvious". The Director of the Interior, Haregot Abay, on the other hand, was less pessimistic and believed in the survival of federation. The greatest difficulty, according to the latter, was the attitude of the Emperor's representative and the various federal department heads in Eritrea. Haregot was "perfectly certain that the Emperor was unaware of the situation" and believed in a positive outcome if the Emperor were to be informed.[2] Both gentlemen believed that the Eritrean government was determined to make the federation work, but Haregot was of the opinion that federation would only work on the condition that the Eritreans themselves held together and did not remain divided.

In a private conversation with Her Majesty's Consulate-General, Tedla Bairu, the chief executive, by and large agreed with Haregot in his diagnosis of the ills of the federation. The chief executive felt sure that "the Emperor wanted to make federation work, and it was not working because of the attitude of the Ethiopian officials in this territory with whom he found it quite impossible to do business".[3] The Emperor's representative was the main culprit, but, according to Tedla, the latter's obstructionism was not intentional.

The views of the Eritrean government leaders on the problems of the federation as well as on the general conditions of the country were not shared by the British advisors, several members of the assembly, and by the opposition. As far as the government's relations with the federal authorities were concerned, the opinion of the British Consulate-General was that the Eritrean government led by Tedla Bairu did not stand firm and demand the strict application of the Federal Act as embodied in the constitution. Tedla Bairu preferred to function as the errand boy of the Emperor's representative rather than as an executive of the Eritrean cabinet and of the assembly that elected him. The judgement of the British Consulate-General strongly emphasised that Tedla Bairu was not up to the heavy responsibilities placed on him.

One who did not share the views of Her Majesty's servant was Wilson Heathcote, the financial advisor. After noting the main sources of revenue, i.e. customs duties, and the need for the reform of income tax laws so as to relieve the population from the weight of heavy taxation and to stimulate the economy, Wilson-Heathcote argued that the main problem lay with the Eritrean govern-

---

[1] WO97/2817. BCA to FO, 2.4.53. Ali Redai was speaking to Wardle-Smith privately at his home. His Majesty's consul advised the president of the Assembly that if the Eritrean parliamentarians "would stand up for what they considered to be their rights", he thought that they would get them.

[2] WO97/2817. Cracknell, D.P.P (Director of Eritrean Police) to BCA, 22.3.53.

[3] WO97/2817. BCA to FO, 4.2.53. Wardle-Smith commented that Tedla Bairu "will make any excuse to avoid doing what ought to be done".

ment in general and its chief executive in particular. His pungent assessment is so revealing that it deserves full quotation:

> The dominating role of the Chief Executive in the Government cannot be over-stressed. The Secretaries have been reduced to the status of clerks who are not permitted to take decisions on comparatively minor matters on their own. The Cabinet has never met despite the provision to that effect in the Constitution, neither has he taken any other steps to make the democratic provisions of the constitution function. On specious excuses he has violated the freedom of the press by suppressing the only independent newspaper, he has prevented reports of the Auditor-General being communicated to the Assembly and has vetoed persons returned in by-elections—all incidentally opposed to him politically. In the light of these facts I consider the thesis that he is a weak man unable to face up to his responsibilities vis à vis the federal government is untenable. The alternative argument that he is deliberately conducting the affairs of his country so that its complete amalgamation with Ethiopia will be an accomplished fact in a short time seems to me to be much more in keeping with the evidence. The deliberate avoidance of pressing for a settlement of the Eritrean share of customs, without which early insolvency is inevitable, the failure to take administrative decisions while keeping the right of decision in his hands all seem to me to point in the same direction. Added to this it is more than possible that he is not politically his own master having given forfeits to the more extreme unionists.[1]

Commenting on the speech made by the Chief Executive accounting for the work of his government, Her Majesty's Consul in Asmara, pointed out once again the unsatisfactory relations between the Chief Executive and his cabinet, on the one hand, and the assembly on the other. There was a widespread feeling, continued the British Consul, that members of the assembly were not allowed to carry out their proper functions and that they were being treated by the Chief Executive in a dictatorial and cavalier manner.[2]

In the sharp and perhaps relentless opinion of the financial advisor, both the problems of the federation and of the Eritrean economy were caused by the inefficiency and deliberate policy of the Chief Executive and his cabinet. Similar views, though expressed in a more abrasive and, what one might call typically Eritrean manner, were aired by Abraha Tessema, the main contender for the office of the Chief Executive. Answering a question put to him by Wardle-Smith, he said the federation was in a hopeless situation and that "annexation was inevitable". For Abraha Tessema, the last hope for postponing the union lay with the Moslems, and he promised that, if they rallied in sufficient strength, he would help them.[3]

---

[1] FO371/102635. Memorandum of Mr. J. Wilson-Heathcote on Eritrean politics and finance, London, 6.5.53.

[2] FO371/102656. BCA to FO, 26.6.53. "To a certain extent", continued Wardle-Smith, "this is true but the situation is much of their [members of the Assembly] own making. [T]hey are a comparatively weak collection of men who time and again let matters go by default and then blame others for the disagreeable result".

[3] BCA to BEAA, 14.5.53. Abraha Tessema had a very interesting comment on Omar Kadi, one of the leaders of the ML. Abraha said that he did not have much faith in the Kadi who was probably trying to build up a sufficient nuisance value in order to recieve a fat bribe from the Ethiopians.

Moslem opposition to the federation, which in fact never ceased, received support from some Christian members of the assembly who went through the frustrating experience of dictatorial treatment by the Chief Executive. The federation was not working because there was no distinction between the Ethiopian government and the federal government. The allegedly federal authorities in Eritrea did not appear to the public to be so, as they were not staffed by an equal number of Eritrean and Ethiopian officials. By June 1953, or nine months after the federation came into force, the leaders of the ML of the Western Province had made up their minds firstly to oppose federation and, in the event of union, to campaign for "the formation of an independent state comprising the Western Province of Eritrea and the Eastern Province of the Sudan".[1]

A surprised and quite worried Wardle-Smith took up his field experience in the Western Province with highly placed American and British Advisors to the Imperial as well as the Federal government in Addis Ababa. The American advisor John Spencer, who did not seem unduly worried, expressed the opinion that, "if the Western Province wanted to go to the Sudan he did not think the Ethiopians would care very much".[2] Similar views were expressed by Frank Stafford, one of the architects of British policy both in Eritrea and Ethiopia, a man who had extensive knowledge of Eritrean politics. Stafford recalled that "the idea of a Beja state was an old story but a true one". He agreed with Wardle-Smith that the Western Province would want to go to the Sudan and that the Ethiopians would not be unduly upset.[3]

By September 1953, opposition movements were beginning to emerge. The first and most articulate was the ML, which had voluntarily disbanded when the federation came into force, and was revived again to safeguard the rights laid out in the constitution.[4] The second was an anonymous group that started its clandestine activities in the wake of the successful visit of the Emperor's Representative to the Western Province in early September. In a widely distributed poster in the market area of Asmara, the "people of Eritrea" were warned that the "Chief Executive together with his supporters has decided to sell you to Amhara by disregarding newspapers and abolishing the federation".[5] From the language of the pamphlet it could be argued that the ML supported the propaganda and that this anonymous group may have been an underground branch of the ML.

---

[1] FO371/102635. BCA to FO, 9.7.53. This was a report of his visit to the Western Province the stronghold of the ML. Wardle-Smith continued, "That the Western Province will not countenance full Ethiopian domination was made clear to me by almost everyone with whom I spoke, and there is no doubt that in the very possible event of total union between Eritrea and Ethiopia the Western Province, failing the achievement of an independent Beja state, would in all probability ask to be incorporated with the Sudan".

[2] FO371/102635. BCA to BEAA, 18.7.53.

[3] FO371/102635. BCA to BEAA, 18.7.53.

[4] FO371/102635. BCA to BEAA, 28.9.53.

[5] FO371/102635. BCA to BEAA, 9.9.53.

The first anniversary of the federation was marked by three events: the absence of the Chief Executive (who was in Addis Ababa); a widespread feeling of unhappiness from the assembly as to the conduct of the Chief Executive; and by the first written appeal to the United Nations calling for the strict application of the United Nations resolution.[1]

By the middle of October, 1953, the leaders of the revived Moslem organizations, i.e. the Moslem League, the Independent Moslem League, and the National Party, addressed an open, signed telegram to the UN. The first in a series of protests, the telegram was most probably seen as a vote of no confidence for the government of Tedla Bairu. It was also one of the first telegrams where the Moslem leaders were primarily concerned with the protection of their rights as Moslems. Notably absent from the list of signatories were the leaders of the ML of the Western Province who were canvassing for support for the formation of an independent Beja state. The ML of the Western Province, a valuable ally of the Unionist Party during the constitutional discussions, was led by Sheik Ali Redai, president of the assembly. For reasons that the British advisors were unable to decipher, the ML of the Western Province chose its own way.

In Addis Ababa Tedla Bairu was openly criticized by Eritreans for not negotiating a higher rank for his office as Chief Executive[2] and for not standing up for the constitutional rights of Eritrea. At home the Chief Executive was harassed by the provocative protests of the Moslem organizations, and faced with the growing opposition from Christian Unionists and former separatists. Still anxious to retain power, the Chief Executive Tedla Bairu began to resort to more flagrant unconstitutional measures. One such act was the arrest of one of his main political enemies, Abraha Tessema on charges of complicity in an attempt on the life of the Chief Executive.[3]

According to the Commissioner of Police, there were indications that the Chief Executive arranged the so-called "attempt on his life in order to discredit the Tessema family and particularly Abraha Tessema against whom he had carried on a vendetta since he defeated him in the election in 1952 for the posi-

---

[1] FO371/102633. BCA to BEAA, 12.9.53. The letter contained four complaints: a) return of internal authority which Ethiopia had taken; b) stopping of the extension of the courts of Ethiopia into Eritrea; c) return of Ethiopian soldiers in Eritrea to Ethiopia; and d) that the Representative of His Majesty should cease to interfere in the internal affairs of Eritrea. The letter is concluded with the warning remark that if immediate action is not taken, the anonymous authors would "surely be against the government of Haile Sellassie which is in turn against individual freedom towards human beings".

[2] The Eritrean Chief Executive was granted the title of Dejazmatch. His critics in Addis Ababa were of the opinion that the title of Ras was appropriate to the highest officer in Eritrea.

[3] FO371/102635. BCA to FO, 27.10.53.

tion of the Chief Executive".[1] Although it was impossible to bring concrete charges against Abraha Tessema, and contrary to the opinion of his advisors, the Chief Executive signed a decree for his indefinite incarceration.[2] Moreover, through the police the Chief Executive proceeded to intimidate the lawyers and family members of Abraha Tessema.[3]

As 1953 came to an end, the Chief Executive and his supporters had managed to increase taxes, to alienate most of the Moslem population, undermine the constitution, extend an authoritarian rule, force the British advisors to resign and bring Eritrea much closer to union with Ethiopia. On December 12, 1953, the Superintendent of Prisons, Major Whaley resigned giving as a reason that the Chief Executive purposely undermined the police force.[4] The next day, The Deputy Attorney-General, discouraged and disillusioned, informed Her Majesty's Consul that he doubted if he could remain in Eritrea much longer. He found it too hard to deal with his being "constantly asked by the Chief Executive to find legal excuses for carrying out unconstitutional acts".[5]

The political history of the Eritrean government was lucidly summed up by Abraha Tessema who was released from detention in the beginning of December (1953). Talking to the British and American Consuls, he made the following points. He described Tedla Bairu as merely the stooge of the Emperor. He said that since there was no freedom of the press and very little freedom of speech, it was difficult to oppose the Chief Executive or to form a properly constituted constitutional opposition. He reiterated what he had stated earlier: that annexation was inevitable and that eventually, Eritrea would become no more than a province of Ethiopia. He believed that after annexation, the Eritrean people would realise that they were doomed and would rise against their masters, and civil war would ensue. Opposition was ruled out because, Abraha Tessema argued, the Eritreans were hopelessly divided by religious and racial divisions. His conclusion was indeed prophetic. He said, "Having succumbed to Ethiopian annexation at some future time they will realise that they are once more an

---

[1] FO371/102635. BCA to FO, 28.10.53. "The so called assailants were Jassu Tessema and Michael Wolela. As you know these two men were arrested by the police outside the cinema and found to be in possession of a revolver and hand grenades. Further, Tedla Bairu's car was outside the cinema but he himself was not there.

    The police investigations to which I have confidential access through the Commissioner, show quite definiteley that Wolela, a well known terrorist in the days of the British Administration and a member of the Andinet Party, was in the house of Tedla Bairu during the evening of Friday, October 23, only 24 hours before the arrest. It is also significant that on the day following his arrest he demanded to be released as his part of the affair had been accomplished.

    With regard to Jassu, he had reason to be angry with the Chief Executive in that he had recently been demoted from District Officer at Addi Quala and given a clerk's job in the inland revenue department". See BCA to FO, 30.11.53.

[2] FO371/102635. BCA to FO, 30.10.53.

[3] FO371/102635. BCA to FO, 4.11.53.

[4] FO371/102632. BCA to FO, 15.12.53. The reasons were: i) that the police would not interfere with his political machinations and ii) because it was a useful field for "jobs for the boys".

[5] FO371/102632. BCA to FO, 15.12.53.

occupied territory", and concluded that this might unite the Eritrean people against the Ethiopians.[1]

Abraha Tessema was a staunch federalist and he strongly believed that his political ideas were as much in the interests of Ethiopia as of Eritrea.[2] According to Abraha Tessema, a strong federation was the only possible solution for Eritrea. Talking about Eritrean attitudes towards Ethiopians, he said that they did not dislike the Ethiopians for racial reasons, but because "they were not going to fill the economic gap" left by the Italians and the British. Abraha Tessema continued and stated that if "the Ethiopians would be generous they would have Eritrea behind them at once...but unfortunately they were not going to get it from the Ethiopians and they [the Eritreans] had not sufficient courage to fight for it".[3] Abraha concluded the dinner evening with the European diplomatic corps with deep regret for the demise of the Italian colonial era and expressed the idea that the departure of every Italian meant an average of three more unemployed Eritreans.

ERITREA, 1953: AUTONOMOUS BUT NOT FEDERAL

From the coming into force of federation in September 1952 until the end of 1953 there were three quite well articulated issues of contention between the Ethiopian and the Eritrean governments. The first and by far the most important issue was that of ascertaining the Eritrean share of the customs duties. A few months before the political transfer, the British had negotiated with the Ethiopians and agreed on a figure of 681,000 pounds (4.1 million Ethiopian dollars). This was communicated to Eritrean politicians. The Ethiopians also agreed to pay this sum to Eritrea in quarterly instalments and in advance.

The problem arose first when the Ethiopians failed to pay regularly and in advance, and secondly, when they began to question the fairness of paying a fixed sum in advance before they themselves had received the customs revenue. The Ethiopians were not at all sure how much of the value of the total imported goods remained in Eritrea and how much was re-exported to Ethiopia. The Eritrean government could not be of any assistance, since they themselves did not have any system of identifying the destiny of imports, i.e. the quantity of goods which remained in Eritrea and the quantity of goods which continued to Ethiopia.

According to its financial advisor Wilson Heathcote, the Eritrean government failed to press the Ethiopian government for a solution of the issue once and for all and the Chief Executive had not taken his responsibility. The issue was, however, more complex. One of the reasons why the Ethiopians were not

---

[1] FO371/108196. BCA to FO, 24.12.53. Confidential.

[2] On the eve of the visit of the UN Commission of Enquiry to Eritrea, Abraha Tessema had disengaged himself from the party of his father (Tessema Asberom leader of the Liberal Progressive Party) and campaigned for a conditional union with Ethiopia.

[3] FO371/108196. BCA to FO, 24.12.53. Confidential.

paying in advance, in addition to different budgetary practices, was that they wanted to establish the exact amount of duties to which Eritrea would be entitled. So while the Ethiopian government continued to pay the amount they were committed to, an inter-governmental committee was set up to find out a means of identifying the destiny of imports.

By the end of 1953, the issue as to the exact sum and mode of payment was still unresolved with the effect that the Eritrean government was constantly on the brink of not being able to pay salaries to its over-staffed bureaucracy.

The second issue, by far more delicate, was that of staffing federal departments, post and telecommunications, the customs, the railways, and the defence institutions. Many Eritreans, and especially those organized by the Moslem organizations, believed that as federal partners Eritreans were entitled to equal representation. Protests in the early months of the life of the federation had in fact caused the Ethiopians to change their intentions of staffing the federal posts with people from other parts of Ethiopia. There were indeed some Eritreans working in the federal departments, but these were by no means in high executive positions. The federal departments, as opposed to the departments of the Eritrean government, remained very distinct and separate, and eventually became symbols of the inefficiency of federal rule.

The third issue that became one of the test cases in the management of relations between the assembly, the Chief Executive and his cabinet and the Emperor's Representative, was the registration of foreign nationals and the issuance of identity cards. The issue was raised when a member of the assembly argued that the issuance of identity cards and collection of subsequent fees were an internal affair of the Eritrean government. The issue was interesting because there could have been something for both parties. The Ethiopian government could have quite easily argued that, according to the constitution as well as the Federal Act, foreign nationals were under the jurisdiction of the Federal authorities. The Eritrean government, on the other hand, could have argued with a great chance of success that the actual issuance of identity cards and the collection of fees (10 Eth. dollars annually) ought to be left to Eritrea as the country of residence of the foreigners in question.

The Ethiopian government had obviously no desire to enter into a dispute with the Eritrean government concerning the division of responsibilities. However, the Emperor's representative would have had no alternative to negotiation, if the issue raised in the assembly had been presented by the Chief Executive as one that deserved dispassionate discussion. The manner in which the Chief Executive handled the motion provided further evidence of the predicaments of the assembly rather than the interfering hands of the Emperor's Representative.

Theoretically, it could be argued that the Eritrean government could have stood up and demanded equal representation at least in the federal departments functioning in Eritrea. As the unfolding of events in the subsequent years would show, the odds against the Eritrean government defending and maintaining the constitution were so overwhelming that the raising of such a question may be considered unprofitable.

By the end of 1953 Eritrean autonomy was severely compromised. The federation existed in name only. Eritrean opposition was weak and divided. The Emperor's Representative with his considerable powers over important aspects of Eritrean politics and economy did indeed contribute his share in the extension of Ethiopian administration to Eritrea. Although both the Emperor and his representative professed to see little difference between federation and complete union,[1] the powers of the Emperor's representative were limited by the constitution and the Federal Act of the United Nations. Nor did the representative possess the means for enforcing his views other than the Federal Act and the Eritrean Constitution.

Eritrean autonomy was compromised because of the social and political alignments that prevailed in Eritrea. The Eritrean Assembly, made up of equal numbers of Christians and Moslems, with few exceptions, consisted of members who could not fully live up to the heavy and delicate tasks placed upon them. The Eritrean Assembly could have supported Abba Habte-Mariam Nugurru when he presented a motion challenging the Ethiopian government not to interfere in Eritrean internal affairs. In theory the Eritrean assembly could have pressed the Chief Executive and his cabinet to be more accountable instead of allowing the Chief Executive to use them as simple clerks.

The Eritrean Assembly, I argue, was paralyzed for three reasons. The first reason was that it was led by an Executive Committee that had campaigned for complete union with Ethiopia. Tedla Bairu, the Chief Executive, was the leader of the Unionist Party that had campaigned for the speedy and complete absorption of Eritrea by Ethiopia. Although not all of the members of his cabinet were of the same political persuasion, they were in no position to challenge him since he did not treat his cabinet in a democratic manner. The cabinet was never called after it was formed in July 1952. The Chief Executive, it appears, preferred to fulfil the wishes of the Emperor's representative rather than the tasks entrusted to him by the constitution and the assembly. The opening statement of his first report to the assembly on the activities of his government is illustrative. Referring to the history of the federation the Chief Executive said, "This decision of the General Assembly of the United Nations which unites Eritrea with Ethiopia was called "Federation".[2] This view of the first leader of an autonomous Eritrea was shared by the British Consul, the British advisors to the Chief Executive, by Abraha Tessema, and by the Moslem League.

---

[1] FO371/108194. BEAA, to FO, 4.2.54. A review of the events of 1953 in Ethiopia and Eritrea. Ambassador Busk wrote, "Although at this interview the Emperor professed to see little difference between federation and complete union, nevertheless my warnings as to the probable attitude of HM Government in the event of federation failing must have been clearly understood".

[2] FO371/102656. BCA to FO, Appendix "A" to Minutes no.169 of 22.6.53. The report is 15 pages long and according to Wardle-Smith it was not received well.

The second factor that further undermined the maintenance of Eritrean autonomy was the contradictory and unenviable position of the Unionist Party. Although the new status of Eritrea as an autonomous unit had begun to win the hearts of the young and the educated, the majority of the Unionist activists saw federation as a temporary hindrance to complete union with the motherland or as a plot by Ethiopian enemies to weaken the country (Redda, 1954). Many of these activists sat in the assembly and had no inclination to encourage the Chief Executive to change track. In many ways, through their periodical appeals (to the Emperor and his representative) for the abolition of federation, the members of the Unionist Party circumscribed the sphere of action of the Chief Executive. By the end of 1953, the Unionist Party had considerable strength which the Chief Executive could not afford to dismiss.

A third undermining factor was the sectarian aspect of Moslem League politics. Coaxed and forced into accepting the federation, the ML factions were always on the brink of breaking away from Eritrea and Ethiopia. In their first anonymous testimony of protest, the Moslem organizations were primarily interested in protecting their interests as Moslems within or outside the federation. Their action in a number of cases gave the impression that they did not fully grasp the real powers entrusted to the Ethiopian government by the United Nations Resolution.[1] In one of the assembly sessions where we have a report, all the Moslem members of the assembly left the building after having been prevented on procedural grounds from raising an issue on the equal treatment of Moslem and Christian holidays.[2] By the end of 1953, the revived Moslem organizations appear to have taken for granted that all non-Moslem Eritreans were in favour of the policies pursued by the Chief Executive and the Emperor's Representative. In fact, the ML was to dominate the political arena for the most of the following year.

THE OFFENSIVE OF THE ML

The year began with the fleeing into exile of Woldeab Wolde Mariam, a courageous opposition leader who was harassed by the Chief Executive and his supporters in the police force. Labour unrest that surfaced in Massawa in the middle of the previous year moved to Asmara in early 1954.[3] While the Asmara strike in the beginning of March was resolved without recourse to the ruthless might of the police, a strike at the Eritrean port of Assab was suppressed at the

---

[1] FO371/102656. BCA to FO, 9.10.53. Discussing the promulgation of Eritrean Notaries and Bailiffs Act, where the heading of the Act began with "Imperial Ethiopian Government: Government of Eritrea", most of the Moslems quite wrongly decided to regard this preamble as an infringement of the Constituion or "even as an invitation to the Ethiopian government to annex Eritrea".

[2] FO371/102656. BCA to FO, 9.10.53.

[3] FO371/108297. BEAA to FO, 4.2.54. The reason for the strike "was the dismissal of ten labourers; but the opinion was officially held that the strike was aimed against one of the directors, Ato Yacob, who was considered to have been hostile to the labourers' interests".

cost of three lives.[1] One of the main reasons for this strike was the arbitrary rejection by the Ethiopians of a 20 per cent pay rise authorized by the Eritrean District Officer.

It had become clear to the politically conscious Eritreans that the ultimate objective of the Imperial federal government was the abolition of the federation in favour of complete union. The Unionist Party, under the reorganized leadership of Gebreselassie Garza and Sahle Ande-Mikael, was a constant reminder of the desire of some sections of the Eritrean people for such a policy. The Chief Executive was also suspected (by some members of his cabinet) of encouraging the UP and thus of undermining the federation.

The Moslem League under the indefatigable leadership of Ibrahim Sultan and Mohamed Omar Kadi continued to complain officially to the Ethiopian government over the violation of the federation. The ML stressed two issues throughout the year. The first was the division of powers between the Eritrean and Ethiopian governments. The second issue dealt with the prerogatives of the Emperor to exempt the people of the Western Province from taxes as a result of bad rains. Convinced that the "Eritrean government, part of the Assembly and its President... are working solidly together in a common campaign for annexation", the ML directed its efforts towards the European consulates and the United Nations.[2]

Whereas the issue dealing with the division of powers was to remain a source of continuous inspiration, the tax issue appears to have been a nervous reaction to the successful policy carried out by the Emperor and his representative of incorporating the Western Province into the empire. The inhabitants of the Western Province who did not show any involvement in politics in Asmara, were more interested in being left alone. The visit by the Emperor's representative in the summer of 1953 and his affirmation of their rights to cross the borders into the northwestern part of Ethiopia to find pastures for their livestock had won them over to the idea of federation. The ML was not happy at all and expressed its dissatisfaction by distributing leaflets in Asmara on the sinister motives behind the representative's visit. The ML reacted in a similar manner when the Emperor's representative repeated his visit in June 1954, and, according to the British consulate, his visit no doubt "helped to placate the hostile attitude of the Moslem population towards the Ethiopian connection".[3] The ML became even more agitated when the Emperor waived the 1954 tax that the inhabitants of the Western Province were liable to pay, thus raising two issues at the same time.

---

[1] FO371/108297. BEAA to FO, 4.2.54. The British ambassador noted that in Ethiopia strike action is rebellion and, not as in more fortunate countries, social conflict. He deplored the fact that the Ethiopian approach had been "ruthless".

[2] FO371/108196. A letter to all the consulates from Ibrahim Sultan, dated Asmara, 19.2.54.

[3] FO371/108197. BCA to BEAA, 30.6.54. The Representative began his journey to the Western Province on June 26.

The first issue was easily dealt with. Since the Emperor, who was then in Asmara, was in a mood to listen, two members of the assembly and a third from the western province were granted an audience to explain their objections. The leaders of the ML might have felt that they achieved their purpose in the sense that they dared to approach the august Emperor and ask him to change his magnanimous decision but their arguments were much poorer than the answer they received.[1] The Emperor is alleged to have replied thus: "I have helped the poor and not the rich and the quota of the rich can go to the hospitals and schools".[2] The ML was on much safer and more secure ground when it continued to accuse the Imperial government of interference in the internal affairs of the Eritrean government.

In a very long note addressed to the Emperor, the leaders of the Moslem organizations took up in great detail the legal and constitutional reasons why the federation was not working and what they stood to lose. In a telegram to the UN, the ML leaders pointed out that the Ethiopian government had failed "to set up organs of federal government whose role and functions have been taken up solely by that of Ethiopia".[3] The main thrust of the unusually long letter of complaint to the emperor was for the need to establish a federal government quite distinct and separate both from the Eritrean and Ethiopian governments.

This was by far the most unchallengeable argument of the ML which the Ethiopians found rather hard to grasp. For the Emperor and his representative in Eritrea federation and unity were synonymous terms. In the middle of 1953, answering one of the first motions calling for the Ethiopian government to cease interference in the internal affairs of Eritrea, the representative pointed out that there were no internal and external affairs as far as the office of the Emperor in Eritrea was concerned. For the representative, a part of Ethiopia was called Eritrea. The Ethiopian view was shared by the Chief Executive and the Unionist Party who, though accepting federation as a transitional phase, used every opportunity to express their wish for a total union.

In its memorandum, the ML pointed out quite clearly that the Ethiopian government had failed to implement a federal constitution as was required by the Federal Act of 1950. It pointed out the obvious: that there was no federal arrangement between Eritrea and Ethiopia as long as the Ethiopian government was part of the federation and acted as the head of the same federation. The memorandum noted the establishment of the Federal Council but pointed out that it had only nominal power and, therefore, was neither heard nor respected.

---

[1] FO371/108196. A letter to all consulates from Ibrahim Sultan, dated Asmara, 19.2.54. In para. 10 of the letter Ibrahim Sultan provides excerpts of the arguments and the Emperor's reply. To the statement, "Your Majesty could have given other help to the Government of Eritrea which might have been used to improve hospitals, schools, agriculture, orphanages or other charitable institutions, but it is not a good thing to excuse tributes", the Emperor replied, "I have helped the poor and not the rich and the quota of the rich can go to the hospitals and schools".

[2] FO371/108196. A letter to all consulates from Ibrahim Sultan, dated Asmara, 19.2.1954.

[3] FO371/108196. The letter addressed to his Imperial Majesty contains a copy sent to the United Nations Secretariat on 12.10.1953.

After pointing out the Imperial Ethiopian government's failure to establish federal executive and judiciary organs, the ML memorandum further illustrated Ethiopian violations of the federation by citing cases where the Ethiopian government arbitrarily extended its legislation to Eritrea without consultation with the Eritrean government.

The ML memorandum continued to list the areas of contention of a more concrete nature, thus in a way setting the tone for the politics of the Eritrean Liberation Front that would emerge just a year before the official demise of the federation. The ML charged that the British Administration had conspired with the Ethiopian government and handed over to the latter both movable and immovable property of the Italian state. Such property should have been transferred to the Eritrean government. In contravention of the Federal Act and the Eritrean constitution, the Ethiopian authorities had taken possession of Eritrean railways, post and telephone communications which were part of internal communications, and, therefore, under the sphere of the Eritrean government.

The memorandum then turned its concern to the role of the Emperor's representative, whose visits to the western province had caused great irritation among the leaders of the Moslem organizations, and they argued that Ethiopia, through the activities of the representative was "working to make null and void the federation and to change it sooner or later into an unconditional annexation".

The memorandum of the ML also pointed out the impact of the extension of the 1931 Constitution of the Empire of Ethiopia to Eritrean Moslems.[1] Summing up, the ML memo stressed that Ethiopia having acted contrary to the decision of the UN, had seized all sources of income of the Eritrean government and created a serious deficit in spite of increased taxation. The ML memo, composed by Ibrahim Sultan, Omar Kadi and Ahmed Abdelkadir Beshi, was almost certainly not forwarded to the Emperor; neither was it distributed in published form since the ML organ, *Voice of Eritrea*, was suppressed in the middle of 1953. There were, however, ample possibilities for the ML organizations to debate and develop the issues raised in the memo, since political organizations were not as yet suppressed.

One reason for the concerted activities of the leaders of the Moslem organizations was, in fact, the success of the visits of the Emperor and his representative to the western province. Whereas, one year previously the majority of the local leaders of the Western Province had been declared anti-unionists, there was, by the beginning of 1954, a marked change in the political climate. During

---

[1] FO371/108196. The memorandum was adressed to his Imperial Majesty on 12.10. 53. The same material was sent to the BCA on 19.2.54. "In fact as a result of the extension of the Ethiopian Constitution in Eritrea it happened that also the Moslem population of Eritrea as wellas that in Ethiopia had been deprived of its civil and religious rights in as much as the Ethiopian Constitution does not recognise for the Moslems of Ethiopia their festivities as public holidays and in consequence the Eritrean Moslem element is under the necessity of recognising, in the same wise as the Moslem element in Ethiopia only those Coptic festivities of Christian denomination as national official festivities".

a visit to the western province, the British Consul reported that he was disappointed to find that of all the senior district officers and officers of the Eritrean Police "only one was a staunch federalist".[1] He was Saleh Hinet from the district of Tessenei.[2] For the most part, continued the British Consul, "the others are waiverers. In other words, they are prepared to be carried by the stream whether it goes towards federation or union". As for the population, the Consul was left with the impression that the chiefs and sheiks took little interest in the Ethiopian question and were far more interested in Kassala and Khartoum than in Asmara and Addis Ababa.

There could also have been an element of self-interest in the campaign by the Moslem leaders to maintain the federation. Omar Kadi was the man who Abraha Tessema described as the one who was making noise in order to be bribed by the Ethiopians. Ibrahim Sultan, the veteran politician who was consistently for the independence of Eritrea, might too have been more interested in his own affairs than in political goals. Four months after the despatch of the ML memo to the United Nations and the Ethiopian Emperor, Ibrahim Sultan was virtually excluded from the leadership of the ML on the grounds that he was working closely with Keshi Dimetros, a well-known unionist, and "he has been seeing the Emperor's Representative a lot lately".[3]

Ibrahim Sultan and Omar Kadi were not the only champions of federation. Most of the members of the assembly from the western province were strict federalists who still believed in its functioning. On May 22, the Moslem members of the assembly were so dissatisfied at the ineffectual report of the Chief Executive on the conditions of the country that they got together and passed two motions calling on Ethiopia to cease interfering in the internal affairs of Eritrea.[4] Their determination to keep the pressure up was further strengthened by the decision of the federal authorities to bring the editors of the ML organ, *Voice of*

---

[1] FO371/108196, BCA to BEAA, 1.4.54. The visit was undertaken in the beginning of March with the object of finding out "the extent to which the Ethiopian scheme of working upon the provincial Eritrean officers in their efforts to bring about union was succeeding".

[2] FO371/108196. Saleh Hinet was despatched to Tessenei by the Chief Executive because of disagreements in matters of policy.

[3] FO371/108197. BCA to BEAA, 12.7.54. The British Consul reported: "The Moslem League instead of taking direct action against Ibrahim Sultan as a result of the discovery of his recent intrigues, has apparently formed a Political Committee of ten persons, one of whom is Omar Akito, a member of the Assembly, to be responsible for the future political policy of the League. From this Committee and its activities Ibrahim Sultan is, of course, excluded".

[4] FO371/108201. BCA to FO, 24.5.54. The motion: "... but deplore the fact that there was no mention in the speech of government policy regarding the action of the federal authorities in their attempt to corrupt the faith of the Eritrean members who represent the people, and of the Eritrean government officials contrary to the letter and spirit of the United Nations Resolution of December 2, 1950, and also deplore their continuous interference in the internal functions of Eritrea injuring thereby the authority of the Eritrean government and impeding its proper functioning.

We also order that His Imperial Majesty, The Sovereign of the Federation, be kept informed of this state of affairs so that he may think fit to take such possible steps in order that the resolution be properly adhered to.

If the assembly does not see such necessary action taken within twenty days we order the Eritrean government to submit this resolution to the United Nations".

Eritrea, to court. Not only was the issue as to whether the federal authorities had jurisdiction over the case very controversial, the editors had already been tried by the Eritrean courts towards the end of 1953 and set free, but their newspaper was closed down by direct orders of the chief executive. Moreover, the decision of the federal authorities raised the issue of the freedom of the press, a right guaranteed by the constitution but not respected by the government of the Chief Executive. The Moslem members of the assembly were, however, unable to raise the matter, since the chief executive fearing the outcome, preferred to exercise his constitutional right and suspend the regular session.[1]

While the proceedings against the editors of the ML newspaper encouraged the Moslem members at the assembly to organize their action, the belated reply of the Emperor to their motions sent through the Eritrean Government appeared to have given them reason to redouble their efforts. All of the 29 Moslem members who signed the motion to the Emperor did not go to the residence of the Emperor's representative to hear the reply.[2] Instead, they declared their intention to reorganize the Moslem League as the main defence of autonomy and to try to buy printing presses with which to continue publication of *Voice of Eritrea*.[3]

The Moslem organizations and the Moslem members of the assembly did in fact succeed in engaging the Ethiopian government in discussions on the relations between the two governments. Their victory over the anti-federalist Chief Executive (in forcing him to forward the two motions from the assembly) and the reply from the Emperor, first denying knowledge of Ethiopian interference in Eritrean internal affairs and, secondly, committing himself to respect Eritrean internal administration, were by far the most notable achievements of the year. Ten days after the Emperor's reply to their motions and while the proceedings against the editors of *Voice of Eritrea* were in progress, the leaders of the Moslem organisations convened a congress in Keren which about 2,500 people were said to have attended. According to what the British Consul was able to learn, it was decided to attempt to unite all the Moslems of Eritrea within the Moslem League to the exclusion of all other parties. It was also decided that the Moslems should not fall into the hands of the Ethiopian government by reacting with violence against the policy of Tedla Bairu's government. Moreover, the congress decided to give the government of Tedla Bairu six months to readjust its attitudes

---

[1] FO371/108197. Her Majesty's Consul reported that the chief Executive's action in suspending a regular session was "due to members insisting upon competence to discuss the pending proceedings in the Federal Court against the independent Newspaper, Voice of Eritrea, whose editors are accused of subversive political activity".

[2] FO371/108197. BCA to FO, 10.9.54. The Imperial message as summarized by the British consul was as follows: "The Emperor denies any knowledge of interference with Eritrean rights. He rebukes the Assembly for unconstitutional behaviour which led to the suspension, and declares the competence of the Federal Court to replace legislation passed by the Federal Government within a sphere defined by the Federal Act. He also stresses the personal order that Eritrean Internal Administration shall, in future, be respected".

[3] FO371/108197. BCA to FO, 10.9.54.

towards the Moslem population after which the Emperor or, if necessary, the United Nations would be officially approached.[1]

THE POLITICAL ALIENATION OF THE CHIEF EXECUTIVE

While the Moslems in the assembly and outside were engaged in a campaign for the maintenance of Eritrean autonomy as a guarantee for the exercise of their rights, Chief Executive Tedla Bairu was more concerned with power and the privileges that emanated from it. As throughout the previous year Tedla Bairu continued to govern Eritrea without the mediating and restraining advice of his cabinet and the assembly. Neither as Chief Executive nor as the leader of the government did he show interest in the growing labour unrest in Massawa and Assab. To the chagrin of the ML and many non-Moslem federalists, Tedla Bairu let the Ethiopian authorities settle the strikes in Massawa and Assab in their own fashion. By the beginning of 1954, Tedla Bairu was alienated from his own cabinet who attempted to recruit the British head of the police, D.P.P. Cracknell, to their side.

Cracknell, the chief of police, had no doubt that the Chief Executive had little support among the police force, where the majority were federalists. In the course of an interview, Cracknell explained for the Chief Executive the reasons why the latter lost popularity among his people. In addition to reasons mentioned earlier, Cracknell mentioned that the Chief Executive had failed to demonstrate a clear policy vis à vis the federal authorities. He also mentioned the vindictive attitude that the Chief Executive pursued against political opponents such as Woldeab Wolde Mariam, Ibrahim Sultan and Abraha Tessema. The Chief Executive was also reminded that his extensive private transactions, and the appointment of old political associates and people from his district to senior posts in the civil service had made the people lose so much confidence that "if he so desired he would have to reassure people by deeds".[2]

In the beginning of 1954, the Secretary of the Interior, Mohamed Said Faki Ali and the newly appointed Director of the Interior, Tesfaldet Gered tried, with some success to enlist Cracknell's support to thwart the policy of the Chief Executive and to "stem the Union tide".[3] Cracknell was asked to keep a special eye on the activities of certain government officials known to sympathize with the Ethiopian move. These were the SDO of Keren, Embaye Habte, the SDO of Serae, Berhane Kiflemariam and the director of public relations, Zerom Kifle. Cracknell, who had long since lost confidence in the commitment and capability of the Chief Executive to maintain the federation, appeared to go along with this

---

[1] FO371/108197. BCA to BEAA, 30.9.54.

[2] FO371/108196. BCA to BEAA, 22.5.54. A report of Cracknell to the British Consul, Wardle-Smith.

[3] FO371/108196. BCA to BEAA, 22.2.54. A report written by Cracknell to the British Consul, Wardle-Smith.

request and even offered to ask the Chief Executive to resign "in the interests of the Eritrean people".[1]

The question has been raised as to whether the Chief Executive was implementing the wishes of the Emperor's representative or his own. The documentary evidence available seems to strongly indicate that Tedla Bairu was determined to abolish the federation much sooner than the Ethiopian authorities were willing to and, it appears, in spite of their good advice. Tedla Bairu paid more attention to the leaders of the Unionist Party than to the substance of the arguments put forward by either the opposition or other federalists.

The first breach with the Emperor's representative occurred in March when Tedla Bairu tried unsuccessfully to force the resignation of the chief justice and president of the Eritrean Supreme Court, Sir James Shearer, and his colleague Mr. O'Hanlon. Apart from the fact that these judges were appointed for a term of seven years, they could hardly bring themselves to resign since resignation would not entitle them to any compensation. A far stronger reason for the judges determination to remain firm, however, was the weakness of the motives calling for their resignation.

As motives for their resignation, the judges were told that there was not "that close co-operation between the Executive and the Judiciary" which Tedla thought was necessary for the good government of the country. The judges were also informed that the Chief Executive regretted to notice that they seemed "to have been unable to adjust to the peculiar needs of the country".[2] Shearer's long reply, copies of which were submitted to the British Consulate, formed the basis of British intervention with the federal authorities both in Asmara and Addis Ababa. As far as the British were concerned, the main reason why Tedla Bairu wanted the British judges removed was because they declared illegal the detention of Abraha Tessema and freed his brother Jassu Tessema from a charge of attempted murder.

If the British had doubts as to whether Tedla Bairu could act on his own, it became clear to them when they approached the Ethiopian authorities on the matter, i.e. the call for resignation of the judges. The Emperor's representative said that the letter by which Tedla Bairu requested the resignation of the judges should have never been sent. Privately the Emperor's representative conceded to the British Consul that Tedla Bairu could be impeached for his unconstitutional action.[3] The Emperor's Representative was, however, unwilling to use his good offices, because as he put it, "he was always accused of interfering in the internal affairs, particularly by the assembly". In the capital, the American advisors as well as the Ethiopian Minister of Foreign Affairs made it clear that

---

[1] FO371/108196. BCA to BEAA, 22.2.54. A report of Cracknell to the British Consul, Wardle-Smith.

[2] FO371/108209. BCA to FO, 19.3.54. The letter to the Supreme Court judges was written on March 18.

[3] FO371/108269. BCA to FO, 15.4.54. The Emperor's representative said that "the [Eritrean] constitution contained provision for the impeachment of the Chief Executive if he did not obey the constitution".

they had nothing to do with Tedla Bairu's arbitrary action and particularly with his disregard for breach of contract. The British, who in the beginning of 1953 saw the Ethiopians as the main culprits for violating the federation and who even went to the extent of reminding the Emperor about it, were now ready to change their minds.

By the first quarter of 1954, the British were convinced that the most serious threat to the federation was the Chief Executive's desire for more power.[1] Thanks to their effective representation, however, the British managed to persuade the Chief Executive to seek a rapprochement with the judges. It was subsequently shown that Tedla Bairu had been engaged in other conflicts with the judges in addition to that concerning the treatment of his political enemies. Tedla had asked the judges to agree that during a state of emergency, sole power would rest in the hands of the Chief Executive. To his chagrin, the judges had replied that they would hear an application on the actions of the executive even during a state of emergency.

While Tedla Bairu's relations with the Emperor's representative might have been rocked by the way the former antagonized British interests, there were further indications that Tedla was losing his base of support. To the Emperor's representative, Tedla was only one of several candidates for high office and the Ethiopians had began to line them up soon after Tedla's debacle with the British judges. By August Ibrahim Sultan was not only working closely with Keshi Dimetros, a well-known unionist member of the assembly, but was also on good terms with the Emperor's representative. Even the arch-federalist Abraha Tessema was won over into the fold of Ethiopianism.[2]

The animosity that Tedla Bairu aroused among people such as Abraha Tessema and Ibrahim Sultan was successfully exploited by the Emperor's representative and with far-reaching implications. Although the ML continued its commitment to uphold the federation, it was no doubt robbed of two versatile and extremely influential leaders. By July 1955, the Emperor's representative confirmed to Her Majesty's envoy J.E.Killick, Chargé d'Affaires, that "the Unionist-Federalist division had largely disappeared".[3] The Emperor's representative attributed this achievement to his own efforts in talking to the Unionists, with whom "he has taken the line that Federation is really only a form of

---

[1] FO371/108269. BCA to FO, 3.4.54. Saying that "it would be disastrous to allow the Chief Executive to get his way", the British Consul reported the following: "With a controlled judiciary in the hands of the Chief Executive, who is giving every indication of being a megalomaniac, there is no knowing what may happen here. Certainly foreigners and foreign interests would receive rough treatment and political opponents would be annihilated. Surely we should make every effort to prevent such a state of affairs coming about. The United Nations representative tells me he has reported to the Secretary General in much the same terms".

[2] FO371/108197. BCA to BEAA, 12.7.54. The Consul wrote: "I am informed that Abraha Tessema, having obviously split irremediably with the present Chief Executive, has drawn closer—perhaps for physical protection—to the Bitwoded [the Emperor's Representative]. The Princess Tenagne Work [daughter of the Emperor and wife of the Representative] recently consented to be the godmother to his grandchild".

[3] FO371/113520. BEAA to FO, 29.7.55.

decentralization of authority" which should be applied to Ethiopia as a whole in due course of time.

Relations with the Office of the Representative were further complicated by Tedla's inability to manage the assembly. On May 22, 1954 the Eritrean Assembly passed two motions as a direct reaction to the fact that the Chief Executive in his yearly speech to the assembly failed to mention Ethiopian interference in Eritrean internal affairs.[1] The Chief Executive was warned that if such necessary action was not taken within twenty days, the assembly would order the Eritrean government to submit this resolution to the United Nations.[2]

Although the British Consul Wardle-Smith did not believe that the anti-Ethiopian motions would be followed up, they were in fact followed up in the sense that they were sent to the Emperor. Further discussions on the matter were, however, successfully thwarted by the Chief Executive who had become fond of suspending sessions of the assembly as a means of not facing criticism.

The victory of the ML members of the assembly over the Executive (in forcing him to forward the two motions to the Emperor) further weakened the position of the latter. The Emperor's representative had found sufficient reason to be dissatisfied with the performance of the Chief Executive. In the assembly, the members of the Unionist Party, led by a prominent member of the Ethiopian Orthodox Church, Keshi Dimetros, began their vicious campaign to oust Tedla from power.

From May 1954 onwards, the assembly that Tedla Bairu had treated as "an assembly of idiots" began to challenge him so successfully that he felt compelled to suspend its regular sessions rather than stand up and justify his actions. In August of the same year, Tedla Bairu suspended the session of the assembly for twenty days when he got to know that many members of the assembly had expressed their intention to discuss the proceedings pending in the federal court against the ML newspaper, *Voice of Eritrea*.[3] Tedla Bairu would certainly have improved his position and perhaps reestablished his tarnished reputation if he had allowed the assembly to discuss the competence of the federal courts to try a case already dealt with by Eritrean courts, or if he had entered into negotiations directly with the federal authorities, or if he had stood up to the assembly in defence of the federal authorities on the matter. His decision to suspend the session of the assembly further confirmed the fears of the ML without satisfying either the Unionist Party or the Emperor's representative. His decision was most probably construed as an act of cowardice.

Alienated from his cabinet and unable to face the assembly, Tedla Bairu appears to have given up all hope of maintaining the federation. As one of the main reasons for his failure, one cannot avoid mentioning his lack of respect for

---

[1] FO371/108201. BCA to FO, 24.5.54. (The motion is quoted above.)

[2] FO371/108201. BCA to FO, 24.5.54. The two motions were put to the vote. The first motion was carried by 31 to 9 and the second by 33 to 7. In both cases there were ten abstentions.

[3] FO371/108197. BCA to FO, 20.7.54.

the concern of the ML members of the assembly. No doubt he was pressured both by the die-hards of the Unionist Party and the Emperor's office in Asmara. However, had he been interested to the same degree as Abraha Tessema, he would certainly have sought allies both in the assembly and in his own cabinet.

A few days after the reply of the Emperor on the two motions passed by the assembly in August was made known, Tedla Bairu made it clear that, if everything depended on him, he would favour complete union with Ethiopia.[1] While Tedla's political position provided an additional argument for the members of the ML to organize themselves even better than they had previously done, it does not appear that his open declaration had contributed to his rehabilitation. His political statement, though in line with the official Ethiopian position, was not appreciated, partly because of the negative reactions that it produced among the ML, and partly due to the fact that Tedla Bairu lost even more of the little leverage that remained for him in the assembly. Between May and September of 1954, the assembly was either suspended or its meetings continually postponed due to lack of a quorum.

Outside of Asmara, the Chief Executive was also losing ground very quickly. Not only did armed bandits (shifta) remain active, the Eritrean government was proving incapable of intervening in land disputes between the largely Moslem Saho and the Tigreans on the southeastern escarpment. Two years after the federation, the Tedla Bairu government issued the Senafe sub-division emergency order,[2] while he himself was in Addis Ababa, probably explaining his controversial speech.

Tedla Bairu's serious breach with the assembly, his frequent absence from Asmara, and the articulated dissatisfaction about his performance from the Emperor, his representative and the Unionist Party were all factors that contributed to his downfall in the following year.

1955 began with a sharpening of the tone between the palace and the Moslem members of the Eritrean Assembly, who on two occasions complained in writing about what they considered as violations of the federation by the federal (Ethiopian) authorities, as well as Ethiopian interference in the internal affairs of Eritrea. Not satisfied by reading the reply of the Emperor (September 9, 1954), the Emperor's representative took the opportunity of clarifying the misunderstanding between the federal government that he represented and the Eritrean government. Addressing the Eritrean assembly on the occasion of the third regular session, the Representative defended his position in a way that

---

[1] FO371/108197. BCA to BEAA, 17.9.54. The occasion was the second anniversary of the Federation as well as the New Year (September 11, 1954). His concluding statement was: "...on the day that the people of 'Mareb Mellasc' after studying the situation should, instead of a federal union, choose to complete union, my joy would be great".

[2] FO371/108201. The Emergency Order of 1954 was issued on September 22 by the Acting Chief Executive in accordance with Articles 77 and 78 of the Constitution. The Acting Chief Executive did not think it relevant to call the Assembly.

was to identify him indelibly as the enemy of federation. The Emperor's representative said:

> Neither I nor my assistants would understand, nor did anyone explain to us the meaning, of the allegation that the Office of H.I.M.'s Representative has intervened in the internal affairs of Eritrea and has attempted to corrupt the faith of the Members of the Assembly. In any case there is no internal or external affair as far as the Office of H.I.M.'s Representative is concerned and there will be none in the future. The affair of Eritrea concerns Ethiopia as a whole and the Emperor. Anything done to the advantage or disadvantage of Eritrea will never fail to affect Ethiopia. We know that Eritrea has internal autonomy but unless a good administration as well as genuine unity is ensured, it will be of no benefit to Ethiopia as a whole and to Eritrea in particular. We will therefore spare no effort to see that all the inhabitants of Eritrea live in peace and harmony.[1]

While the palace presumably blamed the Chief Executive Tedla Bairu for not controlling the assembly, opposition to the chief executive was building up both within the assembly and outside. Although the opposition from the assembly was finally to bring him down, the act that "stung" Tedla Bairu to action was the case against him filed by Abraha Tessema for wrongful imprisonment.[2] By March 1955 Tedla was most probably beginning to feel that he was approaching the end of his career as Chief Executive. In addition to the critical assembly which began the new session with its wounds of the previous year still fresh, the Chief Executive had also to deal with the revival of widespread banditry (shifta).[3] The Chief Executive was unable to deal with the shifta problem partly because his hands were tied with constitutional safeguards and partly due to the fact that he did not appreciate how the revival of shifta activities undermined his authority and power.

Mistrusted by the assembly and snubbed by the Emperor's representative, Tedla Bairu no longer had the power to appoint and dismiss Eritrean civil servants that he seemed to have had soon after he assumed power. His efforts to reshuffle the district governors and to dismiss those whom he either feared or who did not fit into his ethnic plan were counterbalanced by the palace. An incident that illustrates the intentions of Tedla Bairu as well as his vulnerable position vis à vis the palace was the case of Lieutenant-Colonel Tedla Ogbit. In November 1954 on the grounds of redundancy, the Chief Executive dismissed three Eritrean police officers, one of whom was Tedla Ogbit. The motives were

---

[1] FO371/113519. BCA, to FO. Speech from the throne delivered on March 28, 1955 by H.E. Bitwoded Andargatchew Messay at the opening of the First Regular Session of the Eritrean Assembly.

[2] FO371/113519. BCA to BEAA. E.J.Howes, Her Majesty's Consul-General reported that Tedla Bairu took two steps. i) "Through the S.D.O. of the Serae Division, who is a trusted friend, the Chief Executive has begun to send for district chiefs and after entertaining them suitably, he now urges them to support federation". ii) "The other step he has taken is abruptly to transfer a well known unionist from his home area where he has influence into a completely different area where the risk of his being rejected was real".

[3] FO371/113519. BCA to BEAA, 22.3.55. The Chief of Police Colonel Wright was certain though he cannot prove it that "the Palace has instigated some, at least, of the present lawlessness and that the Eritrean authorities are by no means alive to the danger not only to public security, ... but to Federation itself".

most probably a combination of the machinations of the secretary for the interior, Sheik Faki Ali who had the plan of harassing the Unionists, and the chief Executive's desire to put someone from his region as successor to the retiring British head of the Eritrean police. Lieutenant-Colonel Tedla Ogbit resigned from his post rather than accept a transfer to a civilian position, giving as his reason that his dismissal had been due to his strong support for Union. Moreover, Tedla Ogbit claimed that he was the strongest future candidate for police commissioner.

The case of Tedla Ogbit was taken up by the palace, thus forcing the Chief Executive to justify his decision to deny the former a career that he was trained for and apparently enjoyed. The Chief Executive could not, after his own pro-union speech of September 1954, persist with his redundancy argument when the latter claimed that he was dismissed for upholding the same views as the Chief Executive. Apart from the fact that Tedla Ogbit had acquired support from the palace by publicizing his case, his claim that he was the best qualified for the job of Commissioner of Police did not appear to have been challenged. Tedla Ogbit was bound to win. In May 1955, E.J. Howes, the British Consul-General reported that the chief Executive "has been forced by pressure from the palace to appoint Tedla Ogbit Deputy Police Commissioner with the rank of major".[1] Later in his capacity as Commissioner of Police, Tedla Ogbit was to be responsible, more than anyone else, for the dismantling of the federation.

The conflict between the Chief Executive and the Assembly surfaced again only two months after the opening of the regular session. Since the assembly could not directly attack the chief Executive, its members directed their attacks at Ali Redai, the president of the assembly. By the beginning of June, some assembly members were campaigning to collect the votes necessary to get the two-thirds majority in an eventual vote of no confidence.[2] Fully aware of the intentions of the assembly, the Chief Executive resorted to the tactic that seemed to have served him in the past, namely to use his constitutional right and suspend the regular session for twenty days. The Chief Executive, as he explained to the British Clerk of the Assembly, Fergus McCleary, needed time to organize his counter-attack.[3] After having suspended the assembly, however, the Chief Executive did not stay in Asmara to organize his counter-attack but instead left for Addis Ababa. The members of the assembly were thus left free to explore all avenues to bring down not only the President of the assembly but also the Chief Executive himself.

One of the areas that the members of the assembly explored was the possibility of impeaching the chief Executive on the grounds of nepotism, favouritism and

---

[1] FO371/113519. BCA to BEAA, 13.5.55.

[2] FO371/113519. BCA to BEAA, 9.7.55.

[3] FO371/113519. BCA to BEAA. The report continues: "The Assembly was duly suspended, but in the event the 'organization' took the form of the Chief Executive's departure to Addis Ababa next day, while Ali Redai went off to his farm in Tessenei".

general inefficiency.[1] Discouraged by the president of the Supreme Court, Judge Shearer, the members of the assembly bided their time. When on July 6 the chief Executive suspended a regular session of the assembly again, motivating his decision by the "disagreement of grave nature which has arisen among the Honourable members of the Assembly", tempers among the assembly members ran so high that it was with great difficulty that he managed to implement his order.[2]

The respite that the Chief Executive derived by the suspension of the session of the assembly was very short-lived indeed. His efforts to defend himself by supporting the President of the assembly threw him further into the hands of the opposition who now had the evidence they needed to prove interference by the Chief Executive in the internal matters of the assembly. With this last evidence in their hands, the enemies of the Chief Executive first went to the Emperor's representative and demanded the resignation of both the Chief Executive and the president of the assembly. The following day (July 7, 1955) the members of the opposition issued a long statement to the press where they stressed the dictatorial measures of the Chief Executive and the President of the assembly, who was more loyal to the Chief Executive than to the assembly.[3]

Initially the conflict between the chief Executive and the Assembly had a rather well defined political dimension. It was initiated mainly by the ML and by some members of the assembly and the conflict dealt with the relations between the Eritrean government and the federal government. From May 1954 onwards, however, the conflict assumed a more personal character. Parliamentary opposition was directed against the dictatorial attitude of the Chief Executive in his relations with the assembly, and against nepotism and general inefficiency of the Tedla Bairu government. Moreover, a close reading of the press statement, issued on July 7, 1955, gives a strong impression that the issues which engaged the ML strongly were no longer important. On the contrary, the concluding paragraph of the press statement by taking "care to make clearly known

---

[1] FO371/113519. BCA to BEAA, 9.7.55.

[2] FO371/113519. BCA to BEAA, 9.7.55. "During the suspension of the Assembly the situation remained superficially dormant. On July 6 however, when the Assembly was due to resume its meetings, Ali Redai did not present himself in the Chamber. Instead Blatta Demsas, the Vice-President, rapidly read in Tigrinya a letter from the Chief Executive suspending the Assembly (of which I enclose a copy) and hurriedly left the Assembly. For a few minutes after his departure uproar ensued in the Chamber, and McCleary was asked to take the Chair so that a vote of 'no confidence' in Ali Redai could be passed. This he refused to do, on the grounds that his action would be unconstitutional. Meanwhile, strong police forces in steel helmets had been stationed around the Assembly and Ato Mesfin Gabrehiwot, Director General of the Eritrean Administration, gave orders that the Deputies should be expelled from the Assembly, and that the doors of the Chamber and Committee rooms should be locked to prevent any further meeting taking place. McCleary went to see Tedla Bairu, and pointed out to him that since Ali Redai was being attacked as a stooge of the Executive, any violent action would constitute a clear interference with the internal workings of the Assembly, thus putting fresh weapons into the hands of the opposition who, if the matter were taken to the Courts, would be in a strong position. Tedla Bairu eventually saw the force of these arguments, and was dissuaded from using the Police".

[3] FO371/113519. BCA to BEAA, 9.7.55. Statement to the Press by the Majority Group of the Members of the Eritrean Assembly. Issued in the morning of 7.7.55.

the ambiguous conduct of the Chief Executive towards H.I.M. the Emperor",
had no doubt a pro-unionist touch.

After the obstructing decision of the Chief Executive to suspend the session
of the assembly on July 6, events developed in a way that surprised the opposition. The matter was brought before the Emperor. Neither the British who followed the development quite closely, nor the ML raised the possible legal issue
of whether the Emperor and his government had any right to intervene in the
conflict. In as far as the July crisis was concerned, the strategy of both the Chief
Executive and the parliamentary opposition to resort to the Emperor rather than
to the Supreme Court seemed to justify the position of the Emperor's representative on the non-existence of internal and external affairs in the relations
between Eritrea and Ethiopia.

On July 15, the Emperor's representative in Eritrea, Andargatchew Messai,
the chief Executive Tedla Bairu, the president of the assembly Ali Redai and
eight other members of the assembly arrived in Addis Ababa to resolve the
impasse. What exactly transpired in the court of the Emperor will never be
known since the practice of keeping written minutes was uncommon. However,
according to the British Embassy's interpreter who was a very close friend of the
Chief Executive, the latter gave the Emperor what amounted to an ultimatum
"that if Andargatchew Messai remained in office as His Imperial Majesty's representative in Eritrea, he would have no alternative but to resign".[1] The
Emperor and his advisors, on the other hand, interpreted the conflict both as
constitutional and purely internal. The Emperor, therefore, instructed his representative in Asmara to inform the Eritrean Assembly that the suspension of the
regular session was unconstitutional and that the Eritrean assembly had the
power to pass a vote of no confidence in those whom it had in the first place
elected.

On July 24, 1955, soon after his arrival from Addis Ababa, it was reported in
the daily newspaper that Ali Redai, the president of the assembly had handed
in his resignation to the chief Executive. It was also reported in the press that the
chief Executive himself would resign shortly. This happened on July 29 when it
was announced that he was resigning for health reasons.[2]

The circumstances which led to the resignation of the Chief Executive
strengthened the position of the Ethiopian government at the expense of Eritrean autonomy. The Chief Executive had ample opportunity to make the
assembly function. By trying to rule without the assembly and by his unconstitutional attempts to defend the president of the assembly, he contributed considerably to lifting the issue of personalities above the political issues dealing
with the power relations between the Eritrean and Ethiopian governments. At
the height of the crisis of the Eritrean government, the Emperor's representative

---

[1] FO371/113520. BEAA to FO, 29.7.55. The report continues: "...but the final outcome was an outright victory for the Emperor's Representative". Soon after Tedla Bairu and Ali Redai announced
their resignation one after the other.

[2] FO371/113520. BEAA to FO, 29.7.55.

candidly informed Her Majesty's Chargé d'Affaires J.E. Killick, that the Union-ist-Federalist division in the Eritrean Assembly had largely disappeared. By arguing that "federation is only a form of decentralization of authority which should be applied to Ethiopia as a whole", the Emperor's representative per-suaded the Unionists to realise that Eritrea (even in the federal arrangement) was already a province of Ethiopia.[1]

The downfall of the Chief Executive was brought about by a combination of several factors. The first was the inability of the chief Executive to manage the Eritrean assembly that was initially dominated by federalists. They were ready to challenge the Emperor as well as his representative concerning the division of power between the autonomous Eritrea and the federal government led by the Emperor. The intolerance of the Chief Executive and his eventual reluctance to forward the motions of the assembly led to a loss of confidence. The charges of nepotism and dubious means of accumulation of considerable property further widened the misunderstanding between the Chief Executive and the assembly.

The second factor was his inability to respect the independence of the judi-ciary which at that time was heavily dominated by British expatriates. Tedla Bairu's vindictive measures against the Tessema family and later on his at-tempts to dismiss the judges from their posts for no sufficient reason caused the powerful British diplomatic machinery in Eritrea and Ethiopia to align against him.

The third factor was the role of the Emperor's representative, who had a higher rank than the Chief Executive. For the Emperor and His representative, by virtue of the 1950 UN resolution Eritrea had become an integral part of Ethio-pia. "Federation" was according to the Emperor's statement in early 1952, "a foreign concept introduced to divide the people". In May 1954, when the Emperor's representative in Eritrea Andargatchew Messai said that "there are no internal and external affairs as far as the work of the Emperor's activities in Eritrea are concerned", he was indeed expressing what to him was self-evident. Meanwhile, the Ethiopian government, in its capacity as the Federal govern-ment, proceeded to confer power and honorific titles on the descendants of the traditional Eritrean elite.[2]

---

[1] FO371/113520. BEAA to FO, 29.7.55.

[2] The Ethiopian government had the power to appoint Eritreans to the Ethiopian Senate and other offices without having to consult the Eritrean government. The Ethiopian Senate had five Eri-treans, all of whom were committed Unionists and from well established political lineages. Haile Mikael, the son of the notorious Ras Woldemikael of Tsazzega, sat in the Senate with the rank of Ras—a title that was refused to the Chief Executive. Dejach Haile, the son of Dejach Tesfamariam Fessehaye, was also in the Senate. These were people who made their careers, with the exception of Ras Woldenkiel, during the Italian period by their skillful manipulation of their allegiance to Italian colonial rule. When the Italians were replaced by the British and later by the Ethiopians, these people were there to smooth the transfer of power.

1. The exiled emperor with Lorenzo
   Taezaz, Ethiopia's representative
   at the League of Nations

2. Emperor Haile Selassie around 1941

3. Emperor Haile Selassie on Mareb River heralding Federation

4. Unionist Party meeting

5. Unionists from Serae province march to meet the Four Power Commission

6. Women unionists
demonstrate
for reunion

7. Demonstrations by the Moslem League

8. Tedla Bairu, the first
chief executive of the
government of Eritrea

Photos nos. 1-2 from *My Life and Ethiopia's Progress 1882-1937*, autobiography by Emperor Halie Selassie (1973); nos. 3-4 from *Ethiopia: Liberation Silver Jubilee, 1941-1966;* nos. 5-8 from *Ethiopia and Eritrea: The last phase of the reunion struggle 1941-1952* by S. and R Pankhurst (1953)

Chapter Four

The Moslem League and the Dissolution of the Federation 1955–1962

THE MOSLEM LEAGUE AND THE GOVERNMENT OF ASFAHA
WOLDEMIKAEL

On August 8, 1955, Asfaha Woldemikael was elected Chief Executive in a secret ballot with 48 in favour and 17 against. Prior to his election, Asfaha Woldemikael was employed by the Ethiopian (federal) government as vice-representative, of the Emperor. He was the second in power after the Imperial Representative in Eritrea. The views of Asfaha Woldemikael on the issue of the relations between Eritrea and Ethiopia were very well known, not only to the members of the assembly who elected him, but also to those who followed the events from a distance. A striking aspect of the election was that the most implacable enemy of the UP, Ibrahim Sultan, the secretary general of one of the two major Moslem League organizations, voted in favour of Asfaha Woldemikael.[1]

Though born and educated in Eritrea, Asfaha Woldemikael spent most of his adult life in Ethiopia where he was first employed by the Italians as an interpreter. After the liberation of Ethiopia from Italian Fascist rule, Asfaha Woldemikael served the Ethiopian government in various capacities; In 1951 he visited Eritrea as a member of an Ethiopian mission to discuss the Eritrean situation with the departing British Administration; and a year later he was posted to Eritrea as the vice-representative of the Emperor and of the Ethiopian Government.

As its president the assembly elected Sheik Sayid Idris Mohammed Adum. The election of Asfaha Woldemikael as Chief Executive by a two thirds majority epitomized the inherent weaknesses of the ML in particular and the level of political awareness of the members of the assembly. If Tedla Bairu had been ousted from power due to his lenient position on the question of Eritrean autonomy, his replacement ought to be a man known for his steadfastness on the issue. There was no shortage of candidates who were known for their "federalist" standpoints. Yet, the assembly chose to elect a leader who could hardly be expected to put up a fight for the maintenance of the federation.

Reporting the election of Asfaha Woldemikael, Her Majesty's Consul-General, E.J. Howes, stressed that it was impossible in Eritrea to draw a hard line between "Federalist" and "Unionist" as many decisions were taken on the basis

---

[1] FO371/ 113520. BCA to BEAA, 11.8.55.

of purely personal jealousies and rivalries.[1] Fully enjoying the confidence of the
assembly and of the office of His Majesty's representative, the new chief executive lost no time in staffing his cabinet with Unionists. The key position of the
Department of the Interior was put in the hands of Araya Wassie, notorious for
his extremist views within the Unionist Party.[2]

A few weeks later, towards the end of September, the Eritrean Assembly
further facilitated the task of the Chief Executive, by unanimously electing
Dimetros Gebremariam its vice president.[3] With Araya Wassie at the head of the
Department of the Interior, controlling the police and the bureaucracy, and
Dimetros Gebremariam as Vice-President of the Assembly, the Chief Executive
was in a much stronger position to pursue his objective of the integration of
Eritrea into Ethiopia. Another key office, that of the Commissioner of Police was
filled by Tedla Ogbit, a staunch supporter of the Unionist Party.[4]

Not a cohesive and united organization the ML was now in an even more
disorganized state than earlier. The election of Asfaha Woldemikael as Chief
Executive, made possible by the vote of the members of the Moslem League, had
further deepened the division within its ranks. The ML of the Agordat district,
which voted for Asfaha Woldemikael, was no longer in the forefront concerning
the status of Eritrea. Although the government of Asfaha Woldemikael, compared to the earlier one, had a much easier task, the persistent opposition of the
diffusely organised ML continued to constrain its room for manoeuvre; in a
number of cases, the ML compelled the government to withdraw from integra-
tionist policies.

The strategy of the ML was based on the preservation of a separate and distinct Eritrean identity. This strategy was to be achieved by a scrupulous defence
of the United Nations Resolution of 1950 and of the Constitution of Eritrea
which emanated from the UN Resolution.

Only a few weeks after Asfaha had come to office, a group of deputies in the
assembly had proposed the introduction of measures to modify the constitution. The President of the Assembly, Sheik Idris Mohamed Adum deemed this
so serious that he consulted the Clerk of the Assembly Fergus McCleary and the

---

[1] FO371/113520. BCA to BEAA, 11.8.55. The despatch further contains biographical information on
Asfaha Woldemikael. According to the author of the despatch, Asfaha was elected by all those
who voted against the president of the Assembly as well as by 14 out of 15 members of the
Moslem League of the Western Province.

[2] FO371/113520. BCA to BEAA, 10.9.1955. The remaining members of Asfaha's cabinet were,
Gebreyohannes Tesfamariam, head of Economic Affairs; Omar Hassano, head of Law and Justice;
Tesfayohannes Berhe, head of Finance; Said Sefaf, head of Social Affairs; and Mohamed Omar
Ibrahim, head of State Property. Although all the three Moslem members were pro-union, the laat
named Sheik Mohamed Omar Ibrahim, was the most outspoken.

[3] FO371/113520. BCA to BEAA, 27.10.1955. Commenting on the appointment of the pro-unionist
Dimetros and the pro-union sympathies of Asfaha's cabinet, the British Consul-General wrote
that the Ethiopian government "have played their hand strongly; it remains to be seen what use
they will make of the cards as they now lie".

[4] FO371/113520. BCA to BEAA, 26.8.55. Tedla Bairu tried to appoint one of his friends, Ato Seium
Kahsai to the post of Commissioner of Police to replace Colonel Wright.

Attorney-General, F.F. Russell. The proposed changes were the: i) adoption of Amharic as the official language of the country; ii) abolition of the flag of Eritrea; iii) abolition of the official Eritrean seal, and; iv) nomination of the Chief Executive by the Emperor, in place of the existing system of election.[1] To the satisfaction of both the president of the assembly and the Moslem League, the attorney-general in a written statement pointed out that while the first three of the proposed changes could be made by two thirds majority vote, the proposed amendment concerning the appointment of the Chief Executive could not be amended at all since it was contrary to article 16 of the constitution and would thus undermine democracy.

Strengthened by the written opinion of the Attorney-General, the ML petitioned the representative of the Emperor with copies to the Chief Executive, strongly reminding them of the terms of the constitution. The petition was concluded by a warning that if the proposed motion was put forward, the ML would take the next step, that is appeal to the United Nations.[2] While the motion to amend the constitution thus remained buried, the Secretary of the Interior, Araya Wassie took one of the first concrete measures to undermine the federation by in practice putting into effect one of the above-mentioned changes. On the occasion of Emperor Haile Selassie's silver jubilee celebration of the coronation, November 2, 1955, Araya Wassie, Secretary of the Interior and Acting Chief Executive, decided to remove "the Eritrean flag which had been put up in the streets together with the Ethiopian flag".[3]

The reaction of the ML was swift. In a letter that they sent to the Acting Chief Executive, the ML expressed its displeasure at the flagrant action of the Secretary of the Interior against the constitution, and that if this matter were not put right, the petitioners made it clear that they would hold a public demonstration the following day.[4] On the same day, that is soon after the petition was delivered, the government hoisted the Eritrean flag, thereby admitting defeat. Nearly three years would pass before the Eritrean government would try successfully to remove the Eritrean flag. The ML must have felt greatly encouraged by the rehoisting of the Eritrean flag.

A sort of modus vivendi appeared to have reigned in the relations between the ML and the Eritrean and Federal authorities until the middle of April 1956. This time the issues of contention were that some members of the assembly were still attempting to amend the constitution to the effect that Tigrinya be replaced by Amharic and that the Chief Executive be directly appointed by the Emperor. The ML reacted by sending a telegram to the representative of the Emperor, the Chief Executive, the president and members of the assembly, the Supreme Court and the Attorney-General. In this telegram, the ML repeated the opinion

---

[1] FO371/113520. BCA to BEAA, 26.10.55.
[2] FO371/113520. BCA to BEAA, 26.10.55.
[3] FO371/113520. BCA to BEAA, 23.11.55.
[4] FO371/113520. BCA to BEAA, 23.11.55.

rendered several months earlier by F.F. Russell, the Attorney-General and strengthened its argument by warning the recipients of its letter that any amendment "will be considered as a change to the problem of Eritrea which has been already solved".[1] The ML also sent a telegram to the European consulates informing as well as reminding them of their responsibility of the consequences in the event that constitutional amendment limited the rights of the people and the autonomy of the country.[2]

In so far as the defence of the Constitution was concerned, the ML was not only running against time but also against the combined forces of the Unionist Party, the Ethiopian government and a faction of the ML (from Agrodat) that was prepared to vote together with the Unionists. The ML, however, persevered through the courage of its members who were legally and constitutionally supported by the presence of Sir James Shearer, the Chief Justice of the Supreme Court of Eritrea and Colonel Wright, the police commissioner until he was replaced by Tedla Ogbit in September 1955.

Throughout May and June of 1956, the ML engaged the Eritrean government on the legality of the electoral procedure to the Second Eritrean Assembly (to be held in August of the same year) and on the intentions of the government to increase the number of judges in the Supreme Court so as to make it possible to amend the constitution. The ML petitioned the Supreme Court to provide guidelines on both issues.

Sir James Shearer, described by the British Ambassador to Ethiopia as the watchdog of the Eritrean constitution, seemed to have enjoyed his task of demonstrating the supremacy of the Supreme Court as well as of the constitution. The Eritrean constitution had been drafted and granted to the Eritrean people by the United Nations, but was ratified by all parties concerned in Eritrea and Ethiopia. Sir James Shearer pointed out that the Eritrean government was bound by article 45 of the constitution to establish an Electoral High Commission entrusted with the supervision of elections. Sir James Shearer knew that the government of Tedla Bairu and the assembly had a draft before them as early as 1953 but were not in the least interested to act upon it. He also knew that as late as March 1956, the assembly refused to deal with such an important constitutional issue even though the matter was raised by some members of the ML within the assembly.

Both the Eritrean and the federal governments were acquainted with the idea of the establishment of an electoral commission. In pursuance to the 1955 Ethiopan Constitution, the Ethiopian Imperial Government was in the process of establishing such a commission by early 1956. However, as far as Eritrea was concerned, neither the federal nor the Eritrean government felt bound by the

---

[1] FO371/118744. BCA to FO, 17.5.56. Enclosure nos. 1 and 2 to letter no.501. The telegram reached Her Majesty's office in Asmara, most probably, before the end of April, but was not forwarded to London until the 17th of the following month.

[2] FO371/118744. BCA to FO. Enclosure no.2. letter no.501 of May 17, 1956. The copy of the letter was signed by the delegates of the party of the Keren district.

Eritrean constitution, a covenant which they had undertaken to uphold. Sir James Shearer's opinion would not have aroused the indignation of the Eritrean government since the Attorney-General had given the latter permission to go ahead with the elections in accordance with Electoral Proclamation no. 121 of 1951.[1] What irritated the Eritrean government was the wide publicity that the president of the assembly, Sheik Sayid Idris Mohamed Adum gave to the opinion of the Supreme Court.

The reaction of the Eritrean and Federal Governments to the pro-ML activities of the president of the assembly strongly indicates the strength of the Unionist forces and the weaknesses of the ML. Against a rather feeble opposition from the ML, Unionist forces within the assembly easily persuaded Sheik Osman Abdurrahman to put forward a motion for a vote of no confidence in Sheik Sayid Idris Mohamed Adum, the president of the Eritrean assembly.[2] The motion was carried by 43 with no abstentions.[3] As a concession to those Moslems who voted with the government against the recalcitrant ex-president of the assembly, the government gave verbal assurances that it would not undermine the constitution further by packing the Supreme Court with more judges.

After one year in office, the Chief Executive, had succeeded in deepening the division within the ML and thereby strengthening his position. Divided into the Keren and Agordat districts, the ML proved unable to speak and act with one voice. Many of the constitutional issues that the ML repeatedly stressed in its memoranda could have been raised at the assembly. We have, however, no reports of the assembly deliberating on such issues, especially after the appointment of Asfaha Woldemikael to the post of Chief Executive. Apart from the odd fifteen members of the assembly who belonged to the ML, the rest were either uncommitted or favoured the position of the Chief Executive.

THE 1956 ELECTIONS TO THE ASSEMBLY

The 1956 elections were held on September 5 and 6. In contrast to the first election (1952), which was supervised by the departing British Administration, the 1956 elections were managed both by the federal and Eritrean governments. The 1956 elections were held under circumstances where the question of the legality of the 1956 election raised earlier by some members of the ML remained unresolved. The Eritrean Assembly had failed to replace the Electoral Proclamation 121 of 1951 by a new electoral law as stipulated by article 45 of the Eritrean con-

---

[1] The argument of the Attorney-General was based on the existing reality rather than on law. He argued that it was far more important to hold the elections at the end of the mandatory period rather than to postpone elections until the Assembly promulgated an Electoral Law.

[2] FO371/118744. BCA to BEAA, 19.6.56. The motion was passed on June 13, 1956.

[3] FO371/118744. BCA to BEAA, 19,6. 56. "The next day", E.J. Howes, the British Consul-General reported, "with the Vice-President Keshi Dimetros in the chair, the Assembly elected Sheik Hamid Farag Hamid as its President".

stitution. A few months before the elections the ML had petitioned the Supreme Court to declare the 1956 elections unconstitutional on the grounds that the Eritrean government had not established an electoral high commission in accordance with article 45. Apart from mentioning the binding nature of article 45 of the Eritrean constitution, the ML did not argue the advantages of a new electoral commission over the old one either to the Supreme Court or in the assembly.

Although we can understand the reasons for the failure of the ML in its drive for a new electoral law, it is indeed difficult to decipher the reasons why the Eritrean Assembly rejected a draft presented to it as early as 1953. It is most probable that the assembly led by Tedla Bairu felt that there was no need for a new law, and many members may have also believed that there was not going to be another election. Whatever the reasons, the Eritrean government overcame the deadlock, partly by managing to acquire the support of the Attorney-General on the applicability of the proclamation from 1951.

The 1956 elections were followed by Fergus McCleary, the clerk of the assembly and by Judge Clarence Smith. In their communication with Her Majesty's Consul-General, these gentlemen pointed out that the Eritrean police and the federal authorities had between them "frightened off any possible opposition".[1] Although the Eritrean Police, headed by the notorious pro-Unionist Tedla Ogbit, had already begun to harass the opponents of the government in September the previous year, its powers were still circumscribed. Through *habeas corpus* the Supreme Court, headed by Sir James Shearer, could compel the police to justify their action for the continued detention of an appellant. In the event the police failed to show a reasonable basis for detention, the Supreme Court had to order the immediate release of the detainee.

In two remarkable cases the Supreme Court succeeded in protecting candidates from police harassment by showing that, as long as the Supreme Court was staffed by impartial judges, the police were subject to legal scrutiny. The first was the case of Fessha Woldemariam, one of the staunch federalists. Refusing to listen to the threats originating from both the government and the police commissioner, Fessha Woldemariam was arrested just a week before the closing day for nominations. His friends brought his case before Supreme Court Judge O'Hanlon who in turn, ordered the police to produce the detainee. As the police were unable to prove "a reasonable suspicion", the Supreme Court ordered the release of Fessha Woldemariam on bail until such time that the police either withdrew from the case or stated their charges. Probably encouraged by the position of the Supreme Court, Fessha Woldemariam proceeded with the nomi-

---

[1] FO371/118744. BCA to BEAA, 28.8.56. These gentlemen also reported that "the situation in the districts is that only one candidate, and he a pro-Unionist is permitted. Others are ordered to keep to their houses or are hauled before the courts and fined, their conviction automatically disqualifying them from nomination as a candidate".

Commenting the above report, E.J. Howes the Consul-General wrote that "at this rate of progress it should not be very long before the Eritrean Assembly votes for complete union with Ethiopia".

nation formalities, and to the great disappointment of the government and the police, he was elected by a wide margin.[1]

The second case was that of Muhammed Omar Akito, from Assab. Also known for his anti-Unionist views, the Eritrean government and the police first attempted to discourage him from standing for office; a bomb was thrown into his living room as a warning.[2] When he persisted, in spite of concerted harassment, and even won the election in his district, the Eritrean government refused to recognise his victory. The Eritrean Assembly, doing the bidding of the government, also declared his election invalid. Muhammed Omar Akito appealed to the Supreme Court, alleging that the assembly's decision was not based on any satisfactory enquiry. The Supreme Court took up the case, since Omar Akito was entitled by the constitution to direct his appeal to this august body. The case was heard by a panel of five judges, including the president of the Supreme Court, Sir James Shearer. Omar Akito was vindicated; the election was declared valid.[3]

There would hardly be any reason to doubt that the government tried to harass anti-Unionist candidates in the rural areas. Tedla Ogbit, commissioner of police, was in the forefront in harassing anti-unionist candidates. However, the election result showed that police harassment was not as widespread as reported by British observers. Twenty-four out of sixty-four elected members were either known anti-Unionists or had no alignment with either of the positions. In the 1956 elections 188 candidates contested 68 seats. Thirty-two members were newly elected, while the rest were re-elected members.

The 1956 elections were a resounding victory for the Unionist forces. 32 of 68 members were declared Unionists. This was nearly half a dozen more than in the 1952 elections. The election was also a victory in another sense; the versatile and self-designated spokesman of the ML, Ibrahim Sultan, lost to his competitor, Sayid Yossuf Faki Ali.[4]

The 1956 elections were held just before the Ethiopian elections to the first Chamber of Deputies in accordance with the Imperial Constitution promulgated the previous year. According to the principle of proportional representation enshrined in the Federal Act, Eritrea was allocated 14 seats in a chamber of 201 members. It is interesting to note that there were substantial differences between the Eritrean and Ethiopian electoral laws. Whereas the Ethiopian electoral law was based on direct elections where for the first time women were given the right to vote, in Eritrea, with the exception of Asmara and Massawa, candidates were elected by a college of electors, made up exclusively of

---

[1] FO371/118744. A report on Fessha Woldemariam, Asmara, 28.8.56.

[2] FO371/118744. A report on the elections for the Second Assembly of Eritrea. Asmara, 12.9.56.

[3] BCA to BE, 7.2.57. The despatch, unfortunately, mentions only the fact that the majority of the judges were non-British. E.J. Howes, the British Consul in Eritrea was acutely aware that the decision of the Supreme Court on the case of Omar Akito would result in a confrontation between the Court and the Assembly.

[4] FO371/118744. A report on the elections for the Second Assembly of Eritrea, Asmara, 12.9.56.

men. Moreover, neither in Asmara nor in Massawa had women the right to vote. In that sense, the electoral legislation of the Ethiopian government was more progressive than that of Eritrea. Although it would be beyond the scope of this chapter to deal with the issue, it would be appropriate to pose the question as to why the Eritrean Assembly did not at least emulate the programme of the Ethiopian electoral law, thereby extending direct elections to include the districts and also extend the franchise to Eritrean women. No matter how one interprets the history of the period, there was indeed very low awareness among the majority of the population on the importance of the replacement of indirect elections by direct elections and on the involvement of women.

With Asfaha Woldemikael at the helm of power, the unobtrusive process of incorporation began to gain momentum. The Department of the Interior, as well as the office of the commissioner of police, were in the hands of notorious Unionists. Araya Wassie, the secretary for the interior, though an Ethiopian by birth had been very active within the Unionist Party since the early 1940s. Tedla Ogbit, the Commissioner of Police, was awarded his position through pressure from the federal government.[1] Federalists could then be systematically harassed, although the presence of Chief Justice Sir James Shearer as the head of the Eritrean Supreme Court compelled the commissioner of police to act within the law.

Although the irreversible process toward the dissolution of the federation began as early as September 1955 with the election of a committed pro-Unionist to the office of Chief Executive, it took seven years to accomplish the job of uniting Eritrea with Ethiopia. From the beginning of 1956 onwards, both in Addis Ababa and Asmara the British were convinced that the Ethiopian government could produce the necessary majority in the Eritrean Assembly for a vote for complete union with Ethiopia. In other words, the Eritrean Assembly was ready to vote itself out of existence from 1956 onwards. However, neither the UP nor the Eritrean Assembly could vote themselves out of existence without having first made sure that Ethiopia was ready to assume overall responsibility.

For those members of the UP who had campaigned for unconditional union, their main aspiration was to submit themselves to the Ethiopian crown. At this stage it is worthwhile to raise some questions. Were Eritrean leaders (the members of UP) aware of the political consequences of the campaign? Were they knowingly undermining the elaborate constitution which the UN drafted for them? Were they deliberately flaunting a democratic experiment? In my opinion these questions need to be answered in the affirmative. Right from its inception, the UP was committed to an unconditional union with Ethiopia. For

---

[1] Tedla Bairu dismissed Tedla Ogbit from the police on the grounds of redundancy. Ogbit appealed to the Palace where he argued that he was dismissed because of his unionist views. The real reason for his dismissal was, however, that Tedla wanted to give this important position to one of his relatives who obviously did not have either professional or political merit for the job. Tedla was virtually compelled to reinstate Tedla Ogbit with the full knowledge that the latter would succeed the outgoing Commissioner Colonel Wright.

the Christian Eritreans, such instinctive attachment to Ethiopia was a reflection of historical and political links. Eritrean leaders had always been appointed by Ethiopian kings since at least the early decades of the 17th century. The Eritrean Christians were accustomed to the existence and symbol of the Ethiopian crown.

Italian and British occupation, paradoxically enough, strengthened further the symbolic value as well the legitimacy of monarchical rule.[1] It was, therefore, logical that the members of the UP perceived the federation and its elaborate constitutional framework either as a naive foreign imposition or as an act of conspiracy hatched by Italy behind closed doors. From the praxis of the first chief executive and his successor, the federal arrangement had several offensive features. I shall here mention a few. The first offensive aspect of the federation was that the chief executive was elected rather than being appointed by the Emperor. The second offensive statement was the term government of Eritrea, a description which appeared to put Eritrea and Ethiopia on the same level. The members of the UP wanted to change government of Eritrea to administration of Eritrea. Finally, the UP activists found the whole idea of the division of powers between the executive, the judiciary and the legislative quite absurd. Eritrea and its inhabitants had never before been ruled under a political framework with distinct division of powers among the organs of the state.

In the reconstruction of the events of the 1950s, Ibrahim Sultan (the leader of one faction of the ML and who fled to the Sudan in 1959) took full licence to distort and misinterpret both the Federal Act and the Eritrean constitution. He was only correct on one point which concerned the personality and the role of the chief executive Asfaha Woldemikael. Ibrahim wrote: "This particular person who was imposed upon the people of Eritrea …, did his best to violate and transgress the constitution of Eritrea, falsify elections and bring up a group of agents under the name of the "Parliament of Eritrea" to be able to achieve and realise all subjective aims which were always trying to put an end to the self-integrity of Eritrea and its annexation to the Ethiopian empire".[2] Ibrahim Sultan failed to mention the fact that he voted Asfaha Woldemikael into office.

BANDITRY (SHIFTA) AND THE DETERIORATION OF THE ECONOMY

One of the intractable problems that the chief executive Asfaha Woldemikael inherited from his predecessor was the climate of terror that the shifta created on the highly developed highways of the country. The phenomenon of shifta had been quite well known since the late 1940s. Throughout the 1940s and up to the end of 1956, it was widely believed that the shifta were in one way or another

---

[1] Italy was a monarchy until its defeat in the Second World War while British foreign diplomats continued to exercise hegemony as humble servants of Her/His Majesty.

[2] FO371/172818. BEC to FO, 26.4.63. The despatch contains two memoranda by the United Party of Eritrea Democratic Front, Headquarters of the Eritrean Moslem League. These documents were signed by Ibrahim Sultan and Adem Idris Nur.

supported by the Ethiopian government for political ends. In the 1940s the British, the Italians and the Moslem League accused the Ethiopian government of financing shifta bands in order to threaten opposition forces as well as to consolidate its supporters behind the policies of the Unionist Party. This view was no doubt a very simplified one; there were at least three types of shifta activities taking place at the same time.

The first type of shifta activity was that carried out by bandits who ran away for personal or clan reasons. Their activities were not directed against the state but primarily against enemy families or clans. The most notorious among these was Hamid Idris Awate belonging to the Beni Amer ethnic group. The second type of shifta activity was carried out by bandits from northern Ethiopia and was motivated and inspired by the ease with which people could be robbed and property and livestock be stolen in Eritrea. Unlike the Italians, the British had, throughout their stay, not quite managed to establish law and order. These two types of shifta activities were to outlive the British period and continued to create problems for the Eritrean government. The third shifta activity, on the other hand, was carried out by people who openly declared their political motives, i.e. liberation from Italian rule and unification of Eritrea with Ethiopia. With the coming of the federation, the third type (political shiftaism) came to an end.

Yet as late as 1955, the British Embassy officials believed that the Ethiopian government was behind the recrudescence of shifta activity in order to demonstrate that "Tedla Bairu was incapable of keeping order".[1] During the 1952–55 period, the British seriously believed that the Ethiopian authorities were conniving with the shifta in order to embarrass the outgoing Chief Executive Tedla Bairu. As an example they cited the Eritrean Public Security Proclamation of 1955 issued on July 5, 1955, giving draconian powers of collective punishment and wide discretionary powers to the police in their battle against the shifta.[2] A few days after the promulgation of the anti-shifta proclamation, the Emperor issued a general amnesty whereby the shifta were given three months to renounce banditry and resume peaceful lives. The action of the Emperor was taken as a clear act of interference aimed at taking the teeth out of the anti-shifta proclamation issued by Tedla Bairu. Here, however, the British were certainly wrong. It was a usual practice of the Emperor to pardon criminals on his birthday which was in the middle of July. Moreover, we can deduce that there was a festive mood in the country on the occasion of the celebration of the 25th anniversary of the Emperor's accession to power (November 1930–55). We may also mention here that the Emperor was about to promulgate a new constitution. But what is perhaps even more important was that the right of the Emperor to declare amnesty was clearly spelled out in article 22 of the Eritrean Constitution.

---

[1] FO371/118738. Ethiopia. Annual Review for 1955.

[2] FO371/113519. BCA to BEAA, 5.7.55. Howes wrote that the Ethiopian authorities were unlikely "to put any obstacles in his [Tedla Bairu's anti shifta proclamation] way even if, for political reasons, they wish to do so".

Meanwhile, the resignation of Tedla and the coming to power of Asfaha Woldemikael gave the British in Eritrea and Ethiopia the impression that there would finally be an end to the shifta problem. By December 8, 1955 the British appear to have believed the report issued by Tedla Ogbit, the newly appointed Commissioner of Police, that only "16 bandits now remained at large in Eritrea".[1] Neither the unscrupulous use of power by the commissioner of police, Tedla Ogbit, nor the pro-Ethiopian Chief Executive Asfaha Woldemikael were, however, sufficient to put an end to the shifta phenomenon. To the surprise of the British, the shifta activities continued with undiminished intensity and brought the security issue into the fore in the beginning of 1956. The Emperor, we are told, was infuriated when bandit incidents continued to take place at a time when he was himself in Eritrea.[2] Only after the Emperor's order to clear the country from the shifta had failed were the British prepared to view the shifta phenomenon as purely Eritrean.

In a report compiled by the British Embassy in June 1957, it was stated that the shifta were becoming more organized; they had inflicted casualties on the police; and the Ethiopian authorities had very little to do with the shifta question.[3] It is worthwhile to add here that the Ethiopian government would have been able to bring under control the shifta activity if these shifta were in the first place either financed or supported by Ethiopia. However, the involvement of Ethiopia and its institutions in the shifta activities in Eritrea from 1947 onwards, have been coloured by the convergence of interests between the objectives of political shiftas and that of the Ethiopian state. Even there Ethiopia's involvement (first put forward by the Italians) was alleged rather than proved. The shifta activities which caused serious security risks were the first two types described above.

The shifta menace continued unabated throughout the year, thus forcing the government to introduce another much more stringent bill known as the Banditry Bill of 1957. According to this new bill, shifta convicted of more than two crimes of violence could be condemned to death. Stiff penalties were also imposed on communities which in one way or another either harboured bandits or provided them with food, information or shelter. The principle of collective punishment, first introduced by the British Administration, was reintroduced by Tedla Bairu in 1955 and further elaborated by Asfaha Woldemikael in the summer of 1957. Due to the shifta menace Eritrea was becoming ungovernable.

---

[1] FO371/113520. BCA to BEAA, 8.12.55. "These [shifta] were being hunted down and the population could be assured that the situation was in hand".

[2] FO371/118744. BCA to BEAA. Asmara, 27.2.56.

[3] FO371/125539. BEAA to FO, 6.6.57. Continuing his report, P.R.A. Mansfiled, the embassy secretary wrote: "The Ethiopian troops in Asmara (there are about a brigade) do nothing to help the Eritrean Government against the shifta. This may be because they have not been asked, or possibly because they do not want to get involved in such a difficult job. There is no political significance in the increase of shifta activity in itself. Apparently, the usual reason given by the shifta when they are caught, for having turned to this way of life, is that their father or uncle has not given them the piece of land which he should have done and which would have enabled them to make a living".

Although economic hardship and the ease with which some shifta managed to rob travellers were sufficient impetus, internal divisions within the Eritrean government, shortage of manpower within the police, and lack of commitment of the law enforcement institutions appear to be reasons of far more importance.

Internal divisions within the Eritrean government revolved around the personalities in power. Towards the end of 1957, there were three factions within the government in Asmara: the chief Executive's faction, the faction headed by the vice-president of the assembly and that headed by the Secretary of the Interior.[1] These three groups did not work together in harmony, and in some cases factional interests appear to have been more important than national interests.[2] The British diplomatic sources do not enlighten us very much on the damaging impact of the existence of these factions on the implementation of the severe anti-shifta law. It could, however, be easily surmised that the anti-shifta law, with its provisions for collective punishment, was difficult to implement in areas protected by one of the three factional interests.

The lack of commitment on the part of the police and, therefore, the continuation of the shifta problem, appear to have been caused by lack of sufficient legal protection. According to Clarence Smith, the Attorney General, an important reason for the acuteness of the shifta problem was that "the police though they fired their guns during their encounters with the shifta, usually aimed so as to avoid hitting them". This was due to the unfortunate psychological effect of a case where a policeman who had hit and wounded a man during pursuit of shifta suspects, was sued for civil damages by his victim and ordered to pay compensation.[3] Clarence Smith later reported that the Chief Executive's severe lecturing (May, 1957) had greatly improved the record of the police, however, nowhere was it reported that the police could be freed from civil claims by persons who suffered damages. Another reason for the continuation of shifta activity, especially after the middle of 1956, was the supply of Egyptian arms to Eritrean Moslems.[4]

The deterioration of the Eritrean economy was an important contributory factor to the growth of the shifta. By the mid-1950s the Eritrean economy had been reduced to a realistic size and capacity. Gone were the days when the Eritrean economy was stimulated by a huge cash flow from Italy. According to British assessment, Eritrea was "a desperately poor country agriculturally and

---

[1] FO371/125539. BCA to BEAA, 5.9.57.

[2] FO371/125539. BCA to BEAA, 5.9.57. Elaborating the political significance of the competition between the factions, the British Consul included an incident: "[T]he Chief Executive recently instructed the chief of the Eritrean Police to arrest fifty persons in the Adi Ugri area who were known to have shifta associations. ...[O]nly five arrests have been made because the Secretary of the Interior (who is the immediate boss of the Eritrean Police) had ordered that the remaining forty five should be left alone".

[3] FO371/125539. BCA to BEAA, 29.10.57.

[4] FO371/118763. BEAA to FO, 18.5.56. The French authorities in Djibouti informed the U.S. embassy officials of clandestine shipments of arms by the Egyptians via Jedda and Hadeida to points north of Assab on the Eritrean coast.

in other ways".[1] The boom years when Asmara was inhabited by more Italians than Eritreans,[2] and when there were more jobs than job seekers, were gone for good. The end of the Second World War had made redundant the small scale Italian factories which were established soon after the British occupation of Eritrea in 1941.

After the establishment of the federation, the Italian population, which stood at around 17,000 in 1952, was reduced to just 11,000 by the end of 1956. The departure of every Italian may not have literally meant the loss of three Eritrean jobs as it has been rhetorically argued by some pro-Italian Eritreans, but there can be no doubt that the shrinking size of the Italian population had adverse effects on the economy.

During the 1952–57 period the Eritrean economy was dominated by the Italian community. In the beginning of 1958, the Italian population in Eritrea was ca. 10,200. Without exception all of the manufacturing establishments were owned and run by the Italians, most of whom had established themselves during the colonial period. The Eritreans, as in the colonial period, waxed and waned with the economic situation of Italian firms. Although many Italian firms had to close because of the stiff competition from European producers soon after the end of the Second World War, their economic position and performance picked up from 1955 onwards. Some of the notable agro-industrial establishments (De Nadai, Barattolo, and Melotti) experienced their intensive periods of expansion after 1955.[3]

Contrary to the claims and allegations of many of those who have studied the period, the economic situation of Italian firms improved considerably with the implementation of the federation.[4] That the federation had much more to offer to Italian firms than the earlier British Administration can be easily seen from the survey carried out by the British Consulate in Asmara. At the end of 1958, there were 627 industrial activities, as opposed to 456 in 1956.[5]

---

[1] FO371/118744. BEAA to FO, 21.2.56.

[2] Guida dell'Africa Orientale Italiana, Milano, 1938; Castellano, 1939.

[3] Consolato General D'Italia, Gli Italiani in Eritrea nel 1958. Asmara, 1959. The material is available at the Istituto Italo-Africano in Rome, Italy.

[4] In 1939 there were 53,000 Italians and 45,000 Eritreans in Asmara. A considerable part of the Eritrean population were women and children. With the Italian defeat in 1941 and the continuation of the War, the British Military Administration supported and encouraged the Italian community to make use of the material and equipment of the Italian state. The Americans were also actively involved in making use of Eritrea as a repair station for their air force. So until the end of the war, the Italian community and the Eritrean economy were on the upswing. The end of the war and the resumption of ordinary economic activities in Europe and the Middle East soon forced the newly established factories in Eritrea to close down. Many of these factories could not compete with older and better managed factories. The period of decline which ensued after 1945 continued until the end of 1955. The pro-Italian leanings of the chief executive and the pro-industrial policy of the Eritrean government appear to have contributed to the revival of the economy, witnessed by the end of 1956.

[5] FO371/138059. BCA to BEAA, 1.4.59. The report based on an Eritrean industrial census, also contains import and export figures.

Undoubtedly, the Italian dominated modern sector of the Eritrean economy picked up momentum after 1956. However, its impact on the living conditions of the majority of the Eritrean people was not sufficiently pervasive. Italian firms may have altogether provided employment for about 20,000 Eritreans (Consolato Generale d'Italia, 1959). In fact the Eritrean government appears to have provided more jobs than the growing modern sector.[1] The modern sector of the Eritrean economy, impressive indeed when compared with what then existed in Ethiopia, was nonetheless, of such a small scale that it could not absorb the continuously growing population that sought employment. Wages were extremely low and were hardly sufficient for social reproduction without supplementary income from family and lineage farm plots.

FEDERATION ONLY IN NAME: THE ERITREAN ASSEMBLY AND THE
MOSLEM LEAGUE, 1957–1962

By the beginning of 1957, Chief Executive Asfaha Woldemikael had managed to translate into common policy what the representative of the Emperor expressed in early 1955 in response to allegations of Ethiopian interference in the internal affairs of Eritrea. The Emperor's representative had said that there were neither internal nor external affairs as far as the office of His Imperial Majesty's Representative was concerned. Asfaha Weldemikael, who then was vice representative, as far as we can judge from his record as Chief Executive, ought to have been in full agreement with the representative of the Emperor. By the end of 1956, Asfaha Woldemikael had already openly expressed his wish to return to his old job as vice-representative. Throughout most of 1957, Asfaha spent most of his time either in the palace (the headquarters of the representative) as a de facto vice-representative, or in his office in his capacity both as Chief Executive and vice-representative.

From the date of his appointment until the end of 1957, Asfaha had succeeded in securing the support of the Ethiopian government, as well as that of the Italian community. In addition to his being a Catholic, Asfaha's policy of silent incorporation of Eritrea into Ethiopia had endeared his policy to the Italian community as a less evil alternative than the federal status quo, where the Italians were tired of paying taxes and owing allegiance to two governments, the Eritrean and the Ethiopian. The chief enemies of Asfaha remained those who sympathised with the ideals of the Moslem League and the supporters of a newly established group known by the name of Federal Youth League of Eritrea (Partito Giovanile Federalisti Eritrea) in early 1958.

The replacement of Colonel Wright by Major Tedla Ogbit as police commissioner in September 1955 had meant a remarkable deterioration of civil rights. We have earlier seen how the police commissioner tried to harass and persecute

---

[1] FO371/102656. Minutes of the Eritrean Assembly, no.169 of 22.6.53. Appendix A. Report of the Chief Executive to the Eritrean Assembly. According to the report, the Eritrean government employed 7,188 people. Of these 4,023 were in the police force.

those who, in spite of its structural defects, favoured the maintenance and continuation of the federal system. Although free to harass, the police commissioner remained accountable to the Eritrean Supreme Court, which from its inception until the end of 1959 was headed by Sir James Shearer.

The last four years of the federal period, 1958–62, were to witness not so much an offensive from the Ethiopian authorities, but more the emergence of an Eritrean system of rule unencumbered by the presence of British and American advisors. Political power, which was dominated by the Christian Eritreans, became even more so during the last four years of the federal period.

With very few exceptions, the Eritrean Christians found it very difficult to translate the federal system that was embodied in the Eritrean constitution into a workable political framework. From the outset the Ethiopian authorities had made it clear that they did not like the federal solution, but there could be no doubt that they were prepared to give it a fair chance.

As far as the ML and the Moslem community were concerned the UP and its followers were the exclusive beneficiaries. In a letter from the Moslem community to the chief executive of the Eritrean government this view was pointed out clearly. After reminding the government to maintain the use of the Arabic language and continued respect to the Eritrean flag, the authors of the letter "vehemently requested the government to give consideration to all applications submitted by the Moslems' educated youth who want employment". The authors further pointed out that Moslems were being denied business licences and this discrimination was based on religious and ethnic grounds. The most serious allegation was, however, directed against the department of the interior which according to the authors of the letter was exclusively made up of "Christians starting from the secretary down to the messengers".

There was no doubt in the minds of the authors that Moslem elements were deliberately "excluded from this vital department which has a direct connection with the population". The concluding statement was revealing indeed. The authors said that such action of discrimination placed the Moslems as foreigners rather than as citizens. In a typical strategy of the ML, the letter asked the government to restore to Eritrea the departments taken by the Imperial Ethiopian Government under the name of the Federal Government such as railways and ropeways, posts and telecommunications, internal roads and revenue from customs. Furthermore, the authors reminded the chief executive to take measures so that Eritrea "exercises a real participation in a real federal system" applied according to the UN resolution which recommended the establishment of a federal unity between two distinct units known as Eritrea and Ethiopia.[1] Unfortunately the archival sources do not enlighten us on the reactions which the letter might have elicited from the Eritrean government. What appears worth stressing, however, was that the major cause for the malfunctioning of the fed-

---

[1] FO371/118744. Moslem mosques committee to H.E chief executive, Government of Eritrea, 21.5.56.

eration as a whole and the plight of the Moslem community was the UP dominated Eritrean government itself.

In October 1957 one of the self-appointed leaders of the Moslem League,
Mohamed Omar Kadi, and the indefatigable Woldeab Wolde Mariam presented
a petition to the United Nations in New York. In their memorandum, Woldeab
and Omar Kadi commented extensively on how the Federal Act and the Eritrean
Constitution were undermined by the combined efforts of the Ethiopian authorities and the Eritrean government. The memorandum, as the first document
issued abroad formed the basis of the argument of the Eritrean organizations in
the 1960s. In view of its importance it is worthwhile to describe its main points.
The first argument of the memorandum was that the existing constitutional
arrangements of the federation did not fulfil the intentions of the United
Nations. Its second argument was that the federal arrangement was being
infringed by the Ethiopian government. We shall not dwell on the issues raised
in the memorandum dealing with the constitutional arrangement since this was
settled by the UN resolution and the creation of the Eritrean government.
Rather, we shall devote more attention to the allegations and interpretations of
what the memorandum calls Ethiopian infringements of the federation. Stating
that the federation would have worked if it had not been violated by the Ethiopians, the authors of the memorandum proceed to elaborate their case.

Although the Eritrean government was set up according to the UN resolution, "its powers were usurped by the representative of the Ethiopian emperor
who exercised his authority through his occupation army".[1] The authors continued and pointed out that the Eritreans took the necessary steps to show the utter
disrespect for the Eritrean constitution by the Ethiopian government.[2] In what
the authors called a detailed review of Ethiopia's gradual abrogation of the UN
resolution they put the blame both on the UN and the British administering
authorities. They accused the British of handing the property of the ex-Italian
administration to the Ethiopian government instead of handing it to the Eritrean
government as the direct successor state (para. 45). They complained that the
British manipulated the elections to the first constituent assembly (1952) and
thus created a parliament "with a majority of pro-British and pro-Ethiopian
members" (para. 47). Meanwhile, the authors argued, the parties who
demanded Eritrean independence and fought against colonialism were perse-
cuted during the elections and were consequently excluded from debating the
constitution. Further the British, conspiring with the Ethiopians, saw to it that
the Constituent Assembly which was elected in 1952 remained in office for a
period of four years.

---

[1] FO371/131245. The complaint of the Eritrean people against the Ethiopian government, submit-
    ted to the United Nations by Mohamed Omar Kadi and Woldeab Wolde Mariam, October, 1957,
    para. 41.

[2] FO371/131245. The complaint of the Eritrean people, para.42. Here the authors are referring to
    the series of protests filed by the Eritrean assembly and the Moslem League in 1953 and 1954.

After stating that the extension of Ethiopian legislation to Eritrea which took effect by Imperial order no. 6 of 1952 was the gravest encroachment on the autonomous jurisdiction of Eritrea, the authors stressed that the Imperial federal Council—a body intended to discuss federal issues—was also paralyzed even before it became established. "The autocratic system of government", wrote the authors, "does not allow any Ethiopian national to raise proposals to His Majesty the Emperor" (para. 53). Returning to one of their favourite issues, the authors had no qualms at all when they charged the Ethiopian government with appropriating Eritrea's share from customs revenue. The authors state clearly that the Ethiopians continued to provide the Eritrean government with a lump sum of 680,000 pounds sterling yearly. This was equivalent to 4.5 million Ethiopian dollars. The actual sum ought to have been, according to the journalists of the *Voice of Eritrea*, 5.1 million Ethiopian dollars. The conflict was about whether this was all the sum due to Eritrea. Since the Ethiopians refused to allow the Eritreans to verify the customs revenues, they opened themselves up to the wildest criticisms.

The authors then continued to describe the measures taken first by the Eritrean government in suppressing the labour union established by Woldeab Wolde Mariam and then the measures taken by the federal authorities (Ethiopian government) against the Voice of Eritrea. Here they reiterated the actions taken by the Moslem League in 1953 with one notable exception. In 1953, the Moslem League's complaints were not against the Ethiopian government but mainly against the Eritrean government which either failed or conspired with the Ethiopian government in undermining the federation. In the 1957 memorandum, the Eritrean government is absolved of responsibility. The main responsibility for the abrogation of the federation was then placed on the Ethiopian government. It can be noted here that the authors of the memorandum were intentionally or unwittingly engaged in the distortion of events the consequence of which was the growth of Eritrean nationalism.

Under the section headed political liberties, the authors wrote that the Ethiopian government, being worried by the Unionist Party's growing support of the federation, counteracted by creating a party "whose members were only priests and bishops of the Coptic Church" (para. 63). This party was then placed under the leadership of Dimetros Ghebremariam who according to the authors was the spiritual leader of the Unionist Party during the 1940s. Elected vice-president of the Eritrean assembly in 1955, the authors of the memorandum wrote that, "in his capacity of a priest and vice-president of the assembly, he is exercising his strong influence in driving the Eritrean people to union" (para. 63).

According to the memorandum, another personality who played a decisive role in the abrogation of the federation was Asfaha Woldemikael, the chief executive who came to power in the summer of 1955 and "by virtue of his allegiance to the Emperor and in his capacity as a subordinate official in the Ethiopian government, had to be a pigtail of it, and enforce all orders and instructions dictated to him by the Emperor" (para.71). The authors admit that Asfaha had always been against the federation. The authors were indeed fully aware that the nomination of Asfaha as chief executive "was the final step towards undoing the federation" (para. 71).

The memorandum described above is a very interesting document as one of the earliest attempts at a reconstruction of the inevitable dissolution of the federation by Eritreans in exile. All the essential facts are recorded but in a distorted manner with a number of false as well as inaccurate reports. The inaccuracies of their account were partly hidden due to the wide powers of the representative of the Emperor as specified by the Eritrean constitution. The representative of the Emperor was the head of a series of departments, such as defence, interstate commerce, communications, and customs. The powers of the Eritrean government were limited to internal matters. The representative of the Emperor had much more power than the chief executive of the Eritrean government.

The memorandum could be studied as an early model of the uses of the past by an incipient nationalist movement. Written mainly by Mohamed Omar Kadi, the 1957 memorandum dealt with the reactions of the Moslem League to the Eritrean and Ethiopian governments' policies in Eritrea. What is striking is that in the 1957 memorandum, the name Moslem League is replaced by the term the Eritrean people. It has also to be remembered that the authors of the 1957 memorandum had to concentrate on the role of the Ethiopian government if they were going to have any chance at all of being heard by the United Nations. They would have had no case at all if they were to accuse the Eritrean government of violating the federation. Both Woldeab and Omar Kadi were certainly aware of the final report of the UN Commissioner for Eritrea where he appended an opinion by an international council of jurists where they stated that "if the Federal Act were violated, the General Assembly could be seized by the matter". The UN Commissioner for Eritrea Eduardo Anze Matienzo himself shared a similar opinion. He was of the firm belief that the Federal Act as an international instrument, the relationship established by it (the autonomy of Eritrea under the Ethiopian crown) could not be altered without the concurrence of the General Assembly.

It was rather obvious that the UN would hardly be engaged in the Eritrean case if it was brought to its attention by Eritreans complaining against other Eritreans over the violation of the federation. Both Woldeab and Omar Kadi were fully aware that the Eritrean government in power was committed to abolish the federation in favour of union with Ethiopia. The only viable strategy for arousing the interest of the UN on the matter was by accusing Ethiopia of the violation of the federation. It was indeed an ingenious strategy. By putting the entire blame on Ethiopia, the pioneers of Eritrean nationalism could then proceed to describe the Eritrean government in any way they pleased.[1]

The 1957 memorandum could, however, hardly stand a critical scrutiny. Its accusation against the British administration for handing the property of the ex-Italian administration to the Ethiopian rather than the Eritrean government has no basis at all. The British acted according to the Federal Act and according to the division of powers between an autonomous Eritrea and the Ethiopian crown. There was no evidence that the British manipulated the elections of 1952. The division of the country into 68 electoral constituencies, as later census trends were to show favoured Moslem communities.[1] The Unionist Party maintained its position in the elections which were held four years later. The extension of Ethiopian legislation to Eritrea was in accordance with the Federal Act and the Constitution. Both Woldeab and Omar Kadi were no doubt conversant with the Federal Act and the Constitution. As long as there was a single nationality, it was self-evident that Ethiopian legislation, which did not pertain to the domestic affairs of Eritrea had to be extended to Eritrea as well.

The 1957 memorandum was a document drafted by disgruntled leaders who were quick enough to realise that the federation was being slowly but steadily dismantled. Whereas, the objective of Woldeab was to revive once again his goal of an independent Eritrea and Tigrai state, that of Omar Kadi was to establish either an Eritrean state dominated by the ML or to restructure Eritrea along the Bevin–Sforza doctrine.[2]

In the United States, Mohamed Omar Kadi was persuaded by the Ethiopian Ambassador to return to Eritrea.[3] As to Woldeab either he was not offered the chance or he was sophisticated enough not to accept such an offer. Once in Eritrea, Mohamed Omar Kadi, was immediately put under police surveillance. Mohamed Omar Kadi had apparently given the overzealous police commissioner Tedla Ogbit enough rope to hang him. While passing through Cairo, Omar Kadi had in a radio interview said that Eritrea was being ruled by a black colonial power, an act that could easily be interpreted as treason. On the basis of the information supplied by Tedla Ogbit the Federal Attorney General filed a criminal charge against Omar Kadi in the middle of March 1958.

No sooner had the news about the impending criminal charges against Omar Kadi become known, than the main centres of the Moslem League were in hitherto unprecedented turmoil. In Keren, Agordat and Massawa the news of the charges against Omar Kadi were answered by spontaneous demonstrations. In Keren the protest against the treatment of Omar Kadi was so violent that the

---

[1]   The resignation of the first chief executive is described as a consequence of a repressive action of the Ethiopian government. In contrast the second chief executive is described as loyal to the Emperor and an official of the Ethiopian government and was, therefore, ever willing to enforce all orders. See, FO371/172820. The Eritrean Liberation Front introduces: Eritrea in the face of Ethiopian invasion, Mogadishu, September, 1963.

[1]   According to the census of 1939, 54 per cent of the population were Tigreans (Castelano, 1948).

[2]   Woldeab Wolde Mariam remained true to his early idea of the possibility of establishing a state made up of the Tigrean parts of Eritrea and that of the province of Tigrai in northern Ethiopia. By 1957, Omar Kadi and many members of the ML had figured out that the federation was lost. By accusing Ethiopia of violating the federation, Omar Kadi and his supporters within the ML hoped that the UN would intervene and hence create an opportunity to choose a better solution.

[3]   Three years earlier, a prominent Eritrean politician commented that the Ethiopians would bring Omar Kadi in line by financial or political rewards. It is indeed very possible that Omar Kadi might have been offered something more substantial than freedom from harassment. It is otherwise quite difficult to imagine why he decided to return to Eritrea after such a provocative and not entirely correct memorandum.

police felt provoked to shoot, wounding 12 and arresting more than one hundred people.[1] In Agordat, while the police arrested, according to an Eritrean memorandum sent to the Emperor, more than a hundred people, the Eritrean government apparently working in collusion with the police dismissed several chiefs from their posts. The protests in Keren and Agordat were also reinforced by similar protests in Massawa, although the immediate reason given was that the Ethiopian forces rather than the Eritrean police had occupied an area where it was alleged that oil had been found.

In Asmara the protests from the western part of Eritrea led to a general strike between March 10 and March 14. Moreover, the Asmara strike, undoubtedly political, was staged in response to the detention of some of the signatories of the March 5, 1958 memorandum to the Emperor where the signatories complained about the manner in which the police and the government dealt with the protests in Keren and Agordat.

The British Consul-General, commenting on the incidents, wrote that "the troubles in Keren and Agordat would probably have not occurred" if the authorities had been less high-handed with Omar Kadi.[2] While the Eritrean government and the federal authorities were drafting charges against Omar Kadi, the Italian Consulate-General informed his British colleague that "attempts have been made recently at Senafe and Agordat to form two groups of armed dissidents".[3] While, the Agordat group, according to the Italian source, succeeded in becoming established, at Senafe, the attempt collapsed for lack of arms.

The urgent telegrams to the Emperor sent by the members of the ML and the Federalist Youth Association of Eritrea were either not forwarded to the Emperor or the latter had given the Eritrean police a sweeping mandate to deal with the politically inspired protest activities. A few weeks after the quelling of the strike in Asmara, the Federal authorities brought criminal charges against three of the eighteen who signed a telegram to the United Nations on October 1957. The accused were extremely influential personalities within the Moslem community. Omar Kadi was a former member of the Federal Council; Suleiman Ahmed, the brother of the mufti of Eritrea; Imam Musa, was a former president of the Eritrean ML for Asmara and Hamassien, who did not officially resign from his post, although the ML had virtually ceased to function as a political organization. These three public figures were brought before the Federal Court on two charges based on articles 14 and 22 of the Federal Crimes Proclamation which dealt with communication with foreign governments without the author-

---

[1] FO371/131245. BCA to BEAA, 12.3.58. The arrests and shooting of demonstrators are mentioned in some detail in the memorandum of the ML and the newly formed Federal Youth League of Eritrea dated 5.3.58 and sent to the Emperor. For a copy of the memorandum see appendix 11.

[2] FO371/131245. BCA to BEAA, 13.5.58. The Consul-General continued: "... but it seems to me that the only thing the Ethiopians can think of when there is unrest in this territory is to sit down on the lid more firmly than ever".

[3] FO371/131245. BCA to BEAA, 13.5.58.

ity of the federal government and with conspiring to bring accusations against the Ethiopian government.

The case against Omar Kadi demonstrates clearly the degree of cooperation between the Eritrean police and the Federal authorities in stamping out any type of political opinion not to the liking of both governments. Omar Kadi was harassed by the Eritrean police soon after his return from New York in early November of 1957, in spite of the fact that during an audience the Emperor was alleged to have assured him that he would not be harassed by the police. Once in Asmara the federal authorities charged Omar Kadi with an act of treason punishable by ten years imprisonment, in full knowledge of the guarantee that the Ethiopian ambassador to the United States had provided in writing. There could be no doubt that both the Eritrean and the Ethiopian governments wanted to use the case of Omar Kadi to discourage similar activities in the future.

Omar Kadi was sentenced to ten years imprisonment on a charge of making statements abroad tending to bring the Ethiopian government into disrepute.[1] The two best-known leaders of the ML members whose crime consisted of signing a telegram to the United Nations also received stiff terms of imprisonment. Suleiman Ahmed, the brother of the mufti of Eritrea, and Imam Musa, the former president of the ML of Asmara, were each sentenced to four years imprisonment.[2] Only the members of the Federalist Youth Association who together with the members of the ML had sent a telegram to the Emperor in March escaped the net of criminal charges, although five of the signatories were detained during the period of the demonstration (March 10–14) and some were demoted from their positions as a result.[3]

The rigorous terms of imprisonment imposed on Omar Kadi, Suleiman Ahmed and Imam Musa were far beyond the actual "crime" for which these gentlemen were indicted. The charge against Omar Kadi was that he described Ethiopia as an imperialist power in Eritrea, an allegation which could in no way be supported either by facts or by law. Whatever his "crime" it was by no means as grave as to earn him ten years imprisonment. Even if no consideration was taken of the assurances he was given by the Ethiopian ambassador in the United States that he would not be molested for acts committed before his return to Asmara, the judgement was indefensible. The harsh terms of imprisonment were signals on the part of the Ethiopian and Eritrean governments that they would tolerate neither direct negotiation on the workings of the federation nor an appeal by Eritrean organizations to the United Nations.

---

[1] FO371/131245. BCA to BEAA, 12.5.58. The charge itself was based on an article of the Italian penal code made applicable to Eritrea by a clause in the Federal Crimes Proclamation. The evidence consisted of a pamphlet distributed in the Sudan and Egypt where the Ethiopians were accused of "having been guilty of a blacker imperialism than either the British or the Italians".

[2] FO371/131245. BCA to BEAA, 30.5.58.

[3] FO371/131245. BCA to BEAA, 3.4.58. One of the signatories of the March telegram to the Emperor —who was demoted from his post as a prosecution officer to a badly paid job in the Department of State Property was Tseggai Eyassu.

The message of the incarceration of the leaders of the Moslem community, was most certainly grasped by those who were outside of the jails, since the March 5 telegram to the United Nations was the last one to be drafted and dispatched from Eritrea. Through ruthlessly exercising their prerogatives the Ethiopian authorities set an example of the price likely to be extorted from less perceptive individuals. For the Eritrean Moslem community as a whole and for the members of the Federalist Youth Association, it must have become clear that they had to look for other forms of protest. If the activists within the Eritrean Moslem League had not discovered the use of armed resistance as a form of protest by the end of 1957, what happened to Omar Kadi probably led them to explore that avenue.

While the Eritrean police and the federal authorities were engaged in the brutal suppression of legitimate and by and large constructive peaceful protest, the Eritrean government and the assembly were waiting for the opportune moment to dismantle the autonomy of Eritrea. Moslem League resistance heavily crushed and the newly formed Federalist Youth Association deemed to be of little consequence, the Eritrean government, in the person of the Chief Executive, concluded this infamous year by pushing through a law known as The Eritrean Flag, Seal and Arms (Amendment) Act, 1958. The bill established that the Ethiopian flag was henceforth to be the only official flag of Eritrea instead of the distinctive Eritrean flag adopted in 1952. Reporting both to the BEAA and the FO, the British Consul-General in Asmara wrote that "the change will not be popular with the Moslem element of the population or with some Copts, and ... the bill was hustled through the assembly without any advance notice so as to allow the Moslem Deputies no time to reflect".[1]

A few months later on the occasion of the passing of the Penal Code (Extension) Act, where the Italian Penal Code hitherto in effect was repealed and replaced by the newly promulgated Ethiopian Imperial Penal Code, the Eritrean Executive Asfaha Woldemikael wrote:

> [T]he 1952 federation of Eritrea with Ethiopia did not at one blow strike off all the shackles of colonialism or heal the deep wound by which imperialist caprice had slashed our portion of the Fatherland from the greater whole to which its natural affinities, its great historical past, and the yearning of all our hearts have always bound it.[2]

ASFAHA WOLDEMIKAEL: CHIEF EXECUTIVE AND VICE-REPRESENTATIVE

Since his election as Chief Executive of the Eritrean government, Asfaha Woldemikael had not, as was expected of him, renounced his former job as vice-representative of the Federal Imperial Government in Eritrea. There appears to have been a tacit agreement between the Ethiopian government and the Eritrean Assembly that Asfaha would continue to be the link between the two govern-

---

[1] FO371/138027. BCA to FO, 5.1.59.
[2] FO371/138027. BCA to BEAA, 12.9.59.

ments. By the end of 1957 it was an open secret that firstly, the Chief Executive himself had expressed a desire to return to his earlier post as vice-representative. Secondly, it was reported that the Emperor's representative in Eritrea, Andargatchew Messai had assembled his subordinates in the palace in Asmara and reminded them that Asfaha was to be regarded as his deputy. According to the British Consul the Chief Executive of the Eritrean government spent, "two or three mornings every week at the palace presiding over conferences of Ethiopian officials". He further said that when "the chief executive elected by the Eritrean Assembly is also the principal agent in Eritrea of the Emperor, the Eritrean Constitution becomes something of a farce!"[1]

The Eritrean Constitution with its fine demarcations of spheres of authority between the Eritrean and the Ethiopian governments was disregarded, it appears, by consent rather than by design. Towards the end of 1958, a case came to the attention of the British Consul which illustrates the decisive but silent dismantling of the federation. The case dealt with the replacement of the post of the president of the Federal High Court. The Chief Executive asked Judge O'Hanlon, the vice-president of the Eritrean Supreme Court to take over the post of president of the Federal High Court. Constitutionally, it was beyond the power of the Eritrean head of government to directly appoint a person to such a federal position. The Eritrean head of state, however, did not appear to see any conflict of loyalty, probably because it was not the first time that the line of demarcation between the competencies of the Ethiopian and Eritrean governments "so carefully drawn by the United Nations Commissioner ... [was] being disregarded".[2]

By the end of 1958, the chief executive was so powerful and the assembly so toothless that the Eritrean head of state began to sign official documents granting exemption from federal tax, as vice-representative.[3] Since the last weeks of 1958 the constitution had definitely ceased to exist. Only its shadow remained; and it was to remain as long as it pleased the Eritrean head of state and the Ethiopian authorities.

From 1958 onwards the incorporation of Eritrea into Ethiopia was understood to be only a question of time. The conditions in Eritrea were laid down for such action. The Chief Executive, the commissioner of police, and the majority of the members of parliament were ready and willing to do away with the last remnants of federation. In fact a detailed rumour was reported by the Italian Embassy in early September of 1959, to the effect that the Ethiopians were considering securing a resolution by the Eritrean Assembly calling for an end to the federation, revocation of the constitution, and full integration of Eritrea into the Empire.[4] Reacting to the rumour that emanated from the Italian Embassy, the

---

[1] FO371/131292. BCA to BEAA, 26.9.58.

[2] FO371/131292. BCA to BEAA, 26.9.58.

[3] FO371/131292. BCA to BEAA, 29.12.58. The information was derived from the United States Consulate.

[4] FO371/138027. BEAA to FO, 1.9.59.

British Embassy reported from Addis Ababa that the Ethiopians might have come to the conclusion that they could push for full incorporation without having to fear the case being discussed in the UN.

However, the Ethiopians were not in a hurry. As the months turned into years, their position appeared to become more solid. By September 1959 the process of incorporation was coming closer to fulfilment. The Penal Code (Extension) Act which replaced the Italian penal code with the newly pro-claimed Ethiopian penal code was a step in that direction.[1] Another step was the integration of the two taxation systems. A few days before the year came to an end, Andargatchew Messai, the Emperor's representative in Eritrea, was replaced by Brigadier General Abiye Abebe.[2] The vice-representative's Office earlier occupied by the Chief Executive of the Eritrean government, was still vacant. This meant in practice that Asfaha Wolde Mikael, the Chief Executive of Eritrea, continued to carry out the unofficial function of vice-representative.

Neither politically nor economically had conditions changed the following year. While the Moslem community got the message concerning the ruth-lessness of the federal authorities, the members of the Youth Federalist Associ-ation also felt the torturing hand of the commissioner of police. To the climate of political repression was added a serious famine caused by locusts. While prompt American grain relief, distributed freely, was sufficient to alleviate the worst impact of the famine, general conditions were worsening throughout the year. Many politicians were beginning to consider exile thus following in the footsteps of Woldeab Wolde Mariam.

In early March 1959 Ibrahim Sultan, who after 1956 "went into political semi-retirement",[3] escaped from Tessenei to the Sudan. Ibrahim Sultan was joined by a group of ten to twelve people, the most important of whom was Mohamed Idris Adum, the last president of the Eritrean Assembly who had been obliged to resign in 1956.

Towards the end of the year, a British advisor who had contributed consid-erably to the life of the federation left Eritrea. This was Sir James Shearer, the president of the Eritrean Supreme Court and the "watchdog of the Eritrean Constitution".[4] James Shearer was remembered well into the late 1970s as a fear-less judge who managed to control the excesses of Tedla Ogbit, the Commis-sioner of Police.

While the days for the formal abolition of the federation were soon approaching, Ibrahim Sultan and Idris Mohammed Adum were quite busy can-vassing for support in Cairo and the other capitals of the Middle East. Their intensive activity in Cairo was brought to the attention of the British Embassy

---

[1] FO371/138027. BEAA to FO, 3.9.59. Commenting on the logical move of having the same general criminal law, Clarence-Smith, the Attorney General of the Eritrean government is alleged to have described the new Ethiopian Penal Code as an exchange of a mediocre law for a poor law.

[2] FO371/146569. JA1015/2. BCA to BEAA, 29.12.59.

[3] FO371/138027. BCA to BEAA, 16.3.59.

[4] FO371/138027. BCA to BEAA, 9.10.59.

who in turn asked the FO to supply an account of the situation in Eritrea.[1] In their reply to Cairo, the British Embassy officials in Addis Ababa summed up the political and economic history of Ethiopia, which though consistent with earlier summations was even more categorical. They wrote that geographically and culturally Eritrea was distinctly divided into the Afars, the Christian high-landers, and the pastoral nomads. Further reiterating reports of the extreme poverty of the country, the British officials wrote that Eritrea was practically speaking "an Ethiopian police state".[2] Elaborating further, they informed their colleagues in Cairo that the Eritrean assembly and courts obeyed the dictates of the Emperor and that the chief of the efficient and well trained police was pro-Ethiopian. It is perhaps relevant to add that, according to the British reading of events, Ethiopia was "for practical purposes a police state in which, on domestic issues public opinion cannot express itself".[3]

Once in Cairo, Ibrahim Sultan lost no time in composing a memorandum to the UN and the European embassies in Egypt. Mentioning the earlier memorandum authored by Omar Kadi and Woldeab Weldemariam in 1957, Ibrahim Sultan further reiterated that Eritrea was being swallowed up by Ethiopia in direct violation of the United Nations Resolution. He repeatedly stressed that the United Nations resolution could only be changed by the United Nations General Assembly and that neither the Ethiopian nor the Eritrean government possessed the right to change the status and constitution of Eritrea.[4] He then reminded the UN Secretary-General that repressive and savage actions were taken against those who protested against the violation of the federation.

The next step towards the abolition of the constitution took place in the spring of 1960. The Eritrean Assembly approved an amendment to the constitution where the term Eritrean government was replaced by Eritrean administration. The title of Chief Executive was also changed to read Chief Administrator. This took place in May 1960. From then onwards, the administration adopted the inscription "Eritrean administration under Haile Sellassie, Emperor of Ethiopia".[5] The process was closely followed by the Eritrean attorney general who was a British subject. The voting was 43 for the change, none against, and one abstention.

The intriguing issue for the British observers of Eritrean events was why the Ethiopians did not push for a speedy abolition of the federation when they could have done so since the end of 1955. One of the reasons given was that, as

---

[1] FO371/146567. JA1015/7. BEC to FO, 3.3.60.

[2] FO371/146567. BEAA to BEC 28.3.1960.

[3] FO371/146567. JA1015/13. BEAA to FO, 13.6.1960.

[4] FO371/ 172818. BEC to FO, 26.4.63. The memorandum to the UN was dated June 30, 1959. It appears that it reached the British Embassy in Cairo in April 1963. The memorandum was then despatched to London together with another far more detailed document renouncing the abolition of the federation.

[5] FO371/146567. JA1015/10. BEAA to FO, 21.5.60.

the Ethiopians were hoping to tie down Somalia into a similar arrangement, it suited them to await the outcome of their policy. Another reason is that, since the coming to power of Asfaha Woldemikael, the division of powers between Eritrea and the federal authorities had virtually ceased to exist. The head of the Eritrean government functioned as the vice-representative of the Emperor and hence of the federation. In such an arrangement, the Ethiopian government could afford to move slowly and let the constitution wither away by itself.

In addition to the unflinching loyalty of the Chief Executive, the Ethiopian government had also managed to recruit another even more zealous officer as the head of the British trained and extremely efficient police authority. Tedla Ogbit was known for his ruthless suppression of actual and anticipated dissension so that by the beginning of 1960 he had managed to muffle all signs of opposition in the country. The departure of Chief Justice James Shearer in 1959 meant that Tedla Ogbit could jail anyone with impunity.

The second Eritrean Assembly, (elected in 1956) appears to have connived actively against the constitution as much as the Chief Executive and the chief of police. We have earlier seen the unwillingness of the Eritrean government and assembly to act on a drafted electoral law thus precipitating a constitutional crisis. The issue surfaced once again in the spring of 1960 a few months before the elections to the third assembly were due to be held. On the closing day of its session the Eritrean assembly adopted a resolution that the forthcoming general election be held in accordance with proclamation no. 121 of 1951 issued by the British Administration.[1] The 1951 proclamation was based on indirect elections with the exception of Asmara and Massawa, where elections were based on universal male suffrage. Both in 1956 and in 1960 the Eritrean Assembly refused to replace the system of indirect elections, although a recent precedent had been implemented by the Ethiopian government.[2] It seems highly unlikely that the Ethiopian authorities were constantly putting spokes in the wheels of the Eritrean government. According to information collated by the British Consulate at Asmara, the attitude of the assembly members was based on the fear that a new electoral law would probably introduce direct elections, thus depriving them of the control over voting they currently had. Since the Eritrean Assembly members figured out that it was easier to control a few indirect votes, they had no reason to either push or adopt an electoral law as prescribed by the constitution.

With Ibrahim Sultan in Cairo and Omar Kadi in jail, there was little reported opposition against the final and inevitable dissolution of the federation. In their annual report, the British embassy officials simply noted the full incorporation of Eritrea following a vote by the Eritrean assembly to end the federation as the major internal political event. The embassy were of the opinion that the move

---

[1] FO371/145567. JA1015/11. BCA to BEAA, 25.5.60.

[2] The Ethiopian government had for the first elections in the history of the country, established an electoral commission and even granted universal suffrage both to men and women.

"appeared to be welcomed by business opinion in Asmara as ending a period of uncertainty and bringing the hope of more investments in Eritrea".[1]

By the beginning of 1962 while the full integration of Eritrea into the Ethiopian empire appeared to be a matter of formality, a rumour was spread which in its turn led to student demonstrations. The rumour was based on a misunderstanding and can be traced to the early 1950s. According to British diplomatic observers, there was a widespread impression in Eritrea that when the UN decided on the federation with Ethiopia, it also passed a supplementary resolution providing for the review of this arrangement after 10 years, i.e. in 1962. The UN did not pass any supplementary resolution to that effect. Nevertheless, for the greater part of May 1962 all secondary schools in the country were closed due to demonstrations. Although the students did not appear to have a clearly spelled out idea of why they were demonstrating apart from "unmistakable dislike of the Ethiopian connection", they were of such a nature as to provoke the Eritrean police to action. According to British sources, the demonstrators in Asmara demanded that the terms of the Eritrean constitution be observed, and in particular "they demanded that the local Ethiopian (sic) authorities should cease arresting people and holding them for lengthy periods without trial".[2] Some more extreme elements, the British embassy officials in Addis Ababa wrote, demanded the ending of the Ethiopian connection and the founding of an independent republic. Here it may be mentioned that since September of 1961, an armed organization had been established in the north eastern part of Eritrea led by the former members of the Moslem League, namely Ibrahim Sultan and Mohamed Idris Adum.

Although the new representative of the Emperor in Eritrea attempted to dismiss the student demonstrations and the widespread rumour of the supplementary UN resolution calling for a review of the federation, the events of May were taken very seriously by Addis Ababa. Between June 15 and 30, the Emperor visited Eritrea and took the opportunity to give his country's understanding on the matters dealing with Eritrea. In his speech the Emperor expressed his surprise that despite "the Eritreans long and gallant defence of their freedom, he should have found a small band of traitorous hypocrites among them".[3] The Emperor further emphasised that Eritrea had only been separated from Ethiopia for the 60 years of Italian occupation. Finally the Emperor rejected the suggestion that Eritrea suffered economic discrimination as compared with the other twelve regions of the empire. On the contrary the Emperor went to the extent of pointing out that since the establishment of the federation nearly 75 million Ethiopian dollars had been spent on the development of Eritrea.[4]

---

[1] FO371/172831. BEAA to FO, 1.1.1963.

[2] FO371/168302. BEAA, to FO, 12.6.62.

[3] FO371/168302. BEAA, to FO, 3.7.62. D.R. Ashe to R.S. Scrivener.

[4] FO371/168302. BEAA, to FO. 3.7.62.

The fears of the Emperor were substantiated a few months later. In Addis Abeba the Ethiopian authorities arrested twelve Eritreans discovered plotting the assassination of the Eritrean chief executive and the Emperor himself.[1] What was more revealing was that the Eritreans were organised in groups of seven. Altogether nearly a hundred people were involved, engaged in conspiring the assassination of the Ethiopian and Eritrean leaders as a well as in mobilizing support through distribution of subversive leaflets. It is most probable that the organization which the Ethiopian authorities discovered in Addis Ababa was part of the Eritrean Liberation Movement (ELM) which was reputedly established in 1958.

On November 15, 1962 the Eritrean assembly voted unanimously to dissolve the federation and unite Eritrea with the Ethiopian empire. According to British embassy officials, the incorporation of Eritrea into the Empire represented a dramatic step towards the cohesion of the whole country. Although this action, the British embassy officials continued, was of doubtful legality and may well have contained the seeds of trouble owing to its unpopularity in Eritrea, the British in Ethiopia believed that a combination of firm suppression and financial and other persuasions would probably succeed eventually in incorporating Eritrea within the empire at least as firmly as some of the other independent-minded territories.[2]

By the end of 1962, however, there were three rather loose political organizations based in Egypt carrying out political campaigns against the incorporation of Eritrea into Ethiopia and supplying arms to the armed band led by Idris el-Awati. The first was the Eritrean Liberation Movement the activities of which were first discovered in Addis Ababa towards the end of 1962. Abroad the Eritrean Liberation Movement was led by Woldeab Wolde Mariam, Mohamed Saleh Mohamoud and Tsegai Kahsai.[3] The second umbrella organization was known as the United Party of Eritrea Democratic Front. This was a direct successor of the Moslem League and since it was led by Ibrahim Sultan and Adam Idris Nur, it can be said that this was the most intransigent organization. It is interesting to note that although both Ibrahim Sultan and Adam Idris Nur describe themselves as members of the Eritrean Islamic Party, they also added that they belonged to the Coalition Democratic Front and Eritrean Political Delegation Abroad.[4] The third organization was the Eritrean Liberation Front led by Idris Mohamed Adum, Othman Saleh Sabby, Idris Osman Gelaidos (sic) Mohamed Saleh Humad.[5]

---

[1] FO371/168302. BEAA, to FO, 24.10.62.

[2] FO371/172816. BEAA, to FO, 16.1.1963. Annual report for 1962 on Ethiopia.

[3] FO371/172820. BEC, to FO. 15.5.63. One more appeal by the Eritrean peoples to their excellencies the African Heads of States.

[4] FO371/172818. BEC to FO, 26.4.63. To the Prime Minister of the United Kingdom from the United Parts of Eritrea Democratic Front- Headquarters of the Eritrean Moslem League. This is a three page long appeal of the Eritrean people. In the document the authors state that the democratic front is made up of the Islamic party and seven other coalition parties composed of Christians and Moslems.

[5] FO371/172820. BEC to FO, 25.8.63.

THE ECONOMY, 1953–58

The import and export data show that the economic situation did not deteriorate as the critics of the federation alleged. Exports and imports followed the colonial pattern in that goods exported from Eritrea included, in addition to Eritrean products, those originating in Tigrai and north eastern Ethiopia. In 1953, the total value of exports including invisible receipts was in the range of 30 million Ethiopian dollars, while total imports were in the range of 29 million. These figures were derived from the State Bank of Ethiopia, Asmara branch. In 1958, there was a remarkable increase in the value of imports, due largely to food crises brought about by the lack of rain and locusts during the previous year. The value of imports was in the range of 46 million, while exports were about 36 million. Compared to the previous year, the value of exports declined from 47 million to 27 million dollars.

The economy of Eritrea was nearly a third as big as the Ethiopian economy. While Eritrean import payment permits were in the range of 50 million Ethiopian dollars, those for Ethiopia fluctuated between 170 and 185 million dollars.[1] Even if allowance is made for the fact that up to 25 per cent of Eritrean imports were destined for Ethiopia, we can see clearly that the per capita consumption of imported goods was higher in Eritrea than in the other parts of Ethiopia. It has, however, to be recalled that the colonial pattern of consumption had hardly changed; with the exception of cotton textiles and food crops, most of the imported goods were destined for the Italian and other foreign communities in Eritrea (Negash, 1987).

An approximate computation of customs fees based on the ten per cent ad valorum tax would have earned the Eritrean government in the range of six to seven million Ethiopian dollars. According to the Federal Act, customs duties on goods entering or leaving the federation and which had their final destination or origin in Eritrea should be assigned to Eritrea. From the federal authorities the Eritrean government received a yearly lump sum of 4,630,000 Ethiopian dollars. During the federation era, the income from customs constituted from thirty to forty per cent of the total revenue of the country. Taking into consideration that up to 25 per cent of imports were destined for northern Ethiopia and an equal amount of exports originated in Ethiopia, the argument of the Ethiopian authorities concerning the difficulties of establishing Eritrea's share becomes understandable. Their reluctance appears to have been more a result of incompetence rather than any other ulterior economic reason.

Towards the end of 1958, the Eritrean economy, vis à vis that of Ethiopia, was assuming a more permanent and recognizable pattern. With the exception of the Eritrean tobacco monopoly, which was owned by the government, the few manufacturing enterprises were in the firm hands of the Italian community.

---

[1] FO371/165310. BEAA to FO, 4.1.62. Annual economic report on Ethiopia.

These were SAVA, Mellotti, Barattolo, and Incode AMAP.[1] The Eritrean government assisted actively in the purchase of shares as well as in providing long-term and low interest loans.

Since the end of the World War the Italian population had been decreasing due to lack of employment. From 1952 until the end of 1958, more than 3,500 Italians left for Italy, depriving at least an equal number of Eritreans of their livelihood.[2] At the end of 1958, the Italian population in Eritrea was made up of 10,200 adults. There were also around 14,000 half-castes who shared many values and tastes with the Italian community. Most of the Italians and half-castes lived in and around Asmara, thus continuing to give the city its Mediterranean character. By the end of 1962, the Italian population in Eritrea was further reduced to about 7,000 not including the half-castes.

The Italian Consulate General who compiled a study on the conditions of its nationals, noted that, in spite of the hard economic times, the Italian community had succeeded in maintaining its dominant position vis à vis other foreign communities as well as the Eritrean community. This strong position was in all fields of the economy. In agriculture, the Italian community maintained more or less the same amount of land in the highlands as during the Italian period (Consolato d'Italia, 1959:7). In the western and eastern lowlands, on the other hand, Italian concessions had significantly increased. In the eastern lowlands, Italian activity was geared to the production of citrus fruits and some coffee. In the western lowlands, cotton and banana production had reached such a level that the Italian community began to pressure the Eritrean government to protect their markets in Italy and South Arabia (Consolato d'Italia, 1959:50). To these were added the concession for the production of cotton run by Baratolo and the smaller one managed by Casciani. Three other companies were producing fibre from sisal and exploiting the multi-purpose dum palm fruit for buttons.

During the period of the federation, the company which outshone all others was SIA (Società Impresa Africane). Established in the 1920s as a public enterprise, the cotton producing concessionary company was engaged in massive infrastructure activities around the river Gash near Agordat. It was converted into a private company in 1948. The company resumed its agricultural activities which were essentially based on the distribution of cotton seeds to Eritrean farmers. By 1958, there were 2,000 Eritreans producing cotton for the textile factory in Asmara and sorghum for their own needs. The company had by this time 15 Italian technicians.

The principal industries in Eritrea, the Italian consulate report continued, were in the hands of the Italians. The most important of these were the salt mines of Massawa, employing about 300 Eritreans and 23 Italians, and the textile factory of Barattolo, employing 600 Eritreans and 30 Italians. The

---

[1] SAVA was the glassworks-factory owned by Mellotti, the brewery. Baratolo was the textile factory; INCODE, the meat packing factory. AMAP was the matches factory.

[2] The majority of Italians could afford to employ Eritreans as gardners and maids.

Barattolo textile factory was so well established that in 1956 it decided to establish a new concessionary company called SAIDE in order to secure a continuous supply of raw cotton. SAIDE had concessions in Mersa Gulub, about a hundred kilometres north of Massawa, and in Karkabat about 140 kilometres northwest of Agordat. This was made possible by the generous low interest and long-term loan from the Eritrean government.

There was also the citrus production complex of De Nadai which had put Eritrea on the map as a fruit exporting country. It began its activities seriously from 1952. By 1958 the De Nadai citrus farm in Elaberd was exporting over 3,500 tons monthly to the Arabian peninsula and Europe.

The Eritrean Chamber of Commerce, Industry and Agriculture was overwhelmingly Italian as late as 1959. Out of the total membership of 328, 249 were Italians; the rest were non-Italians e.g. Arabs, Indians, Greeks, Jews (Consolato d'Italia, 1959:8). Although we do not have the precise numbers, the Eritrean members could not have been more than a dozen.

The position of Italian economic predominance was further strengthened by the policy of the Eritrean government through its generous loans and purchase of shares. The initial capital of 400,000 Ethiopian dollars for the glassworks company which was run by the Mellotti family was provided as a loan by the Eritrean government. Other companies which had long-term and low interest loans from the government were the palm dum company (200,000 Ethiopian dollars), the Tabacchi ceramic factory (100,000 dollars), SAIDE (300,000 dollars), the Casciani sisal fibre company (300,000 dollars) and the sweater (industria maglieria) company (100,000 dollars). Through a share holding policy, the Eritrean government provided the Barattolo textile company with fresh capital of 315,000 dollars between 1956 and 1961. About thirty per cent of Barattolo's capital was provided in this way by the Eritrean government. Other companies which were able to get off the ground thanks to the readiness of the government to buy huge shares were the Asmara sack company and the African Matches and Paper Factory (AMAP) which were to supply both Ethiopia and Somalia during the 1960s and 1970s. Out of the initial capital of 500,000 dollars, the Eritrean government bought shares for 42,000 dollars (Government of Eritrea, 1962).

Contrary to the nationalist rhetoric that Ethiopia left the Eritrean economy to decay, (Tseggai, 1984; Sherman, 1980; Yohannes, 1991), there was in fact a resurgence of commercial and manufacturing activities. According to the documents originating from the Eritrean Chamber of Commerce, the number of firms dealing with industrial activities increased from 395 (1953) to 627 (1959). Likewise there was a dramatic increase of cottage handicraft enterprises from 745 to just over one thousand during the same period.[1]

Compared to the imperial Ethiopian government budget, the Eritrean budget was more evenly spread. Although both economies were of a very small

---

[1] FO371/138059. BCA to BEAA, 1.4.59.

scale indeed, Eritrea had much more leeway than the federal partner. To take
the expenditure on education as a case, while the Ethiopian government allotted
for the 1962–63 budget year 25 million Ethiopian dollars (3.5 million pounds
sterling), the amount allocated for this purpose in Eritrea was in the range of
two million excluding federal funding of secondary and technical schools. The
total government expenditure for 1961–62 was in the range of 210 million Ethiopian dollars whereas the budget of Eritrea for domestic purposes was nearly 17
million Ethiopian dollars.[1]

Yet the Eritrean economy was faced with structural problems some of which
had more to do with the political changes brought about by the federation. The
most serious weakness of the Eritrean economy was that it was dominated by
Italian capital and management. The establishment of the federation had meant
that Italian firms, if they so wished, could move their plants to the central parts
of the country where markets appeared to be more profitable. By the late 1950s
it was widely known among the Italian community in Eritrea that double taxation (to the Eritrean and federal governments) was causing them to contemplate
moving their plants to other parts of the empire. Moreover, the Eritrean market
was far too small for many of the Italian plants in Eritrea. In order to survive,
they had to sell their products in other parts of the country. The population of
Addis Ababa alone soon surpassed the total population of Eritrea, and thus for
many Italian entrepreneurs it began to make sense to move their activities to
other parts of the country.

The second structural obstacle for the continued development of the Italian-
dominated Eritrean economy was the increasing importance of Assab for the
economy of the central and southern parts of Ethiopia. The more Assab developed, the more it competed with Massawa and the factories dependent on
imported materials. From the 1960s onwards, factories established in the central
parts of the country could compete with those in Eritrea in spite of the 600 km.
distance between Addis Ababa and Assab.[2] Although the Ethiopian government had managed to get a significant position in the Djibouti–Addis Ababa
railway network (established in 1917), throughout its existence it had remained
cumbersome and inefficient. In contrast, Assab was nearer to the central parts of
the country and far more goods could be transported much faster to and from
Assab than on the single line rail-track. From the late 1950s and especially from
the 1960s, the port of Assab began to play a key role in the economic development of the country, thus leaving the greater part of Eritrea, which is far from
Assab, to fend for itself.[3]

---

[1] FO371/158765. BEAA to FO, 24.8.1961. A memorandum on the Ethiopian budget for the year
     1960–61.

[2] Apart from the fact that Italian firms in Eritrea were subjected to several kinds of taxes levied
     since the colonial times, the manufactured products had to be transported to Addis Ababa and
     south which tended to increase their retail price.

[3] Even during the Italian period, the port of Assab was of little importance to Eritrea. After 1953
     Assab was administered by a military officer appointed by the Ethiopian government.

The industries which survived the stiff competition from the factories which were mushrooming in the rest of the country were those which had specialized in products where the raw material was easily accessible. This is true of the Barattolo textile factory with its efficient supply of raw cotton from the Gash River Valley, from Mersa Gulub and Karkabat. This was also true of the Mellotti brewery with its nation-wide clientele and its reputed high quality beer. The glassworks also survived; in addition to the availability of raw materials, it was highly mechanized and, therefore, effectively competitive.

Yet the Eritrean economy did not show the annual increase usually associated with growing economies. Between 300 and 400 Italians were either leaving the colony annually for good or moving to the other parts of Ethiopia, probably enticed by the more liberal economic climate in the rest of the empire. The Italian population dropped from 18,000 in 1952 to approximately 7,000 in 1962 (Killion, 1985:341). The Eritreans might have succeeded after the departing Italians, although it did not appear that they expanded on what they inherited in terms of creating more jobs. Although the documentation shows a very small rate of growth akin to stagnation, the impact of this state of affairs assumed much larger proportions due to the steady growth of job-seeking youth who poured annually into an already stagnating and inflexible economy.

As the study of Thomas Killion (1985) clearly shows increasing unemployment and the virtual inability of both the Eritrean and Ethiopian governments to indigenise the economy gave rise to a series of labour uprisings. The confederation of Eritrean trade unions (Unione Sindacati Liberi dei Lavoratori Eritrei) which reached its apogee of power in 1958 functioned as an outlet for the political and economic disillusionment which followed in the wake of the federation. Initially tolerated, the trade union movement was finally crushed by the Eritrean government, partly due to its own intransigence and partly because it was regarded as an organization harbouring political objectives.

BY DEFAULT OR BY DESIGN: THE DISSOLUTION OF THE FEDERATION

The ML fought hard to preserve the federation without the prerequisite leadership. The Eritrean government did virtually nothing to maintain the federation partly because it was dominated by the Unionist Party and partly because the continuation of the federation meant the upholding of the constitution. The Ethiopians had neither the know-how nor the interest to keep the federation going. It was bound to fail because it had several structurally inbuilt weaknesses. The intriguing issue is not why the federation failed, but the resilience with which the memory of the federal experience was kept alive and handed down to the second generation.

The history of the federation was to a great extent the history of its dissolution. There were some remarkable reactions indeed against the dismantling of the federation both by individuals and small groups, which in turn might have contributed to the collective memory of the period. However, such acts of heroism were not what Eritreans associate with the federation period.

I believe that what has kept the memory of the federation strong and alive was the freedom of opinion which the British initiated and the UN encouraged. This honeymoon was staged carefully with the British holding the reins. It all started towards the end of 1946 when it had become known that Eritrea's fate would be decided by the FPC. Right from the start, the wishes of the Eritrean people were to be given consideration.

Between 1947 and 1952, under the aegis of the British, the Eritreans, ordinary men and politicians alike, lived through a period of political freedom which I believe left behind it a memory strong enough to inspire many people.There was really no time when the federation existed or functioned as was intended by its authors. Its provisions were infringed both by the Eritrean government and the so-called Federal Authority. Serious incursions were made to curb the freedom of the press less than a year after the coming into operation of the federation. Yet, the myth of a federated Eritrea with democratic structures remained very strong throughout the 1970s and 1980s.

The democratic institutions, which the Ethiopian government was accused of dismantling were not institutions created by the Eritreans themselves but were superimposed on the Eritrean society by the UN agencies. The freedom of political opinion which indeed prevailed in Eritrea, once again, came into existence and was made possible by the presence of the BMA. Without the decision of the BMA to engage the Eritreans in the future of their country, and without the presence and supervision of the BMA, there would not have been an open society during the 1947–52 period. To the extent that the structures of a civil society as we experience them in the Western hemisphere are the culmination of processes which began several centuries ago, it would be preposterous to expect the ex-Italian colony to indulge in such an exercise. It would be distortion of a dangerous magnitude to argue that the Eritreans had in fact more advanced political institutions, as many of the propounders of Eritrean nationalism have done.

Eritrean nationalism imagined the colonial period. The Eritrea that the Ethiopian government was alleged to have destroyed was the entity that was created by the Italians and the British. The former were responsible for the economic infrastructure and Mediterranean life style, while the latter were associated with the spread of political freedom and democratic practices. This study has, however, attempted to show that the federation arrangement had very few committed supporters. The first incursions against the Eritrean constitution were not from Ethiopia or the federal authorities but from the Eritrean Assembly and government.

The Eritrean economy continued to be dominated by Italian capital and personnel well into the 1960s giving Asmara, the capital, a distinctive character. As late as 1974, there were up to 6,000 Italians in and around this magnificent capital. However, the British sponsored and the UN underwritten constitution died an abrupt death in spite of the valiant efforts of the few British advisors and civil servants seconded to the Eritrean government. The administration of justice retained considerable autonomy as long as Chief Justice Shearer remained the president of the Eritrean Supreme Court. If there was an independent judiciary in Eritrea, it was greatly due the fact that the administration of justice was in the firm hands of Chief Justice James Shearer.

ETHIOPIA AND THE FEDERAL ARRANGEMENT: MYTHS AND REALITIES

Insofar as Ethiopia was concerned the fate of Eritrea was already decided in December 1950 when the UN resolved that "Eritrea shall constitute an autonomous unit federated with Ethiopia under the sovereignty of the Ethiopian crown". As outlined in the previous chapter, the Ethiopian government had considerable power over the Eritrean autonomous unit. These powers were specified in the Federal Act issued by the UN in 1950. For the Emperor and his advisors, the UN Resolution was sufficient to confirm Ethiopian power in Eritrea.

Before dealing with the powers reserved for the Emperor and his government under the misleading legal term of federation, let us dwell on the real meaning of the term as used in the Federal Act. The only structure that the UN demanded from the Ethiopian government in order to define the relationship between Eritrea and Ethiopia as federal was the following. The Ethiopian government was expected to form an Imperial Federal Council composed of equal numbers of Ethiopian and Eritrean Representatives who were to meet at least once a year to advise the Emperor upon the common affairs of the federation. Moreover, the UN document federating Eritrea to Ethiopia specified clearly that Eritreans should be represented in the executive, legislative and judicial branches of the federal government in the proportion that the population of Eritrea bore to the population of the federation. The Imperial Federal Council had no power other than advisory; it was constructed to be an organ without any power at all. As to the participation and representation of Eritreans in the federal (Ethiopian) bureaucracy, the Ethiopians had since the late 1940s a magnificent record of employing thousands of Eritreans in the civil service.

According to the Federal Act, the jurisdiction of the Ethiopian government dealt with the following matters: defence, foreign affairs, currency and finance, foreign and interstate commerce and external and interstate communication, including ports. The Federal Government had also the power to maintain the integrity of the federation, and the right to impose uniform taxes throughout the federation to meet the expenses of federal functions and services. The jurisdiction of the Eritrean government was to extend to all matters not vested in the Federal Government, including the power to maintain the internal police, to levy taxes to meet the expenses of domestic functions and services, and to adopt its own budget.

Soon after the coming into effect of the federation, the Ethiopian Government established itself in Eritrea with the purpose of exercising its powers. Customs, ports and transport services were immediately put under the control of the Ethiopian authorities also called the Federal Authorities. Currency and finance also came under Ethiopian administration leaving ambitious Eritreans with very little scope for prestigious careers.

Most of these so-called Federal departments were led by Ethiopians, although the majority of clerk and middle level management posts were occupied by Eritreans. Whereas, the Eritrean government and the Unionist Party appeared to have fully understood and accepted the consequences of the Federal Act, the Moslem League raised repeatedly the fact that there were many more Ethiopians working in the federal departments. The Moslem League appeared to have deliberately ignored the fact that Eritreans were to participate according to the proportion that the population of Eritrea bore to the population of Ethiopia. In their turn, the Ethiopian authorities chose to muffle and suppress opposition rather than oppose the inaccurate claims of the Moslem League. Throughout the period, the population of Eritrea was estimated to constitute about ten per cent of the population of the Ethiopian empire.

For all intents and purposes, the relationship between Eritrea and Ethiopia was not in the least federal. Even according to the intentions of the UN, Eritrea was not granted a federal status but only a status of autonomy. Yet the UN and its advisors, including the Commissioner for Eritrea, Anze Matienzo, insisted on using the term federation without having to bother about laying down the appropriate infrastructure for its proper functioning. Two years later British diplomats reminded each other that they really had not believed that the federation would work. In Eritrea, all important parties appeared to have considered the Federal Act and the federation as a reflection of success and vindication of their claims. In Europe and elsewhere the inputs of the UN Commissioner were widely appreciated.

The Federation was doomed to fail because it did not reflect the conception and exercise of power as understood by the UP.[1] The federation and the Constitution survived for some years due to the fact that some key positions were held by former British colonial servants. The opposition of the ML was not based on any notion of democracy but was largely inspired by the consequences of the spread of Abyssinian and Christian power. Confronted with the extensive powers allocated to the Ethiopian government by the Federal Act, and daily witnessing the full collaboration of the UP in the dismantlement of the federation, the ML tried to renegotiate the UN resolution. The 1957 memorandum submitted by Woldeab Wolde Mariam and Omar Kadi can hardly be interpreted in any other way. In my opinion the greatest enemy of the federation, was the UP domi-

---

[1] FO371/172818. BEAA to FO. Reunion of Eritrea with Ethiopia: Federation Dissolved. nd. (November 1962). In dissolving the parliament Asfaha Woldemikael said that "the reunion is a recognition of our being Ethiopians" and added that "the word federation did not even exist in our language".

nated Eritrean government. Although the Ethiopian government might have been equally interested in abolishing, it is inconceivable that this would have succeeded without the full support of the UP and the Eritrean government.

Chapter Five

The Long Road to Independence:
An Outline

THE ERITREAN LIBERATION FRONT (ELF) BEGINS THE ARMED STRUGGLE

The Eritrean Liberation Front (ELF) armed struggle that began in September 1961 was the culmination of two separate but parallel developments which trace their origin to the late 1950s. The first development was the persistent struggle of the ML since the inception of the federation. The second development was the evolution by 1958 of a nation-wide underground movement known as the Eritrean Liberation Movement (ELM) which was active in mobilizing support against the growing erosion of the federation.[1] Organised by Eritrean exiles in the Sudan, the ELM attempted to mobilize opinion inside Ethiopia and abroad against the violation of the federation.[2] Although the diplomatic community might have heard rumours about the existence of the ELM as early as late 1958, it was probably in 1962 that the ELM became known to the Eritrean government.[3] Although the story of the ELM has yet to be written, the sparse and disparate information appears to indicate that its main objective was to revive the federation.[4] Moreover, the ELM was from its inception made up of Eritreans from both religious denominations.

While the ELM was presumably in the process of adapting to the inevitable dissolution of the federation, some other Eritrean exiles in Cairo, the most prominent of whom was Idris Mohammed Adum had after repeated attempts to engage the United Nations on the matter of the federation, decided to form a new organization known as the Eritrean Liberation Front.[5] The exiles in Cairo were inspired as well as influenced by the Algerian Liberation Front that was

---

[1] In an unpublished MA thesis, Richard Taylor wrote that the ELM was organized by Eritrean exiles in Damascus (Syria) and Cairo (Taylor, 1971:25). The evidence, however, is challenged by Tesfatsion Medhanie's more rigorous and comprehensive research. According to Medhanie (1986:27) the ELM was organized inside Eritrea. The ELM might have had some Eritrean followers in Addis Ababa.

[2] According to one of the very few studies which throw some light on the ELM, we read that it was organised by Tsegai Kahsai, Mohamed Saleh Mohamed and Tahir Ibrahim. The ELM was soon joined by Woldeab Wolde Mariam, who was at that time in Cairo. (See Bogale, 1993:65.)

[3] During an attempt to murder the Emperor's Representative in Eritrea Leutenant General Abiy Abebe in July 1962, many of the followers of the ELM were arrested. The Eritrean and Ethiopian governments then learned that the ELM members were organised in cells where each sell had seven members. In Eritrea, the ELM was known as a group of seven. (See Bogale, 1993:66.)

[4] Some of its leaders belonged to the Association of Young Federalists.

[5] The ELF was initially led by Idris Mohamed Adem, Idris Gelawdeos, Othman Saleh Sabby, Mohamed Saleh Ahmed and Osman Idris Kiar. The ELF continued to be led by Eritrean Muslims until the end of the 1960s. (Bogale, 1993:67; Said, 1994:12.)

about to score a remarkable victory over the French. The Palestinian agitation to regain their lost homeland was also a source of inspiration that the Eritrean exiles in Cairo and other Middle Eastern countries, particularly Saudi Arabia, were well acquainted with.

Formed in July 1960, the ELF soon began to recruit men who would carry out the actual fighting (Medhanie, 1986:27–74). A year after its formation, it succeeded in recruiting the notorious Hamid Idris Awate. It has been pointed out by at least one author that Idris Awate was recruited by Idris Mohammed Adum on the basis of kinship, since both of them were from the same ethnic group and related (Pool, 1983:184). A shifta with a long experience and who only a decade earlier roamed over Eritrea with his army of about fifty men, Idris Awate did not appear to have second thoughts. Apart from the knowledge that the Cairo based ELF leadership would provide him with arms and provisions, Awate had other more practical resentment against the Eritrean/Ethiopian state. One of his grievances was the refusal of the latter to return to the Beni Amer (the ethnic group to which Awate belonged) the land confiscated by the BMA. Moreover, Awate was informed that the Eritrean security police in its zealous clamping down on political oppression was ready to jail him. With a dozen other followers, all from his own ethnic group, Awate resumed his shifta activities this time, however, under the formal leadership of the Cairo based ELF. This occurred in late July 1961.

According to an eyewitness narration recorded twenty years later, Awate was soon joined by another dozen Eritreans who had been serving within the Sudanese Army. In the first year of its existence, the Eritrean Liberation Army (ELA) was virtually made up of Beni Amer (Erlich, 1994:153). As late as 1965, the ELF was primarily made up of Moslem Eritreans both at a leadership and grassroots level (Said, 1994:12–16). I shall further mention two cases which stress even more forcefully the links between the Moslem League and the ELF. The first case is that of the Blin, the only ethnic group in Eritrea with an equal number of Christians and Moslems. During the 1940s the political allegiance of the Blin reflected religious and cultural affiliations. The impact of religion on political allegiance continued in the 1960s; Moslem Blin joined the ELF whereas Christian Blin joined the Eritrean and Ethiopian armed forces (Ghaber, 1993:60–64). The second example is from the founders of the organization which later formed the backbone of the EPLF. In their document, translated as *Our Struggle and Its Objectives*, they argue clearly and unambiguously that the ELF was a Moslem organization conducting a Jihad against Christianity (EPLF, 1973:5–23). Moreover, the ELF leaders succeeded quite easily in persuading Middle Eastern states that Eritrea was an integral part of the Arab world and that the nascent ELF was "a main pillar of the Palestinian revolution" (Erlich, 1994:155).

The emergence of the ELF and its armed wing the ELA undermined the effectiveness of the non-violent ELM, which in view of the effective repressive measures of the Eritrean police and the refusal of the United Nations to entertain allegations originating from Eritrean organizations abroad, was doomed to extinction. Before its final demise, however, it was reported that the ELM had realized the necessity of resorting to armed struggle and had in fact done so. In early 1964 a small group was organized by the ELM and made its presence felt in the northern Sahel. No match for the army of the ELF, the ELM group was completely liquidated by the former (Medhanie, 1986:28–29; Bogale, 1993:71). ELF's intolerance, as well as its ambition to be the only organization on the ground, was to be a recurrent theme during the greater part of its existence (Cf. Iyob, 1995:98–107).

During the first decade of its existence, the main objective of the ELF was the liberation of Eritrea from the oppressive rule of Christian Ethiopia. The ELF did not make any distinction between the Eritrean Christians and the Ethiopian state. For the ELF, the Eritrean Christians were not distinguishable from the "Amhara ruling class" of Ethiopia. As an organization dominated by former members of the Moslem League (ML), the ELF perceived itself as a Moslem organization engaged in freeing Eritrea, which it continued to describe as predominantly Moslem and Arab. In the literature of the 1970s and 1980s, the exclusively Islamic nature of the ELF was denied both by the EPLF and by the non-Moslem supporters of ELF. Even those who conceded a pro-Arab and Moslem orientation, did so in an apologetic manner.[1]

The perception of Eritrea as a Moslem country, and therefore, a member of the Arab world was enhanced by factors of culture and geography. Several of the Eritrean ethnic groups in the western part of the country had kinsmen in the Sudan. Moreover, since the 1950s Egypt, Sudan, Syria, Iraq and Saudi Arabia had been the principal outlets for Eritrean Moslems in search of employment and/or political asylum. The founders of the ELF, with the notable exception of the former leader of the LPP Weldeab Wolde Mariam, were all Moslems who found it quite logical to appeal to the spirit of Arab brotherhood for political and material support. Their physical presence in the capitals of African and Middle Eastern Moslem countries and their belief that over 80 per cent of Eritrea's territory was inhabited by Moslems resulted in the growth of the identification of the ELF as a Moslem (Arab) movement (Erlich, 1994).

The extension of Ethiopian "Christian" power in Eritrea, coupled with the Ethiopian government's reliance on Israel in security matters provided the ELF with even stronger evidence for the Moslem and Arab nature of the conflict.

To a great extent, the objectives of the ELF were based on the image of Eritrea that the ML developed in the late 1940s. Partly on the basis of an outdated census and partly due to the fact that up to 80 per cent of the Eritrean countryside was inhabited by Moslems, the ML had persistently argued that Eritrea was

---

[1] Ruth Iyob writes: "The ELF leaders' choice of Arab supporters was more a matter of necessity than a reflection of enduring Arab identity. This is not to minimize the existence of a shared Islamic heritage. ... The collaboration of Eritrean Christians with the emperor during the 1940s and 1950s was highlighted as a key factor leading to the disenfranchisement and discrimination of Eritrean Moslems", p. 110.

a Moslem country.[1] The ELF, as the ML in the 1940s was either unable or un-willing to take into consideration the fact that the Christian Eritreans, although confined to a very small area, constituted slightly more than fifty per cent of the country's population. For this oversight, the ELF was to pay a high price.

From the outset, the ELF was materially supported by Saudi Arabia and Syria (Taylor, 1971:26). While the Saudi support due to its proximity to Eritrea could be interpreted in the same manner as the Ethiopian support to the South-ern Sudanese rebels, Syrian support of the ELF appears to have been based on the latter's perception of the ELF as a Moslem and Arab movement.

The ELF passed through three phases before its demise as a fighting force in the summer of 1981. These phases were: i) the early years of growth, 1961–66; ii) the ideological crisis arising from its inability to deal with the Christian Eritre-ans, 1967–72; iii) the decade of decline characterized by the shift of power from the ideologically Moslem ELF to the emergent EPLF with its more educated and better organized Christian social base, 1972–81.

During the first phase, i.e. the 1961–66 period, the ELF's main propaganda weapon lay in its daring attacks on the symbols of domination, i.e. the police sta-tions. In 1962 alone the ELF carried out about a dozen raids and attacks in the western lowlands and executed several Eritrean civilians whom it described as traitors. However, the action that brought the attention of all Eritreans to the ELF was its armed attack in Agordat on July 17, 1962 aimed at killing the Emperor's representative, General Abiy Abebe, the Eritrean Chief Executive Asfaha Woldemikael, and the president of the Eritrean General Assembly Hamid Ferej.

The ELF armed attacks against mobile police forces and permanent police stations continued throughout 1963. Determined to gain the attention of the first Meeting of the African Heads of State in Addis Ababa in May 1963, the ELF carried out up to a dozen attacks simultaneously. At this stage the ELF believed fully that its continuous armed attacks would eventually attract the attention of the United Nations and the newly formed Organization of African Unity.

By 1963 the ELF may have had as many as 600 men in the field. This rapid growth was almost certainly the reason for the first military meeting held inside Eritrea that led to a new organizational structure. The ELF army was divided into four platoons under the overall leadership of Abubaker Mohamed Idris. The other leaders were Omar Ezaz Nasser, Kibub Hajaj and Osman Mohamed Idris (ELF Newsletter, no.44 of 1.9.81).

The following year (1964) witnessed the intensification of guerilla activities, the intervention of the Imperial Ethiopian Army and the first armed clashes between the ELF and the ill-organized, and ill-equipped forces of the ELM. Up

---

[1] There are significant distinctions between the Moslems of the Eritrean highlands, known as Jeberti and those of the lowlands. The highland Moslems speak Tigrinya and form part of the Abyssinian/Ethiopian culture. The lowland Moslems speak languages different from that used in the highlands and pursue either a pastoral or semi-pastoral mode of subsistence. The difference between the two cultures has not yet been fully appreciated.

to 1964, the Eritrean police which numbered ca. 5,000 dealt with the mobile and intractable ELF guerillas. In March 1964 the Imperial Ethiopian government made the decision to deploy its 6,000 man strong Second Division against the ELF. Although better armed and superior in numbers, the Ethiopian army was less suited to the job than the Eritrean police. Mostly composed of men from provinces outside of Eritrea, the Ethiopian army lacked knowledge of the area and of the people that it was to pacify.[1]

While the ELF could quite rightly regard 1964 as a year of remarkable achievements, its attitude towards the ELM was a sign of its attempts to dominate the struggle for liberation. Very little is in fact known about the ELM. As far as the ELF is concerned, the ELM was "blackening the struggle and attempting to sow discord among the nationalists in the field as well as abroad" (ELF Newsletter, no.44 of 1.9.81). According to at least one author (Medhanie, 1986) however, the ELM was politically a much more advanced organization.

The success of the ELF against the ELM meant that the former continued to portray the nature of the struggle in pan-Islamic and pan-Arab terms. However, as many Eritreans of the Christian faith began to join the armed struggle, the ELF found itself more and more unable to pursue its Islamic and Arabic policies. Although very few Christian Eritreans held top positions, the sheer presence of many of them as rank and file fighters was serious enough for the ELF to begin to experiment with a number of solutions. The first innovation was to divide the country into five military regions. Regions 1 to 4 were in the Moslem areas, whereas the Christians were given the last region. This took place in 1965. The divisions were made along purely religious and regional lines (Pliny the Middle-Aged, 1978:37–45; Medhanie, 1986:29). The main aim of this change was to control more effectively the Christian fighters, as well as to minimise the risk of internal conflicts among the various ELF factions.

The new administrative apparatus was very short lived. The Supreme Council, on the whole, had very little contact with the regional commanders. Moreover, this new structure served to intensify the internal disputes within the ELF. The Christian members of the ELF, who had been harassed from the very beginning, did not benefit from the change of administrative routine. Although organised in a military region of their own, they were completely dependent on the Supreme Council for supplies. They felt discriminated both in the allocation of resources and the formation of policies.

The ELF, by then committed to a pan-Islamic and pan-Arabic goal, was unable to integrate Christian Eritreans. Towards the end of 1967, for instance, more than one hundred Christian fighters opted to surrender to the Ethiopian

---

[1] There is sufficient reason to believe that the Ethiopian government realised the limitations of its army. From 1967 onwards, the Ethiopian government initiated an extensive recruitment of a counter-insurgency force trained by the Israeli army. The Eritrean commandos proved far more effective than the army.

authorities rather than face probable execution by the ELF.[1] According to Eritreans who escaped from ELF persecution in the late 1960s as well as the first document of the EPLF, as many as 300 Christian Eritreans may have been killed by the ELF in an effort to control their inflow.

By 1968 the ELF was incapacitated by internal dissension. The ELF leadership, exclusively made up of people from the historical regions of the Moslem League (western province), was under continual accusation of discriminating against the three remaining regional divisions. Partly arising from internal pressure and partly in order to meet the growing criticism, ELF leadership had agreed to call a nation-wide military conference in the summer of 1969. All the regions were represented and a new leadership known as the ELF General Command was established. The Supreme Council and the Revolutionary Command were abolished. The shift of leadership from the capitals of Middle Eastern countries to a General Command with its home base inside Eritrea was indeed a great innovation. The General Command had 38 members, twenty of whom were from among the staunch supporters of the former Supreme Council and Revolutionary Command.

No sooner had the conference dispersed, than the General Command, which was dominated by the Moslems from regions one and two, began to harass the members from the remaining three regions, detaining and killing several. In Europe up to 1970 the ELF was known as a Moslem organization carrying out the objectives of Arab Revolution in the black continent (*Africa Confidential*, 1970, 2:6) Eritrea was also described as predominantly Moslem (Erlich, 1994:15–64).

THE EMERGENCE OF EPLF

The history of the formation of the EPLF is closely linked with Othman Saleh Sabby, whose ability as a spokesman enabled him to secure the necessary resources. Originating from Massawa region and a member of the Supreme Coun-cil of ELF, Sabby had felt pushed aside by the Beni Amer dominated leadership of the organization. There were several issues of conflict. The first issue was power, where Sabby felt that the ELF leadership obstructed his campaign in the Middle East. The second issue which was of a more fundamental nature involved his understanding of the role of the various regions in an independent Eritrea. This latter issue is more thoroughly discussed by Haggai Erlich (1994). Sabby believed that the Eastern Red Sea region, which he described as the Assab-Massawa-Asmara triangle, was far more important to the Arab world than the Western Eritrean region (Erlich, 1994:160). There is no doubt that Sabby was reacting against the Beni Amer domination of the ELF and was thus bargaining for a sort of autonomy for the people of Massawa and its hinterland by forging links

---

[1] BBCWB/ME 6.11.1967 and 8.11.1967. One of those who surrendered was Weldai Kahsai, the commander of division 5. He is reported to have said that "the so-called Eritrean Liberation Front was prepared to hand over the province to any neighbouring Arab State".

with Asmara and Assab.

A dynamic organizer and a prolific writer, Sabby had by 1969 begun sending his followers to the PLO training camps. Although we do not know when exactly the acronym PLF (Popular and/or Peoples Liberation Forces) was first used, by the early months of 1970 there were three small groups challenging the hegemony of the ELF. These were: PLF 1 led by Sabby, PLF 2 also called the Essayas Afewerki Group, made up of Christian fighters who broke off from the ELF in 1969, and finally, there was PLF 3 also called the Obel Group. In the middle of June 1970, the leaders of these three groups agreed to coordinate their activities vis à vis the ELF. What is striking about the Essayas Afewerki Group is that it gave a religious motive for breaking away. In their programme document, which has had tremendous influence on Christians, they described the ELF as a purely Moslem organization with the goal of establishing a Moslem and Arab state in Eritrea.

In this document by Christians and for Christians, the ELF is portrayed as an Islamic movement and a sworn enemy of Christians. It reiterated the crimes committed by the early ELF leaders against Christian fighters and the peasantry (Medhanie, 1986:35–6). That the early ELF was permeated by Moslem ideas and goals is sufficiently and clearly stated by historians sympathetic to the front. One such author is Tesfatsion Medhanie. In his major study on the Eritrean national question, he described the early ELF in the following words:

> The ELF was launched as a pre-emptive project against the development of the ELM. Its leadership was comprised exclusively of Moslem lowlanders. Even though it included a few intellectuals and other petty bourgeoisie, the leadership was dominated by bureaucrats known to have had strong feudal tendencies.

> The leadership organised the ELA [Eritrean Liberation Army] along sectarian lines, recruiting fighters from the Moslem peasantry in the western lowlands. ... It preached sectarian goals, stressing that Haile Sellassie was a Christian despot and that most of the Christians in Eritrea favoured union with Ethiopia. ...The leadership also pursued a religious oriented foreign policy. It confined its external activities to the Islamic Near East, spreading propaganda which portrayed Eritrea as a Moslem country and part of the Arab world. It presented the Eritrean cause as a Moslem struggle against Christian oppression. (Medhanie, 1986:28.)

I think Medhanie was not exaggerating at all when he wrote that the document issued by the Essayas Group in 1970 was "a clarion call for all Christian Eritreans" to rally behind Essayas against the anti-Christian ELF (Medhanie, 1986:36). Moreover, it was not the least surprising that the Essayas Group resorted to the religious/cultural divide.

David Pool also interpreted the reasons for the breakaway of the Christian group led by Essayas as a result of the ELF's portrayal of Eritrea as a predominantly Arab and Moslem society and the liberation struggle as a fight for Islam and Arabism (Pool, 1983:186). A highly controversial issue which deserves close scrutiny is the extent to which the ELF was already abandoning its Islamic and pan-Arabic ideology a few years prior to the formation of the EPLF. According to Medhanie, the continuous pressure of the Christian and other small Moslem minorities had begun to produce an impact on the workings of the ELF, a view with which Markakis (1987) concurs. The military congress held in 1969 and the establishment of the General Command were taken as steps in the right direction. Between 1969 and 1971, the ELF made repeated efforts to bring together the seceding groupings. Particular attention was directed to the Essayas Group, and the ELF, we are told, recognised some of the grievances as justified. At the ELF-organised First National Congress, which the Essayas Group refused to attend, the ELF resolution called for a negotiated settlement with the Essayas Group, while the same resolution simply ordered the other two splinter groups to return to the fold. Yet the Essayas Afewerki Group refused to seek a solution to the conflict which was unquestionably assuming a religious guise (Medhanie, 1986:37; Markakis, 1987:129).

The General Command of the ELF proceeded with the preparations for the First National Congress as was agreed at the 1969 conference. Its efforts to persuade the three splinter groups, however, proved futile. By the time the ELF was ready for its First National Congress (held in October–November, 1971) the gap between the General Command and the splinter groups had irrevocably widened. There was no doubt that the congress organised by the General Command was fully cognisant of the state of affairs, a fact we can deduce from its resolutions. The congress resolved that "the Command stemming from the congress shall have full powers to take military measures to ensure the unity of the organization and the unity of the revolution". Moreover, the congress resolved that the Eritrean arena could tolerate only one revolution led by one organization and with a single command (Erlich, 1983:30).

The 1971 ELF congress contributed further to the solidification of the differences which were graphically represented by the Essayas Group. The few quite well-known Christians who had joined the leadership ranks of the ELF were not sufficient to persuade Essayas and the other splinter groups. The EPLF continued to stress the fact that there was no substantial change within the ELF.

While the ELF was devising military means of bringing into its fold the recalcitrant splinter groups, the document issued by the Essayas group was being actively used by Eritrean exiles for purposes of recruitment. By 1972, when the ELF began its war of liquidation against the EPLF, the latter turned conveniently to its 1971 document to further substantiate its accusations against the ELF. As far as the EPLF was concerned, ELF remained a Moslem front founded in order to transform Eritrea into a Moslem and Arab state.

The continued success of the EPLF was achieved by the ingenious use of three strategies, which reached their culmination towards the end of 1977. The first strategy was the identification of the Essayas Group as socialist. The socialist objective in turn legitimated and established the EPLF within the anti-imperialist camp in the west. This strategy, it should be pointed out, was more apparent than real. The main document out of which the socialist nature of the Essayas Group was derived contained only a paragraph on the subject. The socialist commitment of the Essayas Afewerki Group was not profound at all, but the few words in the 1971 document were sufficient for Eritrean exiles in the US and Europe to defend the ideological differences between the EPLF and the ELF.

The second strategy that the Essayas Group made extensive use of was the anti-Christian nature of the ELF. The 1971 document described in great detail the atrocities committed by the ELF against members of the organization as well as against the peasantry because these people happened to belong to the Christian faith. Tesfatsion Medhanie argued that the EPLF had exaggerated the list of atrocities committed by the ELF but otherwise agreed with the description. Up to 1974, while the Essayas Afewerki Group continued to recruit Christians only, its supporters in Europe and the US continued to mobilise Eritreans along the framework of the 1971 document, depicting the EPLF as Christian as well as socialist. Since the great majority of Eritrean exiles in Europe and the US were Christians, the process went quite smoothly. By 1976, more than ninety per cent of the Eritreans in Europe and the US were organised behind the EPLF.

The third strategy which the Essayas Group managed extremely well was to keep alive the loose front they established with the Obelites (PLF 3) and the Massawians (PLF 1). Until 1973 the so-called EPLF was made up of three distinct groups jointly represented by the dynamic Othman Saleh Sabby. Apart from the fact that the Sabby connection was the only means of supply, the Essayas Group had very little to fear from the two small and ill-organised Moslem forces. The Obelites were virtually extinct after a heavy onslaught from the ELF and the recruitment base for the Massawians was extremely limited. Whereas the Essayas Group had up to a million Christians to rely on for purposes of recruitment, the Massawians had at most a population base of not more than 100,000.

The operation of the Essayas Group within the loose EPLF structure enhanced the image of the group as an organization that was not inspired by religion. For the great majority of the Eritreans, however, it was very clear that the EPLF was first and foremost an organization formed and dominated by Christians.

From its inception in the end of 1970 until the end of 1974, the EPLF passed through a very critical period. On the one hand, it had to counteract the political and military onslaught from the veteran and well armed ELF. On the other hand, it had to stand firm against cooptive rapprochement from the Ethiopian government. During this initial period, The EPLF connections with the indefatigable Othman Saleh Sabby were no doubt of great importance.

In the beginning of 1974 it was already clear to many Eritrean activists in Europe and North America that the Sabby connection was purely one of convenience. Eritreans in Europe and North America had begun to undermine the position and influence of Sabby by stressing the socialist and anti-Arab nature of the EPLF. From 1974 until the long-awaited break between the EPLF and Sabby in March 1976, there were at least two foreign policies. While Sabby continued to stress Eritrea's close cultural ties with the Middle East, the Eritrean activists in Europe and North America, most of whom were Christians, emphasized the socialist and Marxist orientation of their organization. Although Sabby still managed until the end of the 1970s to secure enough resources from the Middle East, the Eritreans in Europe and North America were slowly but steadily building a base of support by portraying EPLF as the opposite of the Moslem-inspired and pan-Arabist ELF.

The period of precarious survival, as far as the EPLF was concerned, came to a surprisingly favourable conclusion at the end of 1974. The Ethiopian coup leaders, who until the night of November 24 , 1974 had prided themselves on carrying out a bloodless revolution, shocked the world and the Ethiopians alike by the summary execution of more than 60 former government officials. Among those who were killed was the Chairman and leader of the coup, General Aman Andom, who in addition to being an Eritrean by birth, had begun to seek a political solution to the Eritrean problem.

The death of General Aman Andom, the first head of the military junta which overthrew the Emperor in September 1974, had very serious repercussions for the nature of the conflict. Up to the end of 1974, the conflict in Eritrea was to a great extent a local affair handled quite efficiently by the Ethiopian armed forces and the Eritrean police.

The intense struggle for power and hegemony between the prime minister Aklilu Habte Wold and the governor of Eritrea Asrate Kassa (1963–73) did in fact involve, among other things, the conflict in Eritrea. At the bottom of the issue lay the expediency of resolving the conflict either through military means or through the policy pursued by Asrate Kassa, i.e. continued use of military and political options. The prime minister and his supporters (who included most of the leaders of the Ethiopian armed forces) campaigned for a more direct military intervention, and they were thus quick to exploit ELF's military operations as signs of weakness on the part of the Eritrean government led by Asrate Kassa. The governor of Eritrea, Asrate Kassa on the other hand argued for a more sophisticated divide and rule policy where the Eritreans (especially the Christians) would be made to play a more active role (Erlich, 1983:38–39).

By 1973 the centuries-old Ethiopian monarchy proved unable to provide effective leadership to overcome the economic crisis created by the Arab-Israeli October War of the same year. The Emperor had become senile and his loyal servants (Asrate Kassa and Aklilu Habteweld) were divided into factions engaged in obstructing one another rather than in evolving a unified strategy to deal with the successive waves of strikes by workers, students, teachers and members of the armed forces.

By June 1974 the country was for all purposes ruled by an unidentified group (up to 120) of non-commissioned and junior officers of the armed forces. This group came to be called the Derg, meaning the committee. General Aman Andom, an Eritrean by birth and a hero of the Ethio-Somali war of 1964, was put forward as their leader. Since, however, the identity of the Derg was kept secret and the imperial government was still officially in place, for a little over half a year there was a political vacuum in the country which greatly benefited the EPLF.

Between June and mid-November 1974, there was a unilateral cease-fire in Eritrea declared and implemented by the Ethiopian government, by then under the effective control of the Derg and General Aman Andom. The cease-fire was based on two premises. The first, adhered to and argued by Aman Andom, was that the Eritreans could be persuaded to lay down their arms if cease-fire conditions were created for them. The second premise was that, if the Eritrean groups proved to be unheeding, then the Ethiopian armed forces could be re-deployed with greater force and severity.

The cease-fire was used effectively by the EPLF. Firstly, it moved rapidly to the vicinity of Asmara, thus covering most of the Tigrinya-speaking parts of the region. Secondly, the cease-fire made it possible for the EPLF to explain to the ordinary citizens of Eritrea its differences with the ELF. Without mincing words, the EPLF accused the ELF of harassing Christian Eritreans. It portrayed itself as a multi-ethnic and multi-religious organization.

Meanwhile, General Aman Andom and the Derg were watching the developments of the cease-fire in Eritrea. By early November, there were two quite conflicting policies on the agenda. The first policy, advocated by the still un-identified Derg, called for the despatch of an additional 5,000 soldiers to Eritrea to strengthen the army's position, as well as to carry out offensive activities when so needed. The second policy, advocated by Aman Andom, called for the continuation of the cease-fire policy and the search for a political solution, in which the Ethiopian government would concede substantial power to the Eritreans.

The summary execution of Aman Andom, who had refused to relinquish power, and that of 62 officials of the imperial government on the night of November 24, 1974 put an end to the cease-fire experiment as well as to the search for a realistic political solution. For the EPLF but also for the ELF, the death of Aman Andom was received with relief, since it was widely believed that he would have succeeded in convincing the Eritrean people to fight the EPLF and ELF out of existence. His summary execution and the policy that was soon pursued by the Vice Chairman, Lt. Colonel Menghistu Haile Mariam (chairman from February 1977) changed completely the pattern of development from a policy of cooperation with Eritreans to their virtual alienation. After November 1974 the Addis Ababa government appeared to have lost all confidence in the role of the Eritrean civilian population in the political and/or military resolution of the conflict. During November and December 1974, the military authorities in Addis began to terrorise the youth of Asmara. Before the end of the year more than 50 young people were strangled to death, thus creating a climate of panic (Markakis, 1987:240–241: Clapham, 1988:208; Lefort, 1981:71–74).

THE INTENSIFICATION OF THE WAR AND THE RISE OF EPLF TO A POSITION OF HEGEMONY

The new policy implemented by the Derg wrought havoc in Eritrea and among its inhabitants, while paradoxically it strengthened the position of the EPLF. With the Derg in power, the EPLF had no serious need to offer explanations to the western world; the manner in which the Ethiopian military government pursued the war was sufficient to evoke sympathy for the underdog.

Inside Eritrea, the positions of the two fronts were changing quite rapidly. By 1975 both fronts had been replenished with tens of thousands of Tigrinya-speaking young men and women who fled from a political and military climate where they felt they were treated as "guilty until proven innocent". By the end of 1975, it was estimated that there were more than 30,000 men and women in each organization. The tide was, however, clearly turning towards the EPLF, because most of the new recruits were Christians, Tigrinya-speaking, far better educated than their Moslem countrymen, and came from a highly centralised political culture.

By the middle of 1975, the EPLF was not at all interested in discussing a merger with the ELF, although the latter had expressed clearly its readiness. The EPLF appeared to have been aware that it had the upper hand, since it had much easier access to the recruitment of Christian Eritreans. ELF's and Sabby's call for the creation of a single unified organization, therefore, fell on deaf ears. The EPLF had its own plans for creating a unified organization. This plan was based on the withering away of the ELF through a combination of internal and external pressures.

The EPLF could see that the ELF was disintegrating because of the impact of the thousands of Eritrean Christians who had joined it since November 1974. These fresh recruits revolted against ELF's pan-Arabic and pan-Islamic orientation. The EPLF flatly rejected ELF's and Sabby's appeal for merger on the pretext that no merger could take place until the ideological differences between itself and the ELF were sorted out. In reality, the main reason for its refusal was the fact that the EPLF did not want to share power.

In March 1976 Sabby broke with the EPLF on the grounds that the latter had refused to honour the agreement he had concluded with the ELF on a time table for the unification of the two organizations. It has been reluctantly admitted by the EPLF, that a few hundred fighters who without exception were Moslems from Massawa and the Red Sea area had left the EPLF and joined Othman Saleh Sabby. The EPLF was deprived of one of its dynamic fund raisers and spokesmen, but only after it had managed to mobilize the vast majority of Christian Eritreans abroad. From the late 1970s onwards, the Eritrean organizations in Europe and North America were to play a very important role both in supplying materials as well as in functioning as a link between the EPLF and the outside world.

By the end of 1976 the ELF still led by the old guard, but dominated at the lower levels by Christian Eritreans, was crumbling. Many of them pressed the ELF to abandon its pro-Arab and pro-Islam stand to satisfy the EPLF. Although the EPLF belatedly accepted a united front arrangement in October 1977, it was widely speculated that this was a time-winning strategy. By the end of the year several thousand soldiers from the ELF had deserted their organization and joined the EPLF. These were all Christians from the highlands. With a social recruitment base of over a million, which was relatively speaking, well organised and better educated, the EPLF was not in the least prepared to share its power with the ELF. Although the ELF had, due to the immense increase of Christian Eritreans, changed and was by 1976 an organization with neither the intention nor the power to exclude the Christian Eritreans, such a change apparently was not enough to satisfy the EPLF.

Divided into several factions (the remnants of the 1965 regional divisions) and poorly led, the ELF was not a real fighting force when the Ethiopian army resumed its offensive in the summer of 1978. By 1980, the Ethiopians had retaken nearly all the towns from both of the Eritrean organizations. While the EPLF succeeded in keeping the Ethiopian forces away from its base areas around the Nakfa escarpments, the ELF was virtually swept away into the Sudan. Thus weakened by the Ethiopian assault, the ELF was finally driven from the Eritrean countryside by a combined assault carried out by the EPLF and the newly established Tigrean Peoples Liberation Front (TPLF). This took place in the summer of 1981.[1]

The war between the Eritrean nationalist organizations was over ideology, history and hegemony. At the bottom of the conflict between the two organizations was the cultural and religious identity of the country. Although the ELF was undergoing radical changes brought about by the flux of new recruits from the Christian parts of Eritrea, and although the ELF was really in the process of being taken over by young, sophisticated and better educated Christians from the highlands, the EPLF did not deem it strategic to let the ELF alone. As Shumet Sishagne (1992:315) has recently argued it was likely that the EPLF was worried that the ELF would continue to question the fundamental thesis of the issue of conflict between Eritrea and Ethiopia, i.e. Ethiopian colonization of Eritrea. The EPLF was worried that the ELF might come to a separate agreement with the Ethiopian government.

---

[1] The EPLF has been very reluctant to admit that it had jointly with the TPLF waged war against the ELF. Since the EPLF pursued the strategy of silence, the ELF's repeated accusations that both EPLF and TPLF were waging war against it were taken as an additional recrimination. Apart from ELF sources, the TPLF has been forthright enough to present a detailed explanation of its war against the ELF which it jointly carried out with the EPLF. In a very complicated analysis the TPLF argued that it went to war because it was provoked by the ELF. It was only later, towards the end of 1980 that the TPLF joined hands with the EPLF in a joint military action against the ELF. See TPLF, Eritrea: From Where to Where. [Tigrinya Text] April 1986. The official version was that the issue which triggered the war was a boundary dispute between the ELF and TPLF in the south western part of Eritrea (Cf. Medhanie, 1986:116–7).

By early 1980, the veteran leaders of the ELF could very well see that the ELF which they built in the early 1960s had changed beyond recognition. The Christians who in the 1940s and 1950s were instrumental in the creation and in the eventual demise of the federation had by the late 1970s also begun to dominate the ELF. The link between the Moslem League and the ELF, which was very clear until the middle of 1976 was broken after 1976. These ELF veterans could also see that independent Eritrea would no doubt be dominated by the EPLF. It was, therefore, probable that some forces within the ELF were beginning to review the situation and even beginning to entertain a settlement with the Ethiopian state, as a better alternative to a life in a new order led by the EPLF. This is the basic argument of Sishagne with which I fully concur. I would, however, like to elaborate further on the inclination within the ELF to entertain a separate settlement with Ethiopia, which was attempted by some factions of ELF towards the end of the 1980s (Said, 1994:259–275).

The leaders of the Moslem League who eventually established the ELF had two objectives. The first one was to engage the United Nations to review the workings of the federation. Such an intervention would have allowed Eritreans of all walks of life to express their views. The ML would have got a new lease of life and the outcome of such a review could well have been the partition of the country. The second objective was to establish an independent Eritrea dominated by the Moslem League. The independent community of Eritrea which these pioneer leaders imagined was both Moslem and Arab. Therefore, the leaders of the ELF, either those who were abroad or inside Eritrea did not want Eritrean Christians to join the ELF. One of the main reasons for their reluctance was their understanding of the role played by the Christians prior to and during the federation.

Throughout the 1960s and 1970s, the ELF accepted the UN federal resolution as an expression of the wishes of the Eritrean people. Veteran ELF leaders were aware that Ethiopia and the UP fought mainly to unite the Christian parts of Eritrea. It was also known to them that both the UP and the Ethiopian government had accepted the British plan of partitioning Eritrea into two parts (early 1949) and continued with the line that it was up to the Moslem League and the Moslem communities in Eritrea to determine their political future. As far as the ELF was concerned the abolition of the federation was the work of both the Ethiopian government and the Unionist Party.

As more and more Christians joined the ELF, the latter was compelled to modify some of its cruder arguments. As late as 1975, the ELF attempted to exclude Christian participation by giving them a class identification and thus turning them into enemies of Eritrean independence (Negash, 1986:83). Eventually, the survivors of ELF persecution established their own organization, which they named the EPLF and soon posed a serious threat to ELF's hegemony. From 1978 onwards it was probably becoming clear to the ELF that it had very little chance in the impending war between itself and the EPLF. It must have been clear to the ELF that a victorious EPLF would be dominated by the authors of

Our Struggle and Its Objectives, i.e. Christians. Taking such a background into account, in their search for a separate settlement with the Ethiopian government, it can be argued that the ELF leaders were making a choice between two unenviable but inevitable alternatives.

The threat which the ELF posed for the EPLF was more ideological than military. The ELF had to be defeated completely not only because it espoused closer links with the Islamic and the Arab world but primarily because it kept alive memories which the EPLF wanted to forget. As long as the ELF existed as an active organization, it functioned as a constant reminder of the role played by Eritrean Christians in the 1940s and 1950s. The ELF saw very little reason for trusting the EPLF. On the other hand the ELF did not want to share Eritrea with the EPLF. For many years, the ELF did not make a distinction between an Ethiopian and a Christian Eritrean, as long as both of them were adherents of the Christian faith.

Once convinced of the possibility of a military victory, the EPLF pursued a hard line against the ELF—a line which it maintained until full victory. The documentation appears to show a consensus that the war of the summer of 1981 between the two organizations was initiated by the EPLF. It was a war designed to push out the ELF from the Eritrean arena. We can surmise that it was also a war to deprive the ELF of the moral right to represent the Eritrean people and their history. Finally it was a war for the monopoly of historical interpretation.

EPLF LEADS ERITREA TOWARDS INDEPENDENCE

Safely entrenched within Eritrea, the EPLF approached the decade of the 1980s with a determination to win over international public opinion. By 1982 the Eritrean conflict had begun to be known both in Europe and the United States through a number of "scholarly" publications. The first one, edited by Lionel Cliffe and the doyen of modern African Studies, Basil Davidson, was published towards the end of 1980. The Eritrean conflict, also described as the war in Eritrea, had then become Africa's longest war. Yet the real motive for the war remained unclear, especially after the conversion of the Derg to socialism, thereby gaining the political and military support of the Soviet Union and its allies.

The Ethiopian government, which had earlier tried to put a lock on information concerning the rebellion in Eritrea, continued to wage a feeble propaganda campaign solely limited to explaining the implications of the newly adopted socialist ideology for the citizens of the country. The Ethiopian government probably felt that it did not have to worry very much about the war in Eritrea after the victory scored against the Somalian invaders in 1977–78.

For the EPLF the decade of the 1980s appeared daunting indeed. Having driven the ELF out of Eritrea and with Othman Sabby no longer canvassing the Middle East for support, the EPLF was compelled to devise a new survival strategy. Throughout most of the 1980s, neither the EPLF nor the Ethiopian government seriously believed that the war would be resolved militarily, although the latter entertained such an option from 1978 to 1983.

One of the most successful strategies that the EPLF implemented was bringing the right of self-determination to the fore, while toning down the "colonial" nature of the war. Throughout the 1960s and 1970s, both the ELF and the EPLF had described the war in Eritrea as a colonial war between Ethiopia as the colonizing power and Eritrea as the colonized. This was an interpretation developed by the ELF and later adopted by the EPLF. The colonial thesis had some semblance of plausibility as long as the country was ruled as an empire by an emperor in old style imperial fashion. The argument in favour of the colonial thesis, which was never strong, was further weakened by the revolution that swept away the emperor and his imperial ideology.

The strategy emphasizing the right of self-determination as the main cause of the war was much easier to defend than the complex and not quite true allegation that Eritrea had been turned into an Ethiopian colony. Moreover, in Europe and North America, the concept of the right of self-determination was self-explanatory. Nonetheless, the first part of the 1980s was a difficult time indeed for the EPLF. The Soviet Union and its allies were strongly opposed to the movement, which was first and foremost engaged in carving out an independent state and only secondarily interested in the concept and praxis of the right to self-determination. In Africa, the OAU continued to regard the war in Eritrea officially as a secessionist war, thereby denying the Eritrean liberation fronts any sort of support or recognition.

By the mid-1980s, the message that the EPLF was fighting to empower the Eritrean people with the right to determine their own political future gained ground in Europe and North America. Most of the painstaking ground work was carried out by Eritrean exiles in these parts of the world. It should also be mentioned that Eritrean intellectuals who took upon themselves the responsibility of explaining the objectives of the EPLF, did much more in this area than the EPLF itself.

It is tempting to speculate about the timing as well as the factors which created the conditions for the support from Europe and North America. No doubt the determined campaign carried out by Eritrean activists in exile was of considerable importance. Another factor was the resilience of the EPLF in the face of repeated and well-campaigned military expeditions sent to Eritrea by the Soviet armed Ethiopian armed forces. An additional factor, which no doubt was of some importance was that many anti-Soviet Union organizations (both from the left and the right) sympathised with the EPLF in its war against the Soviet-supported aggression. Finally, the process of the dismantling of the Soviet Empire initiated by Michael Gorbatchov (1986) infused new life into the concept of the right to self-determination.

The second strategy adopted by the EPLF was the referendum option for a political solution. The EPLF referendum document (issued in November 1981) stated that the Eritrean people could choose one of three alternatives: i) union;

ii) federation within a regional autonomy framework; or, iii) independence. The OAU and the UN were to be entrusted with supervising the implementation of the referendum. Probably issued to gain international support rather than to convince the Ethiopian authorities, who at that time still believed in the military solution, the referendum document was extremely challenging. The position of the EPLF and its Eritrean supporters in exile on the referendum was very clear. In the event that the referendum option became operative, they would campaign for independence. The Ethiopian government dismissed the EPLF overture, firstly as a sign of weakness, and secondly, on the grounds that the Eritrean people had twice before expressed their wish in a similar exercise in the 1940s. Moreover, the Ethiopian authorities could clearly see that the EPLF was eliminating as traitors those Eritreans who were loyally serving the Ethiopian government in Asmara. Abroad, however, the referendum option was taken as further evidence that the EPLF was genuinely seeking a political solution to the longest war in Africa.

Although no lessons can be learned, it is nevertheless very tempting to raise the question as to what might have happened if the Ethiopian government had acted upon the referendum challenge. The lives of hundreds of thousands of Eritrean and Ethiopian soldiers might have been saved. The leadership of the country could have had some energy left to pursue a people-oriented development policy instead of pouring up to 50 per cent of the state budget into the army. The Ethiopian government would have had ample opportunity to compete with the EPLF for the hearts of the Eritreans. Eritrea and its inhabitants would have been saved the immense destruction of the limited infrastructure that the country possessed.

However, neither the Ethiopian authorities nor the EPLF were ready to give political options a chance. The Ethiopian leaders believed that they could win the war, while the EPLF, it was alleged, was trying to achieve its goal through the back door, since it did not believe that it had the capacity to win the war.

While the EPLF was thus engaged in a war of nerves, a series of events in Ethiopia were facilitating EPLF's ultimate goal. One of the events which weakened the position of the Ethiopian government was the famine that struck the country in 1984. The Ethiopian government did in fact send warning signals on the impending crisis to the international community well ahead of time. These signals were conveniently ignored by the western world. The fact that the famine coincided with the formation of a communist party along the Soviet lines and the extravagant celebration of this occasion further contributed to the isolation of the country from the potential aid donor community, which by and large was made up of Europe and North America.

When the intensity and extent of the famine were finally brought into the homes of ordinary European families, the Ethiopian government was readily condemned for misplacing its priorities. The communist ideology pursued by the government and the war in Eritrea, which by this time was extended into the northern region of the country, were henceforth regarded as the reasons for the famine. To what extent the Ethiopian government of the day could have prevented the 1984 famine, and the extent to which the international community used famine as a political instrument to discredit the government, are certainly issues for debate. What is relevant here is that the 1984 famine resulted in the very close scrutiny of the Ethiopian government's internal policies by the international community. For the first time, the economics of the war began to be widely discussed with the inevitable result that more pressure began to be put on the Ethiopian government to resolve the war in Eritrea peacefully. In the exercise of such pressure, the EPLF, had nothing to lose but everything to gain.

The second series of events which further weakened the position of the Ethiopian government was the manner by which the latter tried to resettle hundreds of thousands of famine stricken families to the more fertile regions in the western part of the country. Resettlement on an individual basis and regulated by push and pull factors had always existed. According to one estimate, as many as one million people had migrated from the northern parts of the country to the central and southern regions. Moreover, the idea of organised resettlement from the ecologically damaged regions of the north had been initially developed by the World Bank.

However, what brought on the wrath of the international community was the authoritarian manner in which resettlement was carried out. Settlement areas were not sufficiently prepared; the people to be settled were not asked about the matter; and there were numerous allegations that the officers who were entrusted with the task were only interested in showing large and increasing numbers of resettled people, without regard for family affiliations and other choices. The resettlement programme was brought to en end by the end of 1986, but only after more than half a million people had been forcibly moved, leaving behind them thousands of people dead either on the long journey to the homes they did not choose or in their new ill-prepared habitat.

The more the international community criticised the Ethiopian government, the more the same community was prepared to entertain the demands of the EPLF. By the beginning of 1987, the position of the EPLF both inside the country and abroad had improved considerably. In Eritrea the Ethiopian government, feeling the pinch of the growing demand for weapons and materials, was becoming increasingly impatient with the army's failure to defeat the EPLF once and for all. In addition to the merciless criticism from the international community, the Ethiopian government had also begun to get warning signals from the new leadership in Moscow. By 1987, the days of the cold war were numbered, and the leaders of the Soviet Empire had already begun to warn the Ethiopians that they could not count on the continued supply of weapons. To make matters even worse, after ten years of small scale harassment, the Tigrean Peoples Liberation Front (TPLF) had reached a rather disturbing stage, forcing the government to deploy more and more soldiers, thus taxing the central government's budget.

In February 1988, the hard-pressed and cornered Ethiopian leadership committed a fatal mistake, which more than any other event contributed to the downfall of the regime and to the victory of the EPLF. The head of the Ethiopian government flew to Eritrea, and after reviewing the military situation, dismissed and later executed the commanding officer of the Ethiopian army. The officer was renowned for his integrity as well as his competence. The dismissal and eventual execution of the commanding officer disheartened the military officers and soldiers in Eritrea so much that, just a month later, they were totally defeated by the EPLF. In the battle of Afabet, not only did the EPLF boost its morale but it became clear to the Ethiopian government for the first time that the military option was out of the question. After the spring of 1988 the EPLF had the upper hand.

In one important respect the coming to power of the EPLF changed the nature of the war. In spite of the rhetoric of the colonial struggle, the EPLF and the Ethiopian leaders had succeeded in limiting the war between themselves. Throughout the 1975–91 period, the Ethiopian authorities maintained a scrupulous distinction between the so-called secessionists (EPLF and others) and Ethiopian citizens from the province (later the autonomous region) of Eritrea. The Eritreans, too, behaved splendidly in their treatment of the thousands of prisoners of war. The war in Eritrea did not assume an ethnic dimension.

The repercussions of the defeat at Afabet were widely felt in the country. While the government began to demand monetary contributions from the citizens to replace the materials and property captured by the EPLF, the professional officers of the armed forces were beginning to see the lack of leadership. Just over a year after the defeat at Afabet, there was an attempt at a coup d'etat in which the majority of the professionally trained generals participated. The coup failed, it is alleged, because of the overconfidence of its leaders. Lt. Col. Menghistu Haile Mariam once again succeeded in suppressing the coup and in the process he further decimated the number of competent generals in his armed forces. From May 1989, the Ethiopian army in the provinces had no leaders who could take action on the dictates of the situations in which they might find themselves. Virtually every operational move had to be cleared through the headquarters in Addis Ababa. According to the assessment of military experts, after May 1989 the Ethiopian army had ceased to be a fighting army.

We will never be able to know how the EPLF would have used the advantage it had vis à vis the Ethiopian government. From the summer of 1989, the Ethiopian government began to face an enemy much more pervasive and intractable than the EPLF. This was the threat coming from the TPLF. The rebellion in Tigrai was initiated in 1975 and remained a small scale guerrilla movement until the famine of 1984. Benefiting from the unpopular resettlement policies of the Addis Ababa government, the TPLF began to increase its forces rapidly. At the time when the Ethiopian forces lost the battle of Afabet (1988), the TPLF had grown to such an extent that the government began to be more preoccupied with it than with the EPLF. The main reason for the preoccupation of the government was the potential of the TPLF to expand beyond the boundaries of Tigray. After having toyed with the idea of creating an independent Tigrai state if necessary, by 1988 the TPLF had identified itself as an Ethiopian organization committed to the principle of the right of nations to self-determination and to the unity of the Ethiopian people on such voluntary basis.

The summer of 1989 witnessed the intensification of the war in Tigray rather than in Eritrea. The year came to an end with the total defeat and expulsion of the Ethiopian forces from Tigray. Although Ethiopian sources of the time stated that Tigray was abandoned rather than lost, the fact remained that Tigray was declared liberated from the oppressive "fascist" regime in Addis Ababa.

For a few months the Ethiopian government felt that the so-called "liberated Tigray" could be a blessing in disguise, since the government could now concentrate all its efforts against the EPLF. This was, however, a very short respite. Soon after the TPLF consolidated its position in Tigray, it managed to create an alliance with a small organization called the Ethiopian Peoples Democratic Movement (EPDM) and thus transformed itself into the Ethiopian Peoples Revolutionary Democratic Front (EPRDF). This new front burst its boundaries in Tigray towards the end of 1989 and by mid-1990 was in more or less permanent control of the central parts of the country. It was now a question of time as well as how and in what form the central government would entertain the demands of the EPRDF which kept expanding its horizons like a savannah fire.

From mid-1990 onwards, well-placed observers could foresee that the epoch of the Derg was coming to an end. The army of the EPRDF began swarming over one region after another with an ease and speed that has yet to be explained. The Ethiopian government army, estimated at about half a million (although 300,000 appears to be more accurate) was ill organised, poorly led and to a large extent immobile. The Ethiopian government army had lost its fighting spirit. By early 1991, through a very long detour the EPRDF had come very close to the capital city of the country and engaged the government in an intense battle in the small but strategic town of Ambo, ca. 120 kms. southwest of the capital.

While the inhabitants and the international community in Addis Ababa were gripped with the horrors of a pitched battle between the government forces and those of the EPRDF, the Americans and the Italians were busily engaged in negotiations for the transfer of power. The chances appeared good, since it was widely known in Addis Ababa that the Ethiopian president had bought a house in Harare, Zimbabwe towards the end of 1990.

On May 20, 1991 Menghistu Haile Mariam, the president of the country and head of the armed forces, fled to Harare. The Americans, who a few weeks earlier had been sounding out the appropriateness of the EPRDF leaders, organised a small meeting in London where they virtually gave the green light for the EPRDF to enter Addis Ababa.

The flight of Menghistu and the entry of the EPRDF into Addis Ababa meant that the Ethiopian army in Asmara had either to continue to fight on its own against both the EPLF and the EPRDF or to raise the white flag. On May 24, 1991 the EPLF entered Asmara peacefully and soon proceeded to disarm the Ethiopian soldiers. Eritrea had, de facto, become independent. At the head of the EPLF was Essayas Afewerki. With the full blessing of the EPRDF government in Addis Ababa, Eritrea became independent on May 24, 1993.

Chapter Six

Conclusion: Future Challenges

THE ERITREANS AND THE MAKING OF THEIR DESTINY

In the course of just a century Eritrea was created, ruled by Italy and Great Britain, federated and later united to Ethiopia and finally after a bitter war of attrition emerged as a sovereign state in 1993. In the last two phases, the Tigreans (Tigrinyans) who formed part of the Abyssinian polity, were the principal political actors. No other group in the Ethiopian region has repeatedly succeeded in shaping its political destiny like the Eritrean Tigreans. In the 1940s, they fought for unconditional union with Ethiopia and won an important albeit partial victory, namely federation. The Eritrean people in general and the Eritrean Tigreans in particular proved that they were far from being pawns either in world or Ethiopian politics. In the 1950s and early 1960s, the Unionist Party and its supporters managed to undermine and eventually abolish the federation in favour of complete union. The preponderant part of the source material used in the study strongly indicates that the federal framework was more hated by the Eritrean Tigreans than by the Ethiopians.

The process of dismantling the federation was opposed by the ML which in the early 1960s transformed itself into an armed organization under the name of ELF. Organised to establish a Moslem and Arab Eritrea, the early ELF elicited three types of responses from the children of the leaders and activists of the Unionist Party. The first response was the desire to re-enact the federation, or failing this, to establish an independent Eritrea. The second response was to fight the ELF out of its pro-Moslem and pro-Arab policies. Getting their figures correct, the founders of the EPLF had as early as 1971 argued that Eritrea was inhabited by more Christians than Moslems. The third and final response was to defeat the ELF out of existence.

As far as the EPLF was concerned, the objective of the ELF was based on a wrong and outdated understanding that Eritrea was predominantly Moslem. This conception of Eritrea was in turn based on a population census carried out at the beginning of this century. Already in the late 1920s the gap was closing; by 1939, the Eritrean Tigreans constituted about 54 per cent of the entire population. The ELF, meanwhile, continued in its belief further supported by the fact that the Moslem communities occupied about 80 per cent of the area of the country. Moreover, either through ignorance or through a deliberate policy, the ELF continued to pursue a pro-Arab and pro-Moslem policy. They were to pay a heavy price.

Between 1972 and 1981, Eritrea's rival organizations (ELF and EPLF) fought more among themselves than against their main enemy, the Ethiopian government. The war between the ELF and the EPLF was in a way a continuation of the political controversy between the ML and the UP with one major exception. While the ELF was to a great extent a direct successor of the ML, the EPLF though originating in Unionist homes, was fighting firstly, to achieve independence and secondly, to keep the ELF out of power. In 1981, with active support of the Tigrean Peoples Liberation Front, the EPLF defeated completely the ELF and thus assumed an uncontested hegemony over the Eritrean region.

CONSTRUCTION OF A VIABLE MULTI-ETHNIC SOCIETY

One of the conclusions that historians can with some certainty draw is that the Eritrean-Ethiopian conflict would have been avoided if the country had been partitioned according to the Bevin-Sforza plan. It is to be recalled that the United Nations had voted in favour of partition, and that the Ethiopian government as well as the Unionist Party had also accepted the UN verdict. It is true that initially most of the opposition parties were against partition but for different reasons. ML opposed partition because of its belief that the greater part of the Eritrean region and the great majority of the population were Moslems. The ML opposed partition because it envisaged ruling Eritrea alone.

The opposition of the ML to partition was, however, transient. With the division of the ML into two factions, the issue of partition surfaced again fully and prominently towards the end of 1949. The new faction calling itself the ML of the Western Province claimed partition and eventual independence for the Western Province. Once again the UP and the Ethiopian government as an interested party reiterated their earlier position and stated that they would respect the partition of Eritrea and the eventual independence of the Western Province if such was the desire of the majority of the inhabitants of the region. Instead, a federal solution was imposed both on Ethiopia and Eritrea.

Independent Eritrea would now have to deal with the legacy of the ML and the ELF. The western parts of Eritrea had during the Italian and British eras enjoyed considerable autonomy. While Italian policy was deliberately pro-Islam, the British Eritrean policy was based on eventual partition. The war between the ELF and the EPLF was in my opinion very strong evidence that the Moslem Eritreans of the Western Province, did not really feel at ease with their Christian and Tigrinya speaking brothers of the highlands. Now the challenge which the EPLF government alone will have to face is that of constructing a viable multi-ethnic society.

Does the military victory of the EPLF mean the total annihilation of the objectives of the ML in general and of the ML of the Western Province in particular? Does the political agitation of the late 1940s and early 1950s have any current social and political relevance? Or have such views been thoroughly superseded by the transformative experience of the armed struggle and the referendum of April 1993 where over 95 per cent of the votes cast were in favour of independence?

The project of keeping Eritrea together, though extremely difficult, is not an impossible task. Admittedly international public opinion now allows and even sanctions the break up of states on grounds of ethnic and cultural incompatibilities. I, however, hasten to add that such a task requires an approach to political and social integration based on respect of cultural diversity, tradition and justice. So far, the EPLF government has put undue emphasis on laying the infrastructure for rapid economic development without too much regard to the wider political and social implications.

Two strategies recently adopted are: i) the redrawing of the provincial boundaries; and ii) the land law proclamation. Although the decision to redraw the boundaries took two years after independence, it does not appear that it was discussed at the grass-roots level. These two strategies are, I believe, illustrative of the high handed manner by which policies are evolved and implemented in Eritrea today. Ever since the creation of the colony, its provincial boundaries have reflected regional diversities and precolonial delimitations. The boundaries of the three highland regions (Hamassien, Akele Guzai, and Serae) are several centuries old and infused with a great deal of symbolism of kinship and solidarity. The Afar region has been indivisible for most of the century. The western part of the country had only been administered as a single unit during the British period. At earlier and later times it had been divided into three sub-regions. Yet the new 1995 boundaries are altogether of a different nature from earlier redrawings. On the new map, the greater part of the former three regions is now designated as the southern province. Peripheral districts are now joined to regions two and four. The regions of western Eritrea have also been affected in the sense that now these regions incorporate the peripheral districts which earlier formed part of the highland regions.

As in Ethiopia, all land belongs to the state where Eritrean peasants hold usufructory rights. This new land tenure proclamation has the effect of depriving villages of their collective rights.

Some unexpected and immediate opposition from the highland regions has been reported (Tronvoll, 1996:330). I fear, however, that due to the high degree of authoritarianism prevailing in Eritrea, it is most likely that such views will be swiftly repressed (for the political milieu see, *Eritrea Profile*, vol. 2. no. 27, September, 1995). As to the type of opposition in the making in the western part of Eritrea, we can only surmise on the basis of historical knowledge of the issues involved.

Beneath the goal of destroying regional feelings, the fact remains that firstly, political power is in the hands of the EPLF and the Eritrean Tigreans. Secondly, although there are no recent census data, it can be surmised that the highland regions are experiencing a rapid increase of population. The new administrative divisions of the country can, therefore, be seen by some of the descendants of the ML as one more device of legitimating the expansion of the highland culture which would remain predominantly peasant and Christian. Both the land law and the redrawing of the boundaries could in fact be interpreted in such a manner.

With the current rate of population growth it will be inevitable that more and more people from the highlands will migrate and settle in the less populated regions of the country. Migration alone, however, is not likely to cause ethnic and regional tensions. There is strong reason to believe that the EPLF has already provoked both the highland peasants and the agro-pastoralists of the lowlands by its land tenure proclamation and the redrawing of the administrative regions. The EPLF would be well advised to frame their social and economic policies with due regard to conceptions of fairness and justice as understood and implemented by the great majority of the population.

Bearing in mind the ca. half million Eritrean Moslems in exile in the Sudan as well as the legacy of the Moslem League and the ELF, it would be wise of the government to review its measures as regards regional boundaries and land tenure. The Eritrean government has a great deal to gain in its goal of creating a viable multi-ethnic society through a slow but steady process of confidence building. The administrative boundaries which were operative prior to the 1995 proclamation, and which reflected ethnic and regional diversity could only be abolished at considerable loss of confidence.

THE CHALLENGE OF A DEMOCRATIC TRADITION

A legacy as well as a challenge facing the EPLF government is the democratic tradition of Eritrea. EPLF and its ideologues had in the past repeatedly argued that the chief reason for the dissolution of the federation was the incompatibility between Eritrean democratic government structure and Ethiopia's autocratic political system. This study has shown that the democratic constitution which was imposed from outside remained foreign and that the Eritrean elite of the period was neither aware of nor interested in democracy. Yet it cannot be denied that the separation of powers did indeed exist. However, in so far as there was democracy in Eritrea, this was limited to the administration of justice. Moreover, it is worthwhile to recall that such a separation of powers was made possible by the presence of Sir James Shearer, as the Chief Justice and President of the Supreme Court of Eritrea from 1952 until 1959.

The Constitutional committee commissioned by the EPLF government in 1994 is in the final process of concluding its work. To judge from the structure of the EPLF government, where executive and legislative powers are in the hands of the president, the constitution due to be announced in early 1997 will hardly come up with a different structure. It is, however, encouraging that the intrinsic value of an autonomous judiciary appears to have been recognised. In my opinion, however, such recognition though important is not sufficient. For many years to come, the government in Eritrea would remain under the firm control of the EPLF, a military organization which owed its success to the barrel of the gun rather than to the ballot box. The transition from a liberation army in power to a political party is painful and in the best of circumstances it might take up to a generation to accomplish such a process.

The Eritrean people are, therefore, likely to judge their government not on the enumeration of rights provided in the constitution but on what the government does in practice. It is indeed tempting to argue that one of the main reasons for the success of colonialism was its ability to administer justice in a fairly impartial manner. Hence, in my opinion, the existence of an impartial administration of justice for the creation and maintenance of confidence between the government and the people can hardly be over-emphasised.

If there is a determination within the EPLF government to establish an autonomous judiciary as the first and most important basis for the democratization of the society, they would then be advised to consider all possible alternatives. One such alternative is to entrust the management of the Offices of the Chief Justice and Attorney-General to foreign, preferably European, experts. These offices would remain in the hands of foreign experts until such time (ca. 20 years) that the Eritrean government and people are sufficiently socialized to the advantages of the democratic way of running political affairs. This will be more so if the reorganization of the Eritrean society along the concept of democracy as understood in the west forms part of the long term objectives of the EPLF government.

It would indeed be unfortunate if such a suggestion is dismissed off-hand as an indictment of the capacity of the present government, or as a blatant proposal against state sovereignty. Inherent to the concept of the separation of powers (between the executive, the legislative and the judiciary) is the limitation of power in the hands of one person as well as the distribution of real, as opposed to nominal, power among several bodies. Given the fact that the EPLF government is essentially a liberation army in power, it could take up to a generation (ca. 25 years) to dissociate the linkage between armed resistance and political power. As in many other sectors of the society, the EPLF government is manned by people with great dedication and determination yet lacking competence. Recruiting foreign experts, not as advisors but as office bearers, is in my opinion a more secure way of dealing firmly with political socialization. I may also add that the argument that the handing over of the judiciary to foreign experts would be tantamount to either a loss of sovereignty or a re-enactment of a new form of colonialism has only a rhetorical value. States unable to feed their citizens are hardly sovereign. A precondition for economic development (where food security is an important outcome) is political stability and accountability of the elite to its citizens. Looked at from this angle, the efforts to establish an impartial judiciary system and tradition is an important precondition.

SUDAN AND THE CHALLENGE OF ISLAM

However, the most daunting challenge facing the EPLF government appears to be that coming from the Eritrean Islamic Jihad Movement. Though formed in 1989, its history goes back to the immediate aftermath of the defeat of the ELF by joint EPLF and TPLF military operations. According to Medhanie (1994: 78–92) on whose account this section is largely based, the founders of the Eritrean Islamic Jihad interpreted the EPLF onslaught against the ELF as a Christian crusade. Already in 1982 two small Islamic organizations were formed. The first one was called the National Islamic Front for the Liberation of Eritrea while the second organization was known as the Islamic Vanguard. Created to arrest what they perceived to be the inevitable Christian/Tigrean march throughout Eritrea, these Islamic organizations remained very small and of negligible significance until EPLF attempted to forcefully recruit women fighters from the predominantly Moslem areas in 1988. By the summer of 1988 two other organizations had been formed (Medhanie, 1994:80). In a unity conference held in November 1988, these four organizations agreed to form the Eritrean Islamic Jihad Movement.

It is indeed striking that the political objectives of the Eritrean Islamic Jihad Movement, are very similar to those of the ML of the late 1940s. The Islamic Movement appears to believe that Eritrea is predominantly Moslem. Its objective of establishing an Islamic Eritrean state governed by the Sharia Laws where the Christians would continue to live as minority citizens is very much reminiscent of the perceptions of the ML and early ELF. Nearly fifty years after the formation of the first political parties and notwithstanding the EPLF's rhetoric on the unifying impact of the 30 year war of liberation, Eritrea appears to be deeply divided.

At present the threat from the Islamic Jihad Movement does not appear to threaten the hegemony of the EPLF, although the alleged EPLF and Israel military links appear to have been designed to thwart future threats. Even though the National Islamic Front of the Sudan (which at present has the hegemonic position in the government) might have functioned as a demonstrative example, the circumstances which gave rise to the emergence of the Eritrean Islamic Jihad Movement have to be looked for inside Eritrea. First as a neighbour and secondly as a country of asylum for about half a million Eritrean Moslems, the Republic of Sudan will continue to assume a prominent position in Eritrean foreign affairs. However, the crucial factor concerns the policies of the Eritrean government vis à vis Eritrean refugees in the Sudan.

It would require considerable political imagination rather than refugee repatriation funds to deal with the huge Eritrean exile community in the Sudan. The scope and dimensions of regional and cultural autonomy in the areas predominantly inhabited by Moslems need to be thoroughly explored. It is in such a context that the administrative boundaries which existed prior to 1995 become relevant. Moreover, the long term advantages of village and collective rights to land tenure in the maintenance of peace and stability need to be weighed far more carefully.

ERITREA AND ETHIOPIA

The war in Eritrea had neither the colonial character as witnessed in other parts of Africa nor that of a war fought against a foreign dominator. It was more of an internal war for power sharing or control of state power. Throughout the duration of the conflict, the Ethiopian government managed to keep the war strictly to that between its army and the armed insurgents in Eritrea. Nationalist rhetoric notwithstanding, the Eritrean war did not go to the extent experienced in Yugoslavia and in some African states such as Burundi, Rwanda, Somalia, and Liberia.

This is best illustrated by the very warm relations which developed in the aftermath of the collapse of the Menghistu regime. The Eritrean government estimates that the war had created an exile population of ca. 700,000. The great majority of these exiles are Moslem Eritreans and are to be found in the Sudan and the Middle East. This figure, the Eritrean government notes, does not include the ca. 300,000 Eritreans living in Ethiopia. Eritreans residing in Ethiopia are considered as if they are in Eritrea. One can hardly come up with stronger evidence to show that the Eritrean war was not between the Ethiopian and Eritrean peoples but mainly between the Ethiopian army and the armed insurgents in Eritrea.

The Eritreans would one day express their gratitude to the Ethiopian people for their refusal to get involved in the war carried out by the forcibly recruited soldiers of the Ethiopian military government. During the final stages of the conflict the Menghistu regime had tried to transform the war into an ethnic one, but without success. The country's deep-rooted humane political culture, the widespread belief that the Eritreans were as good as other Ethiopians and that the war was essentially over the enjoyment of the spoils of power, were important factors in regulating the dimensions of the war.

Even the Ethiopian leaders had during the greater part of the conflict acted in the belief that the war in Eritrea was instigated by a few secessionists misled into acts of treason by foreign (Arab) money and ideologies. The remaining civilian population in Eritrea and in other parts of the country were, throughout the war, treated as Ethiopians. From the Eritrean side, the EPLF and the ELF responded by treating their Ethiopian prisoners of war according to the UN convention although the Ethiopian government continued to deny that its soldiers had been captured in the war in Eritrea.

As long as Eritrea's resources remain what they are, Ethiopia will remain the most important partner. The commercial exploitation of oil (Tesfagiorgis, 1993) and thermal energy may, of course, change the pattern of relations. Throughout this century, Eritrea has had few exportable resources and has been dependent for its food imports on Ethiopia. This fact was very well understood by the colonial rulers; i.e. Eritrea was of little importance without its Ethiopian hinterland.

Immediately after the end of the war (1991) Eritrean intellectuals and political leaders have been exploring actively the nature of future relations between Eritrea and Ethiopia. Although the rhetorical framework for Ethio-Eritrean relations is made within the context of the Horn of Africa, the principal states (or the core regions) are Eritrea and Ethiopia. An eloquent outcome of this exploration is an anthology (Tekle, 1994). Though conceived in 1989, the chapters for the book were written in 1993 after Eritrea had become independent. The recurrent theme of the anthology is a plea for economic integration which would subsequently be the basis for political integration. While Eritrean intellectuals were rationalizing the mutual advantages of economic and political association, the Eritrean and Ethiopian governments took actions along the same lines which they finalised in September 1993. Although the details of what came to be called the Asmara pact are not made officially known, both governments have entered into an agreement to cooperate in a wide range of activities, one of which is a defence pact. As recently as July 1996, the president of the Provisional Government of Eritrea was quoted as saying that both governments were developing their relations where boundaries would be meaningless. The Eritrean Ambassador to Ethiopia was even more explicit. In a recent interview he stated that, "forming an independent state was never the ultimate goal of our long struggle". Further elaborating on the theme, the Ambassador said that "integration will be easier with Ethiopia as we share common history and culture and have also lived together under a common political system" (*The Reporter*, Addis Ababa, vol. 1, no. 2, 18.9.96). It appears that the Eritrean government has come to appreciate what the Italian and British colonisers had known all along, i.e. Eritrea can hardly survive without Ethiopia as its hinterland.

It is indeed tempting to agree with the widespread view in Ethiopian circles that the Eritreans have got more than what they had bargained for. Eritreans in Ethiopia enjoy the same rights as other Ethiopians and are free to settle and invest as before. In the international arena Eritrea maintains its status as a beneficiary of foreign aid. This currently satisfactory state of affairs is made possible by the friendly attitude of the present government in Ethiopia, a friendship greatly conditioned by the fact that the leaders of both countries are from the same ethnic group, i.e. Tigreans.

It would be wise of Eritrean leaders, now when they enjoy an opportune moment, to concentrate their energies on building Eritreo–Ethiopian relations on a firmer basis. As things now stand, a change of government in Ethiopia may bring with it a change of policy which could directly affect the security of Eritreans in Ethiopia and Eritrea's access to Ethiopia. A vivid example that friendly relations can suddenly go sour is that of Eritreo-Sudanese relations.

In the few years that Eritrea has been independent, the dimension of the ties which bind the two countries has become even clearer. These ties are not only economic but as in the 1940s, they encompass culture and history. It is hardly an exaggeration to state that during the past three years Eritrea, more than Ethiopia, has been anxious to keep open its access to Ethiopia. The sea ports of Massawa and Assab (now under Eritrea) are presented as bait for Ethiopian cooperation. These ports are indeed important but their value, contrary to the belief of some Eritrean policy makers, ought not to be exaggerated. For the greatest part of its history Ethiopia was landlocked; it was only with the federation that it acquired direct access to the sea. Even during the 1952–1991 period when Ethiopia controlled the Eritrean sea ports, Djibouti maintained its position as the most important port for the needs of the country. Assab came second and remained important as long as the federation lasted. Ethiopia has, if it wishes to make use of them fully, other options at its disposal to ward off undue dependence on Eritrea and its ports, options such as Zeila in northern Somalia and the Kenyan port of Mombasa.

Some disgruntled voices notwithstanding, the Ethiopian people as a whole have accommodated Eritrea and Eritreans. It is, however, relevant to ask whether in view of the close links between the two countries, and recent statements of the Eritrean government officials, the long drawn out war (described as Africa's longest) was worth the heavy price which it elicited. This is a question that is being increasingly asked by a growing number of people of both countries. The past cannot be undone; it can only be hoped that a sober re-reading of the past might enrich and widen the scope of policy options at the disposal of the civil societies of both countries.

Bibliography

Archival Sources

Public Record Office, Foreign Office Files (FO371) London, United Kingdom.
Public Record Office, War Office Files (WO230/168) London, United Kingsom.
Public Record Office, War Office Files (WO97) London, United Kingsom.
Archivio Storico dell'Africa Italiana, Archivio Eritrea (ASMAI, AE) Rome, Italy.
Archivio Storico dell'Africa Italiana (ASMAI), Affari Politici, Direzione Generale, 1942–46.
Archivio Storico dell'Africa Italiana (ASMAI), Direzione Africa Orientale, 1946–50.
Archivio Storico del Ministero degli Affari Esteri (ASMAE), Affari Politici, 1946–50.
Institute of Ethiopian Studies, Addis Ababa University, (IES, Nega Haile Sellassie Papers).

Contemporary periodicals

Eritrean Weekly News (EWN), 1942–1953.
Zemen Biweekly, 1953–55.
Ethiopia Weekly, 1947–50.
New Times and Ethiopia News, 1947–56.

Select Bibliography

Adou, A. Abdullah, 1993, *The Afar: A Nation on Trial*. Stockholm.
Africa Confidential, 1970,2:6.
Amar, Wolde Yesus, 1992, *Eritrea: Root Causes of War and Refugees*. Baghdad: Sindbad Printing Company.
Arén, Gustav, 1978, *Evangelical Pioneers in Ethiopia: Origin of Mekane Yesus*. Stockholm: EFS Förlaget.
Association of Eritrean Intellectuals, 1949, *Some Notes on the Peoples of Eritrea in Support of their Strife for Independence*. Asmara.
Association of Eritrean Students in North America, 1978, *In Defence of the Eritrean Revolution*. New York.
Battaglia, Roberto, 1958, *La prima guerra d'Africa*. Torino: Giulio Einaudi Editore.
Bogale, Alemseged, 1993, *Ye Ertra Enqoqulish* (The Eritrean Riddle). Addis Ababa.
Calchi Novati, Giampaolo, 1994, *Il corno d'Africa nella storia e nella politica: Etiopia, Somalia e Eritrea fra nazionalismi, sottosviluppo e guerra*. Torino: Società editrice internazionale.
Castellano, Vicenzo, 1948, "Il censimento del 1939 della popolazione indigena della Eritrea storica in un cinqunatennio di amministrazione italiana", in *Rivista italiana di demografia e statistica*, 2:2, pp. 264–290.
Clapham, Christopher, 1988, *Transformation and Continuity in Revolutionary Ethiopia*. Cambridge: Cambridge University Press.
Consolato Generale d'Italia, 1959, *Gli italiani in Eritrea nel 1958*. Asmara.
Conti Rossini, Carlo, 1916, *Principio di diritto consuetudinario dell'Eritrea*. Roma: Tipografia dell'Unione Editrice.
Conti Rossini, Carlo, 1935, *Italia ed Etiopia. Dal trattato di Uccialie alla battaglia di Adua*. Roma: Instituto per L'Oriente.

Cuddus, Yibarek, 1993, "Prospects of Petroleum Exploration and Production in Eritrea", in Gebre Hiwet, Tesfagiorgis, (ed.), *Emergent Eritrea*, 248–252.

Da Nembro, Metodio, 1953, *La missione dei minori cappuccini in Eritrea*. Roma: Institutum Historicum Ord.Fr. Min. Cap.

Davidson, Basil and Lionell Cliffe, (eds.), 1988, *Eritrea: The Long Road to Independence*. New Jersey: Red Sea Press.

Del Boca, Angelo, 1976, *Gli italiani in Africa Orientale. Dal unitá alla marcia su Roma*. Milano: Laterza.

Del Boca, Angelo, 1984, *Gli italiani in Africa Orientale: Nostalgia delle colonie*. Milano: Arnaldo Mondadori Editore.

Dilebo, Getahun, 1975, "Historical Origins and Development of the Eritrean Problem, 1889–1962", in *Current Bibliography on African Affairs*. Ametyville, New York: Baywood Publishing Co.

Dinstein, Yoran, (ed.), 1981, *Models of Autonomy*. New Brunswick and London: Transaction Books.

ELF, 1967, *The Ethiopian Unilateral Abrogation of UN Federal Resolution*. Damascus.

ELF, 1968, "Eritrean Tragedy: A Brief Memorandum by the Eritrean Liberation Front". *Mimeographed*. Sent to the World Council of Churches assembled in Uppsala, Sweden.

ELF, 1968, *The Struggle of Eritrea*. Damascus.

ELF, 1971, *The Eritrean Revolution: A Programmatic Declaration*. Approved by the First National Congress held inside the liberated areas, October 4 to November 12.

ELF, 1975, *The Second National Congress of the ELF*, n.p. May.

ELF, 1981, "ELF, 20 Years", in *The Eritrean Newsletter: Anniversary Issue* no. 41.

ELF, 1982, "An Inside Story", in *The Eritrean Newsletter*, Issue no. 42.

ELF-PLF, 1971, *Eritrea: A Victim of UN Decision and of Ethiopian Colonial Aggression*. An Appeal of the Eritrean People to the 26th session of the UN General Assembly. New York.

Ellingson, LLoyd, 1986, *Eritrea: Separatism and Irredentism, 1941–1985*. East Lansing: Ph.D. thesis, Michigan State University.

EPLF, 1973, "Our Struggle and its Objectives", in *EFLNA, Liberation*, 1:3, pp. 5–23.

EPLF, 1975, *Hafeshawi Poletikawi Timiherti* (General Political Education), n.p.

EPLF, 1977, *National Democratic Programme of the EPLF*. n.p.

EPLF, 1978, *Memorandum: The National Question in Eritrea, and the Right of the Eritrean People to Self-Determination*, n.p.

EPLF, 1987, *Ertran K'alssan* (Eritrea and her struggle) n.p.

Erlich, Haggai, 1981, "The Eritrean Autonomy, 1952–62: Its Failure and Contribution to Further Escalation", in Yoran Dinstein, (ed.), *Models of Autonomy*. New Brunswick, N.J.: Rutgers University Press, 171–182.

Erlich, Haggai, 1982, *Ethiopia and Eritrea during the Scramble for Africa: A Political Biography of Ras Alula, 1875–1897*. East Lansing and Tel Aviv: Michigan State University and Center for Middle Eastern and African Studies, Tel Aviv.

Erlich, Haggai, 1983, *The Struggle over Eritrea, 1962–78. War and Revolution in the Horn of Africa*. Stanford: Stanford University Press.

Erlich, Haggai, 1994, *Ethiopia and the Middle East*. Boulder and London: Lynne Rienner Publisher.

Ethiopian Revolution Information Centre, 1979, *Class Struggle and the Problem in Eritrea*. Addis Ababa.

Eyassu, Gayim, 1993, *The Eritrean Question. The conflict between the right of self-determination and the interests of states*. Uppsala: Uppsala University.

Gebre Sellassie, Zewde, 1975, *Yohannes IV: A Political Biography*. Oxford: Oxford University Press.

Gebre-Medhin, Jordan, 1989, *Peasants and Nationalism in Eritrea*. New Jersey: Red Sea Press.

Ghaber, Michael, 1993, *The Blin of Bogos*, Baghdad.

Gilkes, Patrick, 1991, "Eritrea: Historiography and Mythology", in *African Affairs*, vol. 90, no. 361.

Government of Eritrea, Office of the Auditor General, 1962, *Audit Report and General Account for the year ending on the tenth of September 1961*. Asmara.

Grassi, Fabio, and Luigi Goglia, 1981, *Il colonialismo italiano da Assab ad Adua*. Bari: Laterza, 1981.

Gray, J.C. and L. Silberman, 1948, *The Fate of Italy's Colonies. A Report to the Fabian Colonial Bureau*. London: Victor Gollancz.

Greenfield, Richard, 1965, *Ethiopia: A New Political History*. New York: Praeger.

Guida dell'Africa Italiana, 1938. Milano: Officine Fotolithografiche.

Habte Sellassie, Bereket, 1980, *Conflict and Intervention in the Horn of Africa*. New York and London: Monthly Review.

Habte Sellassie, Bereket, 1989, *Eritrea and the United Nations*. New Jersey: Red Sea Press.

Habtu, Hailu, 1983, *British Military Administration and the Evolution of Political Parties in Eritrea, 1941–47*. London: M.A. thesis, School of Oriental and African Studies.

Hagos, Fesshaye, 1963, *Tintawina Zemenawi Tarik. Ye Etiopiana Ye Ertra* (Ancient and Modern History of Ethiopia and Eritrea). Asmara: Il Poligrafico.

Halliday, Fred and Maxime Molyneaux, 1981, *The Ethiopian Revolution*. London: New Left Books.

Iliffe, John, 1987, *The African Poor. A History*. Cambridge:Cambridge University Press.

Iyob, Ruth, 1995, *The Eritrean Struggle for Independence. Domination, Resistance and Nationalism, 1941–1993*. Cambridge: Cambridge University Press.

Keller, J. Edmond, 1990, "Constitutionalism and the National Question in Africa: The Case of Eritrea", in Marina Ottaway (ed.), *The Political Economy of Ethiopia*. New York: Praeger.

Killion, Thomas, 1985, *Workers Capital and the State in the Ethiopian Region*. Stanford: Ph.D thesis, Stanford University.

Lefort, René, 1981, *Ethiopia. An Heretical Revolution?* London: Zed Press.

Lewis, I.M., (ed.), 1983, *Nationalism and Self-Determination in the Horn of Africa*. London: Ithaca Press.

Lobban, Richard, 1976, "The Eritrean War: Issues and Implications", in *CAS*, 10:2, pp. 335–346.

Lobban, Richard, 1972, "Eritrean Liberation Front: A close-up view", in *Munger African Library Notes*, 113.

Longrigg, H. Stephen, "The Future of Eritrea", in *African Affairs*, vol.45, no.80.

Longrigg, H. Stephen, 1945, *A Short History of Eritrea*. Oxford: Oxford University Press.

Louis, W. Roger, 1977, *Imperialism at Bay*. Oxford: University Press.

Luther, Ernest, 1958, *Ethiopia Today*. Oxford: Oxford University Press.

Marcus, Harold, 1983, *Ethiopia, Great Britain and the United States, 1941–74, the Politics of Empire*. Los Angeles: University of California Press.

Markakis, John, 1987, *National and Class Conflict in the Horn of Africa*. Cambridge: Cambridge University Press.

Markakis, John, 1988, "The Nationalist Revolution in Eritrea", in *Journal of Modern African Studies*, 26:4, pp. 51–70.

Markakis, John, 1995, "Eritrea's National Charter", in *ROAPE*, no. 63.

Martini, Ferdinando, (ed.), 1913, *L'Eritrea economica*. Novara.

Martini, Ferdinando, 1935, *Nell'Affrica Italiana*. (10th. edition, 1935). Milano.

Martini, Ferdinando, 1946, *Il Diario Eritreo, 1897–1907*. Firenze.

Medhanie, Tesfatsion, 1986, *Eritrea: The Dynamics of a National Question*. Amsterdam: B.R. Grüner.

Medhanie, Tesfatsion, 1994, *Eritrea and Neighbours in the New World Order: Geopolitics, Democracy and Islamic Fundamentalism*. Hamburg: Bremer Afrika-Studien Band 15, LIT verlag.

Meron, T. and A.M. Pappas, 1981, "The Eritrean Autonomy: A Case Study of a Failure", in Dinstein, Yoran, (ed.), *Models of Autonomy*, 183–212.

Mesfin, Araya 1990, "The Eritrean Question: an Alternative Explanation", in *JMAS*, 28:1, pp. 79–100.

Mesfin, Araya 1991, "Colonialism and Natural Economy: The Eritrean Case", in Northeast African Studies, 13:2&3, pp. 165–185.

Nadel, S.F., 1945, "Notes on the Beni Amer Society", in *Sudan Notes and Records*.

Nadel, S.F., 1946, "Land Tenure in the Eritrean Plateau", in *Africa*, 21:1, pp. 1–21.

Negash, Tekeste, 1986, *No medicine for the bite of a white snake: Notes on nationalism and resistance in Eritrea, 1890–1941*. Uppsala: Uppsala University.

Negash, Tekeste, 1987, *Italian Colonialism in Eritrea: Policies, Praxis and Impact, 1882–1941*. Stockholm: Almqvist and Wiksell International.

Negash, Tekeste, 1994, "The Eritrean Unionist Party and its Strategies of Irredentism, 1941–52, in Bahru Zewde, et al. (eds.), *Proceedings of the Eleventh International Conference of Ethiopian Studies*. Addis Ababa: Institute of Ethiopian Studies.

Negash, Tekeste, 1995, "Competing Imaginations of the Nation: The Eritrean Nationalist Movements, 1953–81", in Tekeste Negash and Lars Rudebeck (eds.), *Dimensions of Development with Emphasis on Africa*. Uppsala: Nordiska Afrikainstitutet and Forum for Development Studies.

Negash, Tekeste, 1996a, "Eritrea and the Battle of Adwa". A paper read at the International conference on the Centenary of Adwa, Addis Ababa and Adwa, February 26–March 2.

Negash, Tekeste, 1996b, "The Eritrean Catholic Community and the Political Debates in the Late 1940s". A paper read at the International Symposium on the Missionary Factor in Ethiopia, Lund University, August 7–10.

Norwegian Institute of Human Rights: 1993, *The Referendum on Independence for Eritrea*. Oslo.

O'Connor, Anthony, 1991, *Poverty in Africa. A Geographical Approach*. London: Bellhaven Press, 1991.

Ogbazghi, Yohannes, 1991, *Eritrea. A Pawn in World Politics*. Gainesville: University of Florida Press.

Pankhurst, Richard, 1962, "The Foundation of Education, Printing and Newspapers in Ethiopia", in *Ethiopia Observer*, 6:3.

Pankhurst, Richard, 1969, "The Ethiopian Patriots and the Collapse of Italian Rule in East Africa", in *Ethiopia Observer*, 12:2.

Pankhurst, Sylvia, 1952, *Why Are We Destroying the Ethiopian Ports?* Woodford Green, England: Lalibela House.

Pankhurst, Sylvia, 1952, *Eritrea on the Eve: The Past and Future of Italy's "first-born" Colony, Ethiopia's Ancient Sea Province*. Woodford Green, Essex: New Times and Ethiopia News Books.

Pankhurst, Sylvia, 1953, *Ethiopia and Eritrea, 1941–52*. Woodford Green, England: Lalibela House.

Pankhurst, Sylvia and Richard Pankhurst, 1953, *Ethiopia and Eritrea: The Last Phase of the Reunion Struggle, 1941–52*. Woodford Green, England: Lalibela House.

Paul, A, 1971, *A History of the Beja Tribes of the Sudan*. Cambridge: Cambridge University Press.

Perham, Margery, 1948, *The Government of Ethiopia*. London: Faber-Faber.

Pliny the Middle-Aged, 1978, "Eclectic notes on the Eritrean Liberation Movement: E Pluribus Unum", in *Ethiopianist Notes* 5:2, pp. 37–45.

Pollera, Alberto, 1935, "L'Italia e le popolazione dell'Eritrea: Conseguenze morali ed economiche che la colonizzazione italiana in Eritrea ha avuto nella evoluzione delle popolazione locali e delle regione finitime", in *Annali del Regio Istituto Superiore Orientale di Napoli*, 8:1.

Pollera, Alberto, 1935, *Le popolazione indigene della colonia Eritrea*. Firenze.

Pool, David, 1980, *Eritrea: Africa's Longest War*. London: The Anti-Slavery Society.

Pool, David, 1983, "Eritrean Nationalism", in Lewis, I.M., (ed.), *Nationalism and Self-Determination in the Horn of Africa*. London: Ithaca Press.

Poscia, Stefano, 1989, *Eritrea: Colonia tradita*. Roma: Edizioni Associate.

Puglisi, Giuseppe, 1952, *Chi é dell'Eritrea*. Asmara.

Rainero, Romain, 1971, *L'anticolonialismo italiano da Assab ad Adua*. Milano.

Redda, Asghedom, 1954, *Ertra Kuratie*. (1961–62 Gregorian calendar). Addis Ababa.

The Reporter vol. 1, no.2, 18.9.1996. Addis Ababa.

Rossetti, Carlo, 1910, *La storia diplomatica del Etiopia*. Torino: Società Tipografica-Editrice Nazionale.

Rubenson, Sven, 1962, "The British in Eritrea. A Review of Eritrea, A Colony in Transition by G.K.N. Trevaskis", in *JAH*, 3:2, pp. 528–530.

Rubenson, Sven, 1976, *The Survival of Ethiopian Independence*. London: Heinemann.

Sabby, Othman Saleh, 1975, *History of Eritrea*. Beirut.

Said, M. Alamin, 1994, *Säwra Ertra* (The Eritrean Revolution: Progress and Setbacks). (Tigrinya text). New Jersey: Red Sea Press.

Sforza, Carlo, 1952, *Cinque anni a palazzo Chighi. La politica estera italiana da 1947 al 1951*. Roma: Atlante.

Shehim, K., 1985, "Ethiopia, Revolution and the Question of Nationalities: The case of the Afar", in *JMAS* 23:2.

Sherman, Richard, 1980, *Eritrea: The Unfinished Revolution*. New York: Praeger.

Sishagne, Shumet, 1992, *Discord and Fragmentation in Eritrean Politics, 1941–1981*. Urbana-Champaign: Ph.D. thesis, University of Illinois at Urbana-Champaign.

Smith, J.A.Clarence, 1955, "Human Rights in Eritrea", in *The Modern Law Review*, 18:484–486.

Sorenson, John, 1991, "Discourses on Eritrean Nationalism and Identity", in *JMAS* 29:2: pp. 301–317.

Spencer, John, H., 1983, *Ethiopia at Bay: A Personal Account of the Haile Sellassie Years*, Michigan: Reference Publications Inc.

Steer, G.L., 1942, *Sealed and Delivered. A Book on the Abyssinian Campaign*. London: Hodder and Stoughton.

Taddia, Irma, 1986, *Eritrea–Colonia, 1890–1952*. Milano.

Tamrat, Tadesse, 1972, Church and State in Ethiopia, 1270–1520. Oxford: Oxford University Press.

Tareke, Gebru, 1984, "Resistance in Tigray (Ethiopia)", in *Horn of Africa*, 6:4, pp. 15–29.

Tareke, Gebru, 1991, *Ethiopia, Power and Protest: Peasant Revolts in the Twentieth Century*. Cambridge: Cambridge University Press.

Taylor, B. Richard, 1971, *Eritrean Separatism and the Eritrean Liberation Front*. London: MA thesis, School of Oriental and African Studies.

Tekle, Amare, 1964, *The Creation of the Ethio-Eritrean Federation. A Study in Post-War International Relations*. Denver: University of Denver, Ph.D. thesis.

Tekle, Amare, (ed.), 1994, *Eritrea and Ethiopia: From Conflict to Cooperation*. New Jersey: Red Sea Press.

Tesfagiorgis, Gbere Hiwet, (ed.), 1993, *Emergent Eritrea: Challenges of Economic Development*. New Jersey: The Red Sea Press.

TGE, 1991, *Transitional Period Charter of Ethiopia*. Addis Ababa.

Tigrai Federal State, *Bisrat, 2:1* (1996 Gregorian calendar).

Tiruneh, Andargachew, 1981, "Eritrea, Ethiopia and Federation", in *NEAS*, 2:3:99–119.

TPLF, 1986, *Ertra Kabei Nabey* (Eritrea: From Where to Where).

TPLF, 1986, "On Our Differences with the EPLF", in *People's Voice*. Special Issue, n.p.

Trevaskis, G.K.N., 1960, *Eritrea: A Colony in Transition, 1941–1952*. Oxford: Oxford University Press.

Trimingham, J.S., 1952, *Islam in Ethiopia*. Oxford: Oxford University Press.

Tronvoll, Kjetil, 1994, "Camel-Dance and Balloting: The Afar Factor in the Referendum on Independence for Eritrea", in *The Horn of Africa Review*, 2:2.

Tronvoll, Kjetil, 1996, *Mai Weini. A village in highland Eritrea*. Oslo: Ph.D thesis, University of Oslo.

Tseggai, Araya, 1984, "Ethiopian Economic Policy in Eritrea: The Federation Era", in *Northeast African Studies*, vol. 6 1984, pp. 1–2.

Tseggai, Araya, 1988, "The History of the Eritrean Struggle", in Davidson, Basil and Lionel Cliffe, (eds.), *Eritrea: The Long Road to Independence*. New Jersey: Red Sea Press

United Nations, 1950, *Report of the United Nations Commission for Eritrea*. General Assembly Official Records supplement no. 8(A/1285). Lake Success, New York.

United Nations, 1950, *Yearbook of the United Nations, 1948–49*. New York.

United Nations, 1952, *Final Report of the United Nations Commissioner in Eritrea*. General Assembly Official Records supplement no. 15 (A/2188). New York.

United Nations, 1952, *Year Book of the United Nations*. New York.

With, A.K. Peter, 1987, *Politics and Liberation: The Eritrean Struggle, 1961–85*. Aarhus: Institute of Political Science, University of Aarhus.

Zemen Biweekly, 6.2.53.

Appendices

1. Text of resolution 390 A (V) adopted on December 2, 1950 by the General Assembly of the United Nations

390 (V) ERITREA: REPORT OF THE UNITED NATIONS COMMISSION ON ERITREA; REPORT OF THE INTERIM COMMITTEE OF THE GENERAL ASSEMBLY ON THE REPORT OF THE UNITED NATIONS COMMISSION FOR ERITREA

A

Whereas by paragraph 3 of Annex XI to the Treaty of Peace with Italy, 1947, the Powers concerned have agreed to accept the recommendation of the General Assembly on the disposal of the former Italian colonies in Africa and to take appropriate measures for giving effect to it,

Whereas by paragraph 2 of the aforesaid Annex XI such disposal is to be made in the light of the wishes and welfare of the inhabitants and the interests of peace and security, taking into consideration the views of interested governments,

Now therefore

The General Assembly, in the light of the reports* of the United Nations Commission for Eritrea and of the Interim Committee, and

Taking into consideration

(a) The wishes and welfare of the inhabitants of Eritrea, including, the views of the various racial, religious and political groups of the provinces of the territory and the capacity of the people for self-government,

(b) The interests of peace and security in East Africa,

(c) The rights and claims of Ethiopia based on geographical, historical, ethnic or economic reasons including in particular Ethiopia's legitimate need for adequate access to the sea,

Taking into account the importance of assuring the continuing collaboration of the foreign communities in the economic development of Eritrea,

Recognizing that the disposal of Eritrea should he based on its close political and economic association with Ethiopia, and

Desiring that this association assure to the inhabitants of Eritrea the fullest respect and safeguards for their institutions, traditions, religions and languages, as well as the widest possible measure of self-government, while at the same time respecting the Constitution, institutions, traditions and the international status and identity of the Empire of Ethiopia,

A. Recommends that:

1. Eritrea shall constitute an autonomous unit federated with Ethiopia under the sovereignty of the Ethiopian Crown.

*See *Official Records of the General Assembly*, Fifth Session, Supplements, Nos. 8 and 14.

2. The Eritrean Government shall possess legislative, executive and judicial powers in the field of domestic affairs.

3. The jurisdiction of the Federal Government shall extend to the following matters: defence, foreign affairs, currency and finance, foreign and interstate commerce and external and interstate communications, including ports. The Federal Government shall have the power to maintain the integrity of the Federation, and shall have the right to impose uniform taxes throughout the Federation to meet the expenses of federal functions and services, it being understood that the assessment and the collection of such taxes in Eritrea are to be delegated to the Eritrean Government, and provided that Eritrea shall bear only its just and equitable share of these expenses. The jurisdiction of the Eritrean Government shall extend to all matters not vested in the Federal Government, including the power to maintain the internal police, to levy taxes to meet the expenses of domestic functions and services, and to adopt its own budget.

4. The area of the Federation shall constitute a single area for customs purposes, and there shall be no barriers to the free movement of goods and persons within the area. Customs duties on goods entering or leaving the Federation which have their final destination or origin in Eritrea shall be assigned to Eritrea.

5. An Imperial Federal Council composed of equal numbers of Ethiopian and Eritrean representatives shall meet at least once a year and shall advise upon the common affairs of the Federation referred to in paragraph 3 above. The citizens of Eritrea shall participate in the executive and judicial branches, and shall be represented in the legislative branch, of the Federal Government, in accordance with law and in the proportion that the population of Eritrea bears to the population of the Federation.

6. A single nationality shall prevail throughout the Federation:

(a) All inhabitants of Eritrea, except persons possessing foreign nationality, shall be nationals of the Federation;

(b) All inhabitants born in Eritrea and having at least one indigenous parent or grandparent shall also be nationals of the Federation. Such persons, if in possession of a foreign nationality, shall, within six months of the coming into force of the Eritrean Constitution, be free to opt to renounce the nationality of the Federation and retain such foreign nationality. In the event that they do not so opt, they shall thereupon lose such foreign nationality;

(c) The qualifications of persons acquiring the nationality of the Federation under sub-paragraphs (a) and (b) above for exercising their rights as citizens of Eritrea shall be determined by the Constitution and laws of Eritrea;

(d) All persons possessing foreign nationality who have resided in Eritrea for ten years prior to the date of the adoption of the present resolution shall have the right, without further requirements of residence, to apply for the nationality of the Federation in accordance with federal laws. Such persons who do not thus acquire the nationality of the Federation shall be permitted to reside in and engage in peaceful and lawful pursuits in Eritrea; The rights and interests of foreign nationals resident in Eritrea shall be guaranteed in accordance with the provisions of paragraph 7.

7. The Federal Government, as well as Eritrea, shall ensure to residents in Eritrea, without distinction of nationality, race, sex, language or religion, the enjoyment of human rights and fundamental liberties, including the following:

(a) The right to equality before the law. No discrimination shall be made against foreign enterprises in existence in Eritrea engaged in industrial, commercial, agricultural, artisan, educational or charitable activities, nor against banking institutions and insurance companies operating in Eritrea;

(b) The right to life, liberty and security of person;

(c) The right to own and dispose of property. No one shall be deprived of property, including contractual rights, without due process of law and without payment of just and effective compensation;

(d) The right to freedom of opinion and expression and the right of adopting and practising any creed or religion;

(e) The right to education;

(f) The right to freedom of peaceful assembly and association;

(g) The right to inviolability of correspondence and domicile, subject to the requirements of the law;

(h) The right to exercise any profession subject to the requirements of the law;

(i) No one shall be subject to arrest or detention without an order of a competent authority, except in case of flagrant and serious violation o f the law in force. No one shall be deported except in accordance with the law;

(j) The right to a fair and equitable trial, the right of petition to the Emperor and the right of appeal to the Emperor for commutation of death sentences;

(k) Retroactivity of penal law shall be excluded;

The respect for the rights and freedoms of others and the requirements of public order and the general welfare alone will justify any limitations to the above rights.

8. Paragraphs 1 to 7 inclusive of the present resolution shall constitute the Federal Act which shall be submitted to the Emperor of Ethiopia for ratification.

9. There shall be a transition period which shall not extend beyond 15 September 1952, during which the Eritrean Government will be organized and the Eritrean Constitution prepared and put into effect.

10. There shall be a United Nations Commissioner in Eritrea appointed by the General Assembly. The Commissioner will be assisted by experts appointed by the Secretary-General of the United Nations.

11. During the transition period, the present Administering Authority shall continue to conduct the affairs of Eritrea. It shall in consultation with the United Nations Commissioner, prepare as rapidly as possible the organization of an Eritrean administration, induct Eritreans into all levels of the administration, and make arrangements for and convoke a representative assembly of Eritreans chosen by the people. It may, in agreement with the Commissioner, negotiate on behalf of the Eritreans a temporary customs union with Ethiopia to be put into effect as soon as practicable.

12. The United Nations Commissioner shall, in consultation with the Administering Authority, the Government of Ethiopia, and the inhabitants of Eritrea, prepare a draft of the Eritrean Constitution to be submitted to the Eritrean Assembly and shall advise and assist the Eritrean Assembly in its consideration of the Constitution. The Constitution of Eritrea shall be based on the principles of democratic government, shall include the guarantees contained in paragraph 7 of the Federal Act, shall be consistent with the provi-

sions of the Federal Act and shall contain provisions adopting and ratifying the Federal Act on behalf of the people of Eritrea.

13. The Federal Act and the Constitution of Eritrea shall enter into effect following ratification of the Federal Act by the Emperor of Ethiopia, and following approval by the Commissioner, adoption by the Eritrean Assembly and ratification
by the Emperor of Ethiopia of the Eritrean Constitution.

14. Arrangements shall be made by the Government of the United Kingdom of Great Britain and Northern Ireland as the Administering Authority for the transfer of power to the appropriate authorities. The transfer of power shall take place as soon as the Eritrean Constitution and the Federal Act enter into effect, in accordance with the provisions of paragraph 13 above.

15. The United Nations Commissioner shall maintain his headquarters in Eritrea until the transfer of power has been completed, and shall make appropriate reports to the General Assembly of the United Nations concerning the discharge of his functions. The Commissioner may consult with the Interim Committee of the General Assembly with respect to the discharge of his functions in the light of developments and within the terms of the present resolution. When the transfer of authority has been completed, he shall so report to the General Assembly and submit to it the text of the Eritrean Constitution;

B. *Authorizes* the Secretary-General, in accordance with established practice:

1. To arrange for the payment of an appropriate remuneration to the United Nations Commissioner;

2. To provide the United Nations Commissioner with such experts, staff and facilities as the Secretary General may consider necessary to carry out the terms of the present resolution.

2. The Constitution of Eritrea, adopted by the Eritrean Constituent Assembly on July 15, 1952.*

Preamble:

In the name of Almighty God,

Trusting that He may grant Eritrea peace, concord and prosperity,

And that the Federation of Eritrea and Ethiopia may be harmonious and fruitful,

We, the Eritrean Assembly, acting on behalf of the Eritrean people,

Grateful to the United Nations for recommending that Eritrea shall constitute an autonomous unit federated with Ethiopia under the sovereignty of the Ethiopian Crown and that its Constitution be based on the principles of democratic government,

Desirous of satisfying the wishes and ensuring the welfare of the inhabitants of Eritrea by close and economic association with Ethiopia and by respecting the rights and safeguarding the institutions, traditions, religions and languages of all the elements of the population.

Resolved to prevent any discrimination and to ensure under a regime of freedom and equality, the brotherly collaboration of the various races and religions in Eritrea, and to promote economic and social progress.
Trusting fully in God, the Master of the Universe.
Do hereby adopt this Constitution as the Constitution of Eritrea.

Part I. General

Article 1

Adoption and ratification of the Federal Act

1. The Eritrean people, through their representatives, hereby adopt and ratify the Federal Act approved on 2 December 1950 by the General Assembly of the United Nations.

2. They undertake to observe faithfully the provisions of the said Act.

CHAPTER I. STATUS OF ERITREA

Article 2

Territory of Eritrea

The territory of Eritrea, including the islands, is that of the former Italian colony of Eritrea.

Article 3

Autonomy and federation

Eritrea shall constitute an autonomous unit federated with Ethiopia under the sovereignty of the Ethiopian Crown.

Article 4

Legislative, executive and judicial powers

The Government of Eritrea shall exercise legislative, executive and judicial powers with respect to matters within its jurisdiction.

* Source: UN, 1952.

Article 5

Matters coming within the jurisdiction of Eritrea

1. The jurisdiction of the Government of Eritrea shall extend to all matters not vested in the Federal Government by the Federal Act

2. This jurisdiction shall include:

(a) The various branches of law (criminal law, civil law, commercial law, etc.);

(b) The organization of the public services;

(c) Internal police;

(d) Health;

(e) Education;

(f) Public assistance and social security;

(g) Protection of labour;

(h) Exploitation of natural resources and regulation of industry, internal commerce, trades and professions;

(i) Agriculture;

(j) Internal communications;

(k) The public utility services which are peculiar to Eritrea;

(l) The Eritrean budget and the establishment and collection of taxes designed to meet the expenses of Eritrean public functions and services.

Article 6

Contribution by Eritrea to the expenses of the Federal Government

1. Eritrea shall bear its just and equitable share of the expenses of Federal functions and services.

Assessment and levying of Federal taxes

2. The Government of Eritrea shall assess and levy in Eritrea, by delegation from the Federal Government, such taxes as are established to that end for the benefit of the whole of the Federation.

Revenue from customs duties

3. Within the revenue which accrues to Eritrea shall be included the customs duties on goods entering or leaving the Federation which have their final destination or origin in Eritrea, in accordance with the provisions of paragraph 4 of the resolution of 2 December 1950 of the General Assembly of the United Nations.

Article 7

Representation of Eritrea in the Imperial Federal Council

1. The Eritrean representatives in the Imperial Federal Council, composed of equal numbers of Ethiopians and Eritreans, shall be appointed by the Chief Executive with the approval of the Assembly. They shall be formally invested in office by the Emperor.

Participation of Eritreans in the Federal Government

2. Eritreans shall participate in the executive and judicial branches and shall be represented in the legislative branch, of the Federal Government, in accordance with law and in the proportion that the population of Eritrea bears to the population of the Federation.

Article 8

Eritrean citizenship

Persons who have acquired Federal nationality in Eritrea under the Federal Act (Section A, paragraph 6 of the General Assembly Resolution 390 A (V)) and have been granted Eritrean citizenship in accordance with the laws of Eritrea shall be citizens of Eritrea.

Article 9

Rights of Federal nationals who are not Eritrean citizens

1. On the basis of reciprocity, Federal nationals who are not Eritrean citizens shall enjoy the same rights as Eritreans.

2. Federal nationals shall enjoy political rights in accordance with the Eritrean Constitution and laws on the basis of reciprocity.

CHAPTER II. REPRESENTATION OF
THE EMPEROR IN ERITREA

Article 10

The Emperor has a representative in Eritrea

There shall be a representative in Eritrea of His Imperial Majesty, the Emperor of Ethiopia, Sovereign of the Federation.

Article 11

Rank of the Representative of the Emperor

The Representative of the Emperor shall, on all occasions, have the place of precedence at official ceremonies in Eritrea.

Article 12

Administering of the oath of office to the Chief Executive before the Representative of the Emperor. Formal investment of the Chief Executive in office

The Chief Executive, elected by the Assembly in accordance with Article 68, shall take the oath of office in accordance with the provisions of Article 72. The Representative of the Emperor, having noted that the Chief Executive has been elected by the Assembly, shall formally invest him in office in the name of the Emperor, Sovereign of the Federation.

Article 13

Opening and closing of sessions of the Assembly

At the opening and closing of sessions of the Assembly, the Representative of the Emperor may deliver the speech from the throne in which he will deal with affairs of common interest to the Federation and to Eritrea.

Article 14

Transmission of legislation to the representative of the Emperor

1. When draft legislation has been voted by the Assembly, the Chief Executive will transmit it immediately to the Representative of the Emperor.

2. If the Representative of the Emperor considers that draft legislation voted by the Assembly encroaches upon Federal jurisdiction, or that it involves the international responsibility of the Federation, he may transmit a request to the Chief Executive within twenty days after the vote by the Assembly for reconsideration of the draft legislation by the Assembly, indicating his reasons for doing so.

Article 15

Promulgation of legislation

The Representative of the Emperor will promulgate legislation in the manner laid down in Article 58.

CHAPTER III. DEMOCRATIC GOVERNMENT IN ERITREA

Article 16

The principles of democratic government

The Constitution of Eritrea is based on the principles of democratic government.

Article 17

Respect for human rights

The Constitution guarantees to all persons the enjoyment of human rights and fundamental freedoms.

Article 18

Organs of government are provided for by the people and shall act in the interests of the people

1. All organs of government are provided for by the people. They are chosen by means of periodic, free and fair elections, directly and indirectly.

2. The organs of government shall act in the interests of the people.

Article 19

Rule of law

1. The organs of government and public officials shall have no further powers than those conferred on them by the Constitution and by the laws and regulations which give effect thereto.

2. Neither a group of the people nor an individual shall arbitrarily assume the exercise of any political power or of administrative functions.

3. Public officials shall perform their duties in strict conformity with the law and solely in the public interest.

4. Public officials shall be personally answerable for any unlawful acts or abuses they may commit.

Article 20

Franchise

The electorate shall consist of those persons possessing Eritrean citizenship who:

(a) Are of male sex;

(b) Have attained the age of twenty-one years;

(c) Are under no legal disability as defined by the law; and

(d) Have been resident for one year preceding the election in the constituency where they shall vote.

Article 21

Federal flag

1. The Federal flag shall be respected in Eritrea. Flag, seal and arms of Eritrea

2. There shall be a flag, seal and arms of Eritrea, details of which shall be decided upon by law.

CHAPTER IV. HUMAN RIGHTS AND FUNDAMENTAL FREEDOMS MS

Section I. Provisions reproduced from the Federal Act

Article 22

Provisions reproduced from the Federal Act

The following provisions of paragraph 7 of the Federal Act shall be an integral part of the Constitution of Eritrea:

"The Federal Government, as well as Eritrea, shall ensure to residents in Eritrea, without distinction of nationality, race, sex, language or religion, the enjoyment of human rights and fundamental liberties, including the following:

(a) The right to equality before the law. No discrimination shall be made against foreign enterprises in existence in Eritrea engaged in industrial commercial, agricultural, artisan, educational or charitable activities nor against banking institutions and insurance companies operating in Eritrea;

(b) The right to life, liberty and security of person;

(c) The right to own and dispose of property. No one shall be deprived of property, including contractual rights, without due process of law and without payment of just and effective compensation;

(d) The right to freedom of opinion and expression and the right of adopting and practising any creed or religion;

(e) The right to education;

(f) The right to freedom of peaceful assembly and association;

(g) The right to inviolability of correspondence and domicile subject to the requirements of the law;

(h) The right to exercise any profession subject to the requirements of the law;

(i) No one shall be subject to arrest or detention without an order of a competent authority, except in case of flagrant and serious violation of the law in force. No one shall be deported except in accordance with the law;

(j) The right to a fair and equitable trial, the right of petition to the Emperor and the right of appeal to the Emperor for commutation of death sentences;

(k) Retroactivity of penal law shall be excluded."

Section II. Other provisions

Article 23

Freedom and equality before the law
Everyone is a person before the law

All persons are born free and are equal before the law without distinction of nationality, race, sex or religion and, as such shall enjoy civil rights and shall be subject to duties and obligations.

Article 24

Prohibition of torture and certain punishments

No one shall be subject to torture or to cruel, inhuman or degrading treatment or punishment.

Article 25

Right to freedom of movement

Everyone resident in Eritrea has the right to freedom of movement and to the choice of place of residence in Eritrea subject to the provisions of Article 34.

Article 26

Freedom of conscience and religion

The right to freedom of conscience and religion shall include the right of everyone, either alone or in community with others and in public or private, to manifest his religion or belief in teaching, practice, worship and observance.

Article 27

No discrimination to the detriment of any religion

No economic, financial or political measure of a discriminatory nature shall be taken to the detriment of any religion practised in Eritrea.

Article 28

Recognition of religious bodies as persons before the law

Religious bodies of all kinds and religious orders shall be recognized as possessing juristic personality.

Consequently, any religious denomination or any group of citizens belonging to such denomination shall be entitled:

(a) To establish and maintain institutions for religious, educational and charitable purposes;
(b) To conduct its own affairs in matters of religion;
(c) To possess and acquire movable and immovable property;
(d) To administer its property and to enter into contracts.

Article 29

Religious instruction and worship in public schools

No pupil attending a public school shall be required to take part in any religious instruction at such school or attend any religious service at such school.

Article 30

Freedom to express opinions

Everyone resident in Eritrea shall have the right to express his opinion through any medium whatever (Press, speech, etc.) and to learn the opinions expressed by others.

Article 31

Right to education and freedom to teach

1. Everyone resident in Eritrea shall have the right to education. The Government shall make every effort to establish schools and to train teachers.

2. The Government shall encourage private persons and private associations and institutions, regardless of race, nationality, religion, sex or language, to open schools, provided that they give proof of the required standards of morality and competence.

3. The instruction in the schools shall conform to the spirit of the Constitution.

Article 32

Associations and companies

1. Everyone resident in Eritrea shall have the right to form associations or companies for lawful purposes.

2. Companies or associations shall enjoy fundamental freedoms in so far as their nature permits.

3. Such companies or associations shall be regarded as persons before the law.

Article 33

Protection of working conditions

1. Everyone resident in Eritrea, regardless of nationality, race sex, or religion, shall have the right to opportunity of work, to equal pay for equal work, to regular holidays with pay, to payment of. dependency allowances, to compensation for illness and accidents incurred through work and to a decent and healthy standard of life.

Trade unions

2. Everyone resident in Eritrea shall have the right to form and to join trade unions for the protection of his interests.

Article 34

Control by law of the enjoyment of human rights and fundamental freedoms

1. The provisions in the last sub-paragraph of paragraph 7 of the Federal Act apply to the whole of Chapter IV of Part I of the Constitution. This sub-paragraph reads as follows:

"The respect for the rights and freedoms of others and the requirements of public order and the general welfare alone will justify any limitations to the above rights."

2. In applying the aforementioned provisions, the enjoyment of human rights and fundamental freedoms may be regulated by law provided that such regulation does not impede their normal enjoyment.

Article 35

Duties of individuals

Everyone shall have the duty to respect the Constitution and the laws, and to serve the community.

CHAPTER V. SPECIAL RIGHTS OF THE VARIOUS POPULATION GROUPS IN ERITREA

Article 36

Personal status

Nationals of the Federation, including those covered by subparagraphs (b) and (d) of paragraph 6 of the Federal Act, as well as foreign nationals, shall have the right to respect for their customs and their own legislation governing personal status and legal capacity, the law of the family and the law of succession.

Article 37

Property rights

Property rights and rights of real nature, including those on State lands, established by custom or law and exercised in Eritrea by the tribes, the various population groups and by natural or legal persons, shall not be impaired by any law of a discriminatory nature.

Article 38

Languages

1. Tigrinya and Arabic shall be the official languages of Eritrea.

2. In accordance with established practice in Eritrea, the languages spoken and written by the various population groups shall be permitted to be used in dealing with the public authorities, as well as for religious or educational purposes and for all forms of expression of ideas.

PART II. THE ASSEMBLY

CHAPTER I. COMPOSITION AND ELECTION OF THE ASSEMBLY

Article 39

Creation of an Assembly representing
the Eritrean people

1. Legislative power shall be exercised by an Assembly representing the Eritrean people.

2. Members of the Assembly shall represent the Eritrean people as a whole, and not only the constituency in which they are elected.

Article 40

Number of members of the Assembly

1. The Assembly shall be composed of not less than fifty and not more than seventy members.

2. Within the limits prescribed in the preceding paragraph, the number of members shall be fixed by law.

Article 41

Constituencies

1. The territory of Eritrea shall be divided into electoral constituencies, each electing one representative.

2. These constituencies shall be established in such a way that they will be approximately equal in population. The boundaries of the constituencies shall be fixed by law.

Article 42

Eligibility

All members of the electorate shall be eligible for election to the Assembly provided that:

(*a*) They have reached the age of thirty;

(*b*) They have been resident in Eritrea for three years and have been resided in the constituency for two years during the last ten years;

(*c*) They are not disqualified for any reason laid down by law; and

(*d*) They are not officials of the Eritrean or Federal Governments, unless they have resigned at the time of presenting their candidature.

Article 43

The two voting systems

1. The members of the Assembly shall be elected either by direct or indirect ballot.

2. The system of voting to be used in any given constituency shall be laid down by law.

3. Voting by direct ballot shall be personal, equal and secret.
For this purpose, a roll of qualified voters shall be drawn up, and revised from time to time.
The system for establishing electoral rolls shall be fixed by law.

4. The first stage of voting by indirect ballot shall be conducted in accordance with local custom. At the second stage, voting shall be personal, equal and secret.

Article 44

Election by direct ballot and election at second stage in the case of indirect ballot

1. If a candidate for the Assembly obtains an absolute majority of the votes cast he shall be declared elected.

2. If no candidate obtains an absolute majority, as defined in paragraph 1, a second ballot shall be held, and the candidate who then obtains the greatest number of votes shall be declared elected.

Article 45

Electoral High Commission

1. An electoral High Commission consisting of three persons appointed by the Supreme Court established under Article 85 shall be responsible for supervising all electoral proceedings (including the compiling of electoral rolls), and for preventing or putting a stop to irregularities.

2. The High Commission shall appoint, in each constituency, from among the electors of that constituency, a representative to act under its authority.

3. The said representative shall be assisted by an advisory election committee, consisting of members chosen by him from among the electors of that constituency.
As soon as an election period has been declared open in accordance with the law every candidate shall be entitled to be represented on the committee.

4. The implementation of the present article shall be prescribed by law.

Article 46

Disputed elections to the Assembly

1. At the opening of the session following an election, the Assembly shall confirm its members. All members whose elections are unchallenged shall be confirmed simultaneously.

2. In any case where an election is challenged, the Assembly shall decide, by a two-thirds majority of the members present, whether the challenged election is valid, provided that such two-thirds majority shall be not less than one half of the members of the Assembly in office.

3. In the event of a member's election not being confirmed, he may, within three days following the adoption in the decision by the Assembly, appeal to the Supreme Court established under Article 85, but shall not take his seat until the Supreme Court has given its decision.

Article 47

Term of the Assembly

1. The Assembly shall be elected for a term of four years.

2. Members shall be eligible for reelection.

3. If there is a vacancy during the term of an Assembly, a by-election shall take place. No by-election can, however take place within six months of the election of a new Assembly.

CHAPTER II. SESSIONS AND MEETINGS

Article 48

Regular sessions

1. The Assembly shall hold two regular sessions each year.

2. The Assembly shall meet in regular session on a date to be specified by law. This session shall continue for at least one month.

3. The opening date of the second regular session shall be fixed by the Chief Executive after consulting the President of the Assembly.

This second session shall be devoted primarily to voting the budget and the Assembly shall consider no other matter until the budget has been voted. The session shall not close until the budget has been voted as prescribed in Article 60.

4. The closing date of regular sessions shall be fixed by the Chief Executive after consulting the President of the Assembly.

5. With the consent of the President of the Assembly, the Chief Executive may suspend a session for a period not exceeding twenty days.

Article 49

Special sessions

1. The Chief Executive may convene the Assembly to a special session.

2. The Chief Executive shall convene the Assembly to a special session whenever a written request is submitted by not less than one-third of the members.

3. When the Assembly is convened to a special session by the Chief Executive on his own initiative, only the questions set forth in the notice convening the Assembly shall be discussed. The Chief Executive shall fix the closing date of the session.

4. When the Assembly is convened to a special session at the request of not less than one-third of its members, it shall determine its own agenda. The Chief Executive shall fix the closing date of the session in agreement with the President of the Assembly.

Article 50

Quorum

Two thirds of the members of the Assembly shall compose a quorum.

Article 51

Rules of procedure

The Assembly shall adopt its own rules of procedure.

Article 52

Officers of the Assembly

The Assembly shall elect its officers at the opening of the first regular session of each year or at the beginning of a new Legislature. The officers shall consist of a President, a Vice-President and, if the Assembly so desires, other officers.

CHAPTER III. STATUS OF MEMBERS OF THE ASSEMBLY

Article 53

Swearing-in of members

Before taking up their duties, members of the Assembly who have not served in the previous Legislature shall take, in accordance with the faith and the customary practice of the individual concerned, the following oath before the President of the Assembly:

"I undertake before Almighty God" (or an invocation conforming to the faith and the customary practice of the member of the Assembly concerned) "to respect the Federation under the sovereignty of the Imperial Crown, loyally to serve Eritrea, to defend its Constitution and its laws, to seek no personal advantage from my office, and to perform all my duties conscientiously."

Article 54

Parliamentary immunity

1. Members of the Assembly shall not be liable to prosecution for opinions expressed or votes cast by them in the performance of their duties.

2. Members of the Assembly shall not be arrested or prosecuted without the authorization of the Assembly, save that in case of flagrant delict they may be arrested, but the prosecution, even in this case, shall be authorized by the Assembly.
When the Assembly is not in session, such authorization may be given by its officers. The Assembly may subsequently decide that proceedings shall be discontinued.

Article 55

Remuneration of members of the Assembly

1. Members of the Assembly shall receive a remuneration fixed by law.

2. No increase of remuneration shall take effect until the term of office of the Assembly voting it has expired.

CHAPTER IV. POWERS OF THE ASSEMBLY

Article 56

General powers of the Assembly

The Assembly shall vote the laws and the budget, elect the Chief Executive and supervise the activities of the Executive.

Section I. Legislative functions

Article 57

Drafting and adoption of legislation

1. Draft legislation may be introduced into the Assembly by members of the Assembly or submitted to the Assembly by the Chief Executive.

2. Such legislation shall be considered, discussed and put to the vote as provided in the Assembly's rules of procedure.

Article 58

Request for a reconsideration

1. Draft legislation adopted by the Assembly shall be immediately transmitted by the President of the Assembly to the Chief Executive.

Approval of legislation by the Chief Executive

2. The Chief Executive will transmit it as soon as received to the Representative of the Emperor who may request, in accordance with the provisions of Article 14, that it be reconsidered by the Assembly.

Publication

3. If the Representative of the Emperor, exercising the prerogatives for which provision is made under Article 14, has transmitted a request to the Chief Executive for reconsideration, giving his reasons for doing so, the Assembly must take a further vote. The draft legislation must obtain a two-thirds majority vote to be adopted.

4. If the draft legislation has been adopted after reconsideration, as provided in the preceding paragraph, or if the Representative of the Emperor has not exercised his prerogatives under Article 14, the Chief Executive must within twenty days after the vote taken by the Assembly, either approve the draft legislation and transmit it to the Representative of the Emperor for promulgation within five days of its receipt, or return it to the Assembly with his comments.

5. If the Chief Executive shall have returned the draft legislation to the Assembly, the Assembly shall reconsider the draft legislation and take a further vote on it. If the draft legislation is then adopted by a two-thirds majority, the Chief Executive shall transmit it to the Representative of the Emperor for promulgation within five days of its receipt.

6. All draft legislation adopted in accordance with the provisions of this article but not promulgated within the time limit laid down in paragraphs 4 and 5 of this Article, shall come into effect after publication by the Chief Executive.

Section II. Budget

Article 59

Submission of the draft budget by
the Chief Executive

1. At least one month before the opening of the second regular session of the Assembly, the Chief Executive shall submit a draft budget for the next financial year.

2. The draft budget shall cover the whole of the revenue and expenditures of the Government of Eritrea for the next financial year.

Article 60

Examination and adoption of the budget by the Assembly

1. During the month preceding the second regular session of the Assembly, the Assembly Finance Committee shall examine the draft budget submitted by the Executive and report to the Assembly.

2. A general debate on the draft budget shall be held at the beginning of the second regular session of the Assembly.

Within ten days following the closure of the debate, the Executive shall submit a revised draft budget including the amendments it may decide to make to its first draft as a result of the observations made by the Assembly.

3. The Assembly shall then proceed to examine the various items of the budget:

(a) It shall first adopt the expenditure estimates with or without amendments, only the total estimate for each Executive Department being put to the vote.

The Assembly may not increase the estimates proposed in the draft budget unless increase is balanced by corresponding estimates of revenue and has received the consent of the Executive.

(b) The Assembly shall then adopt, with or without amendments, the revenue estimates chapter by chapter, each of which shall be put to the vote separately.

4. The complete budget shall be adopted before the beginning of the financial year; otherwise, the amended draft budget submitted by the Executive as provided in paragraph 2 above shall be deemed to be adopted, provided the Executive has itself observed the time-limit laid down in Article 59 and in the present article.

Article 61

All taxation and expenditure must be authorized by law

No tax shall be levied and no expenditure shall be incurred unless authorized by law.

Article 62

Form of the budget

A law shall be enacted governing the form in which the budget is to be submitted and voted on each year.

Article 63

Credit for urgent expenditure

1. When voting the budget, the Assembly shall include a credit for urgent expenditure.

2. The amount of this credit shall not exceed 10 per cent of the expenditure estimates.

3. At the beginning of the following session of the Assembly, the Chief Executive shall report on the use he has made of this credit. The Assembly shall take a vote on this report.

Article 64

Accounts for past financial years

1. Within eighteen months following the close of each financial year, the Executive shall submit the accounts for that financial year to the Assembly for approval.

2. An Auditor-General, independent of the Executive, shall be elected by the Assembly.

3. The principal function of the Auditor-General shall to examine the annual accounts, and to make a report to the Assembly containing his observations on them at the time of their presentation to the Assembly.

4. The method of election and the matters within the competence of the Auditor-General shall be established by law.

Section III. Election and supervision of the Executive

Article 65

Election of the Chief Executive

The Assembly shall elect the Chief Executive as provided in Article 68.

Article 66

Supervision of the Executive by the Assembly

1. Members of the Assembly may submit questions in writing or short questions orally to the Executive, which shall reply.

2. At the request of ten members of the Assembly, a debate may be held on the Executive's policy.
The Executive shall be entitled to intervene both in the course of the debate and before its closure.

PART III. THE EXECUTIVE

CHAPTER I. COMPOSITION AND APPOINTMENT

Article 67

Composition of the Executive

The Executive shall consist of a Chief Executive assisted by Secretaries of Executive Departments.

Article 68

Election of the Chief Executive

1. The Chief Executive shall be elected by the Assembly by secret ballot; if a candidate obtains two thirds of the votes cast he shall be declared elected. If no candidate obtains the requisite number of votes the candidate receiving the least number of votes shall be removed from the list and the Assembly shall vote again on the remainder repeating the process if necessary until a candidate obtains the required number of votes.

2. Only Eritrean citizens having attained the age of thirty-five years and in possession of their political rights shall be eligible for the office of the Chief Executive.

3. The Assembly shall elect a Chief Executive at the opening of each new legislature.

4. In case of death or resignation of the Chief Executive, the Assembly shall elect a successor within fifteen days. If the Assembly is not in session, the President of the Assembly shall convene it to a special session.

The newly elected Chief Executive shall remain in office until the expiry of his predecessor's term.

5. The Chief Executive shall be eligible for re-election.

Article 69

Appointment of Secretaries of Executive Departments

1. The Chief Executive shall have power to appoint and dismiss Secretaries of Executive Departments, who shall be responsible to him.

2. Only persons qualified to be members of the Eritrean electorate shall be eligible to hold office as Secretaries of Executive Departments.

3. The Chief Executive shall select the Secretaries of Executive Departments in such a way as to ensure as far as possible a fair representation in his council of the principal groups of the population and the various geographical areas of the territory.

4. The number and the functions of Secretaries of Executive Departments shall be prescribed by law.

Article 70

Incompatibility

The office of the Chief Executive or of Secretary of an Executive Department is incompatible with the holding of any other administrative or judicial office.

Article 71

Acting Chief Executive

The Chief Executive, on being elected, shall designate one of the Secretaries of Executive Departments to act for him if he is temporarily prevented from discharging his duties or, if his post fall vacant, until such time as a new Chief Executive is elected.

Article 72

Swearing-in of the Chief Executive

Before taking up his duties, the Chief Executive shall, according to his faith and customary practice, take the following oath in the Assembly before the Representative of the Emperor:

> "I undertake before Almighty God" (or an invocation conforming to the faith and the customary practice of the Chief Executive) "to respect the Federation under the sovereignty of the Imperial Crown, loyally to serve Eritrea, to defend its Constitution and its laws, to seek the welfare of the Eritrean people in the unity of its inhabitants bound together by ties of brotherhood, whatever their race, religion or language, and to seek no personal advantage from office."

Article 73

Swearing-in of Secretaries of Executive Departments

Before taking up their duties, Secretaries of Executive Departments shall, according to their faith and their customary practices, take the following oath publicly in the Assembly before the Representative of the Emperor:

> "I undertake before Almighty God" (or an invocation conforming to the faith and customary practice of the individual concerned) "loyally to respect the Federation under the sovereignty of the Imperial Crown, loyally to serve Eritrea, to respect its Constitution and its laws, to seek no personal advantage from my office and to perform all my duties conscientiously."

Article 74

Council of the Executive

The Chief Executive shall from time to time summon a council of the Secretaries of Executive Departments. This Council shall advise the Chief Executive on matters of general policy and on any questions he may submit to it.

Article 75

Removal from office of the Chief Executive

1. The Chief Executive shall not be answerable for any act performed by him in the course of his duties except for a grave violation of the Constitution. He shall be answerable for failure to dismiss any Secretary of an Executive Department committing a grave violation of the Constitution.

2. In such circumstances,the Chief Executive may be impeached by a two-thirds majority of the members of the Assembly in office, and tried by the Supreme Court established under Article 85.

3. If the Supreme Court finds the charge to be proved, it shall order the removal from office of the Chief Executive. It may, furthermore disqualify him from performing any executive function or legislative duty.

4. Removal from office shall be without prejudice to any proceedings which may be instituted if the acts committed by the Chief Executive constitute offences under criminal law.

CHAPTER II. POWERS OF THE EXECUTIVE

Article 76

Enumeration of powers

1. The Chief Executive shall ensure that the Constitution and the laws are enforced. He shall have responsibility for the direction of the Executive and Administrative Departments and public services. He shall be Chairman of the Civil Service Commission for which provision is made in Article 82, and shall make appointments in accordance with the Constitution and the laws.

2. He shall be responsible for the internal police of Eritrea and, to this end, he shall issue regulations conforming to the Constitution and the laws to ensure the maintenance of public order and security.

3. He shall convene the sessions of the Assembly as provided in Articles 48 and 49 of the Constitution.

4. Each year, at the opening of the first regular session, he shall give an account to the Assembly of his conduct of affairs and report on the general situation of Eritrea.

5. He shall have the power to propose legislation. He may request the Assembly to reconsider draft legislation. He shall publish the laws after their promulgation or under the provisions of Article 58.

6. He shall submit to the Assembly a draft annual budget and the accounts for the preceding financial year, as provided in Articles 59, 60 and 64.

7. He shall have access to and the right of addressing the Assembly. He may be represented in the Assembly and its Committees by the Secretaries of Executive Departments.

8. He shall issue the regulations required to implement the laws.

9. He shall issue orders as provided in Article 77.

10. He may temporarily limit certain provisions of the Constitution as provided in Article 78.

11. He shall take the necessary measures for the suppression of brigandage, as provided in Article 79.

12. Official documents issued by the Chief Executive must be counter-signed by the Secretaries of the Executive Departments concerned.

Article 77

Power of the Chief Executive to issue orders when the Assembly is not in session

1. In the interval between sessions of the Assembly the Chief Executive shall have authority to issue, when necessary, orders governing any matter within the jurisdiction of the Government of Eritrea except matters dealt with in Chapter IV of Part I of the Constitution provided that such orders are compatible with the Constitution and the laws in force.

2. Such orders shall be submitted to the Assembly which must approve or repeal them within a period of two months from the opening of the session following their promulgation.

3. Failing a decision by the Assembly within the above mentioned period, orders issued by the Chief Executive shall be deemed to be confirmed.

Article 78

Limitation in time of emergency of certain constitutional provisions

1. In the event of a serious emergency which endangers public order and security, the Assembly may, on the proposal of the Chief Executive, adopt a law authorizing him to impose, under the conditions provided for in Article 34, temporary limitations on the rights set forth in Chapter IV of Part I of this Constitution.

2. The authorization thus given by law shall be valid for a maximum period of two months. If necessary, it may be renewed under the same conditions.

3. During the interval between sessions, the Chief Executive may, if it is urgently necessary, issue an order prescribing the measures referred to in paragraph 1.

In such cases, a special session of the Assembly shall be convened, as soon as possible and, at the latest, within twenty days following the promulgation of the order, to adopt a law approving, amending or repealing the said order.

Article 79

Suppression of brigandage

1. If public order and the security of persons and property in Eritrea are threatened by organized brigandage, the Chief Executive shall, after making a proclamation to the people, adopt the exceptional measures necessary to suppress such brigandage.

2. The Chief Executive shall inform the Assembly of the measures he has taken.

CHAPTER III. THE ADMINISTRATION

Article 80

Conditions of appointment of officials

Officials shall be chosen for their ability and character; considerations of race, sex, religion or political opinion shall not influence the choice either to their advantage or to their disadvantage.

Article 81

Status of officials

1. The general status of administrative officials shall be fixed by law.

2. The special status of the various categories of administrative officials shall be fixed by regulations.

Article 82

Civil Service Commission

1. A Civil Service Commission, under the chairmanship of the Chief Executive or his representative, shall be created.

2. This Commission shall be responsible for the appointment, promotion, transfer and discharge of officials and for taking disciplinary action against them.

3. The composition of this Commission, the procedure for the appointment of its members, and the conditions under which it will function will be determined by law.

Article 83

Local communities

1. The Constitution recognizes the existence of local communities.

2. Municipalities shall be accorded the management of their own affairs.

3. Officials responsible for the administration of village and tribal communities shall be selected from persons of those local communities.

4. The conditions for the application of the preceding provisions may be determined by law.

PART IV. THE ADVISORY COUNCIL OF ERITREA

Article 84

Advisory Council of Eritrea

1. An Advisory Council of Eritrea is hereby established.

2. The function of the Council shall be to assist the Chief Executive and the Assembly, with a view to achieving economic and social progress in Eritrea. To this end it may:

(a) Draw up plans for the development of the country's resources and for the improvement of public health and hygiene;

(b) Put forward proposals concerning finance and the budget and the organization of the administration and the public services;

(c) Give advice on draft laws submitted to the Assembly;

(d) On the request of the Chief Executive or of the Assembly, prepare drafts of laws, regulations or orders.

3. The composition and organization of the Council shall be fixed by law.

PART V. THE JUDICIARY
SOLE CHAPTER

Article 85

Judicial power

Judicial power shall be exercised by a Supreme Court and by other courts which will apply the various systems of law in force in Eritrea. The organization of these courts shall be established by law.

Article 86

Qualifications required of judges

1. Judges shall be chosen from persons of the highest moral reputation and known to be well versed in the customs and legislation peculiar to the various systems of law which they are required to apply.

Oath

2. Before taking up office, judges shall, according to their faith and their customary practice, take the following oath:

"I swear before Almighty God (or an invocation conforming to the faith and the customary practice of the judge concerned) to be a faithful guardian of the law and to administer it impartially and independently in order to ensure that justice shall reign supreme in Eritrea."

Independence of the judiciary

3. The judiciary shall be independent and must be free from all political influence. The Assembly and the Executive shall not give orders or injunctions to the judges, nor shall they bring any pressure to bear on them.

Status of judges

4. The status of judges shall be established by law.

Article 87

Appointment of judges

1. Judges shall be appointed by the Chief Executive on the recommendation of the President of the Assembly who shall be supplied with a list of candidates by a Committee composed of the President of the Supreme Court and two judges chosen by the members of the Supreme Court and of the court or courts immediately inferior thereto.

2. The President of the Assembly shall recommend to the Chief Executive two candidates for each appointment.

3. The list of candidates drawn up by the committee provided for in paragraph 1 must include at least three names for each appointment.

Article 88

Responsibility of judges

The Supreme Court provided for in Article 85 shall have jurisdiction in respect of criminal or disciplinary responsibility of judges for acts in connection with the discharge of their duties.

Article 89

Composition of the Supreme Court

1. The Supreme Court shall consist of not less than three and not more than seven judges. On the proposal of the Court, the number of judges may be decreased or increased by law.

2. Judges shall be appointed for a period of seven years, which period may be renewed.

Article 90

Jurisdiction of the Supreme Court

The Supreme Court shall have jurisdiction in the following matters:

(1) As a court of last resort with respect to appeals from final Judgements on points of law, and also to the extent provided by law with respect to appeals both on questions of law and fact.

(2) Conflicts of jurisdiction between courts.

In the event of a question involving conflicting jurisdiction, proceedings shall be suspended and the issue shall be presented to the Supreme Court, which shall determine the competent jurisdiction.

(3) Disputes concerning the constitutionality of laws and orders.

If the constitutionality of a law or order is challenged before a Courts proceedings shall be suspended and the issue shall be presented to the Supreme Court which shall decide whether such act is constitutional.

(4) Actions based on administrative acts brought against the Government of Eritrea or other public bodies, unless courts have been established by law to try such cases.

(5) Criminal and disciplinary responsibility of judges as provided in Article 88.

(6) Responsibility of the Chief Executive as provided in Article 75.

PART VI. AMENDMENT OF THE CONSTITUTION

Article 91

Compliance with the Federal Act and the principles of democratic government

1. The Assembly may not, by means of an amendment introduce into the Constitution any provision which would not be in conformity with the Federal Act.

2. Article 16 of the Constitution by the terms of which the Constitution of Eritrea is based on the principles of democratic government, shall not be amended.

Article 92

Amendments to the Constitution

1. Any amendment to the Constitution must be submitted in writing either by the Chief Executive or by a number of members of the Assembly equal to one quarter of the actual number of members.

2. A period of twenty days must elapse between the submission of an amendment and the opening of the Assembly's discussion thereon.

Article 93

Conditions governing the adoption of amendments

1. If an amendment is approved by a majority of three quarters of the members of the Assembly in office, the amendment shall be declared adopted.

2. If an amendment is approved by two successive legislatures by a majority of two thirds of the members present and voting or by a majority of the members in offices the amendment shall be declared adopted.

Entry into effect of amendments

3. Any amendments to the Constitution adopted by the Assembly according to the provisions of the foregoing paragraphs will enter into effect after ratification by the Emperor, Sovereign of the Federation.

PARTVII. TRANSITIONAL PROVISIONS

Article 94

Entry into force of the Constitution

1. This Constitution shall enter into effect following ratification of the Federal Act by the Emperor of Ethiopia, and following approval by the United Nations Commissioner, adoption by the Eritrean Assembly and ratification by the Emperor of Ethiopia of the Eritrea Constitution.

2. The Administering Authority shall continue to conduct the affairs of Eritrea until the transfer of power to the Government of Eritrea has taken place.

Article 95

Laws giving effect to the Constitution

1. Any laws giving effect to the present Constitution, adopted by the Eritrean Assembly convened by the Administering Authority, shall enter into effect simultaneously with the Constitution.

2. Such laws shall conform strictly to the principles and provisions of the Constitution.

Article 96

Legislation remaining in force when the Constitution comes into effect

1. Laws and regulations which were in force on 1 April 1941, and have not since been repealed by the Administering Authority and the laws and regulations enacted by that Authority, shall remain in force so long as they have not been repealed and to the extent that they have not been amended.

2. In the event of conflict between such laws and regulations and this Constitution, the Constitution shall prevail in accordance with Article 90 (3).

Article 97

Respect for obligations contracted on behalf of Eritrea

1. Obligations of any kind regularly contracted by the authorities administering Eritrea up to the date on which the Constitution enters into force shall remain valid for the Government of Eritrea and must be respected provided that such obligations relate to matters within the jurisdiction of Eritrea.

2. As from the date of the entry into force of the Constitution any undertaking regularly concluded by the Executive Committee established by the Administering Authority before the date of the entry into force of the Constitution shall remain valid and must be respected.

3. The provisions contained in paragraph 1 shall not apply to obligations terminated by the Peace Treaty with Italy of 10 February 1947 or by the Resolution adopted by the United Nations General Assembly on 29 January 1952.

Article 98

Retention of officials in office

Administrative officials and judicial officials whether Federal nationals or not, holding office when the Constitution enters into force, shall continue in office. They may be dismissed only on three months' notice.

Article 99

Term of the first Assembly

The Assembly responsible for adopting the Constitution shall exercise the powers of the Assembly as provided in the Constitution for a period of four years after the Constitution enters into force.

3. FO371/118738. Eritrea: Annual Review for 1955

The year 1955 has done little to fulfil the golden dreams aroused at the time of Eritrea's attainment of independence three years ago. After a quite start, a period of increasing tension between the country's first elected Chief Executive and the Assembly culminated in July in the former's resignation under somewhat unheroic circumstances. His successor, while possessed of a fair reputation for administrative efficiency, is well-known for his whole-hearted support of ultimate union with Ethiopia, and in all fields of public activity the end of the year saw a considerable advance of the more extreme Unionist elements, who are now well-placed to be of the maximum use in this summer's Eritrean elections. On the economic side an increasing shortage of liquid capital, the failure of the part of the Ethiopian authorities to provide adequate attractions for foreign investors, and the continuing difficulties created for foreign business men by the customs authorities, have led to a further diminution of the European colony, and thus of purchasing power generally throughout the country.

2. The fall of Tedla Bairu, and his succession by Asfaha Woldemikael, was due to a combination of arrogance and over-confidence on the part of Tedla, slowness by the members of the Assembly to grasp a situation which they themselves had created, and a not unexpected quickness on the part of the local Ethiopian representatives to take advantage of the changed circumstances. Since his election as Chief Executive in September, 1952, Tedla Bairu had treated the Assembly with increasing off-handedness; he seldom appeared at its meetings, and the Secretaries of the Executive Departments frequently failed to turn when important bills regarding their Departments were being discussed. In addition, ugly rumours of nepotism and personal corruption on the part of Tedla himself had gained wide currency. The Deputies chose to attack the Chief Executive through Ali Redai, the President of the Assembly and in June, in face of an attempt by his opponents to pass a vote of "no confidence" in the President, Tedla Bairu suspended the Assembly for 20 days, an action which, in certain circumstances, is permitted by the Eritrean Constitution. At the end of this period Tedla ordered a further 20 days suspension; suddenly realising that a real danger to his position existed, Tedla now began a feverish campaign of self-justification, including newspaper interviews, personal visits to provincial towns and a published speech in one of Asmara's largest cinemas. But by this time it was too late. His opponents had appealed to the Emperor, through his Imperial Majesty's Representative in Asmara, against the Chief Executive's actions and the Emperor let it be known that he considered the suspension illegal. While it appears that under the constitution this action, however unwise, was in fact permissible, it was now clear that the highest Ethiopian authorities were no longer prepared to give Tedla Bairu their support. Tedla accordingly resigned, and left for Addis Ababa, where he now lives in a villa outside the town, reputedly financially assisted by the Emperor himself.

3. It would be a mistake to regard Tedla Bairu as a martyr on behalf of Eritrean independence. He had himself long been identified with the Unionist Party and, although he may since have attempted to justify himself with the Federalists, in order to strengthen his internal position within Eritrea itself, it does not appear that this was the cause of his rejection by the Ethiopians. Rather, the latter seem to have come to the conclusion that because of his growing local unpopularity, Tedla's usefulness to them was now ended. They therefore seized the opportunity offered to them by the disarray of Tedla's opponents—who, once the cause of their animosity had actually been displaced, seemed to have no clear ideas as to whom they wanted to replace him—to install as Chief Executive a man even more closely bound to Unionist interests. Asfaha Woldemikael, the former Vice-Representative of the Emperor in Eritrea, has been careful to avoid his predecessor's mistakes, and has treated the Assembly with some show of outward deference. While

undoubtedly working for Union in the long run, he is unlikely to make any rash or ill-considered moves in that direction. As expected the Jubilee, (25 years since the emperor ascended the throne) passed off without any substantiation of the rumours that Union might be proclaimed to mark the occasion.

4. It is extremely difficult however to assess the degree of resistance which may exist within Eritrea to any moves in the direction of closer Union with Ethiopia. When at the time of the Jubilee the extreme Unionist Secretary of the Interior, Araya Wassie ordered that only the Ethiopian flag should be flown in Asmara, the Moslem League were able, by means of an unwontedly vigorous protest, to secure the display of the Eritrean flag. On other occasions during the year they have threatened to protest to the United Nations against alleged Federal interference in Eritrean internal affairs. It seems doubtful however whether the Moslems and their Christian allies in the Federalist cause would in fact do anything more positive to resist a move for Union. Meanwhile, strong Unionists have been placed in positions where they can influence to the utmost the forthcoming election (in August); apart from the Secretaries of the Executive itself, the Vice-President of the Assembly, the Chief of the Police and many of the district officials are now prominent members of the Unionist Party. While it is of course most improbable that the election would be fought on outwardly Unionist versus Federalist lines, candidates amenable to Government influence may well be returned in a large proportion of constituencies, and the new Assembly will no doubt contain a substantial majority of members who would supinely vote for any motion which was presented to them. At the same time, precipitate action is likely to be avoided, in view of the Ethiopian desire to make a good impression on world opinion in 1960, when the future of the former Italian Somaliland will raise itself in an acute form.

5. Strenuous efforts were made during the Jubilee period by local Unionist to whip up popular enthusiasm for the Ethiopian royal family. These endeavours met with little real success however, and Eritrean reactions to the affront to local susceptibilities over the flag have been described above. His Imperial Majesty accompanied Marshall Tito [president of Yugoslavia from ---- and one of the founders of the third world non-alignment movement] on his official visit to Asmara and Massawa at the end of the year, but here again, apart from school children who had been dragooned to line the streets, there was little genuine enthusiasm as the visitors passed. The Emperor took the opportunity to have a week's holiday in Massawa, where early in the New Year he inaugurated the new Imperial Naval College.

6. After an uneasy lull which lasted into the beginning of the year, shifta activity flared up pace more in the spring, when there was a series of ugly incidents. Finally the Chief Executive decided to invoke a proclamation, originally published during the British Administration, which would have conferred wide powers of arrest and search upon the Eritrean police. By this time however Tedla Bairu was already on his way out, and lack of Ethiopian support for him was reflected in an amnesty which was proclaimed by the Emperor only few days after the Eritrean Government's action. During the three months conceded by the Amnesty, a total of 188 shiftas surrendered. At the end of this period the Acting Commissioner of Police (Tedla Ogbit] (the first Eritrean officer to be appointed to this post) announced that only 16 bandits now remained at large in Eritrea, and that they were being actively hunted down. This sanguine estimate has not since been brone out, however, and a further series of incidents has continued right into the New Year. Distinct suspicions were current during the first outbreak that the shifta were being actively encouraged from south of the border, with the object of demonstrating that the Eritrean Government were incapable of maintaining law and order, with the inference that this could only be assured by the presence of Ethiopian forces within the territory. This im-

pression was reinforced by the Emperor's undermining of Tedla Bairu's authority, referred to above, and hopes were felt that, with the advent to power of their own nominee, Asfaha Woldemikael would receive more active and open support from the Federal authorities. To protests against the recent incidents, the local authorities are unanimous in protesting that the culprits are no longer professional shifta, with the political connotation carried by this word, but merely local villagers who are earning an extra penny in their time off from their legitimate occupations. The police have announced plans for dealing with the latest outbreak. It is too early as yet to say how effective these will be. Meanwhile, the incidents have had an unsettling effect on the local—and particularly European population.

7. On the economic side, the run-down of Eritrea continued throughout the year on its gradual but seemingly inexorable way, with inevitable repercussions on local purchasing-power and, thus, on market possibilities for importers. The vagaries of the Customs services, with its capricious assessment of duties payable, are enough to discourage all but the most resolute traders, while liquid capital is in very short supply, with the consequence that many bills are outstanding for long periods. The leader of the American economic mission, which visited Eritrea in November, pointed out in a frank interview with the local government paper that new investments of foreign capital could not be expected to come forward until adequate guarantees were offered by the Federal authorities. Meanwhile the Italian exodus from the country continues; there has hitherto been no comparable shift of purchasing power to the native population, with the consequence that markets for importers, particularly of consumer goods, become ever more restricted. By itself, Eritrea has of course probably never been economically viable, and the inflated standard of living achieved by circumstances, and faced by the necessity of dealing with two sets of officials and of supporting through their taxes two governments, many of the Italian business men still remaining in Eritrea appear, in spite of their misgivings, to be resigned to full Union between Eritrea and Ethiopia as the only way out of their difficulties.

8. Finally, the departure of British advisors to the Eritrean Government on the expiry of their contracts, or by semi-voluntary resignation, continues, and, so far, none of them have been replaced. Those who have gone this year are:

a) Colonel C.W.Wright, Commissioner of Police.

b) Mr. C.Crowson, Advisor to the Railways and Ropeway Administration.

c) Mr.E. Allen Smith, Financial Advisor to the Eritrean Government.

d) Captain D.W. Dix, Port Manger, Massawa.

On the positive side Mr. Steed Pope, Advisor, Posts and Telegraphs, who left in September 1954, has now returned at the request of the Ethiopian authorities to sort out the mess into which affairs had fallen since his departure.

**4. FO371/118744. Memorandum submitted by the Moslem League to
H.I.M. The Emperor of Ethiopia, Asmara, 3.1. 1956 corresponding to
20 Jamad Awal, 1375**

To: H.I.M. The Emperor of Ethiopia, Sovereign of the Federation. Through: H.I.M Representative in Eritrea.

With due respect to your Imperial Majesty, the Moslem League in Eritrea has the pleasure to welcome your fourth visit to Eritrea. The Moslem League in this opportunity begs to submit to Your Imperial Majesty the following:

1. The Moslem League considers its first duty to see that the Federation and the autonomy of Eritrea under the Sovereignty of Your Imperial Crown are safeguarded.

2. The outstanding problems of the Rights of Eritrea in the domestic and Federal fields constitute the prime concern for the Eritrean people. Their immediate solution is but an urgent necessity. Your Majesty, undoubtedly remembers the letter which has been submitted to You at the end of January, 1953, and the Memorandum submitted by the people on February 1954 in this regard. The Moslem Conference which was held on first and second December, 1955 had also submitted to H.E. The Chief Executive, to H.E. The President of the Eritrean Assembly, and to the members of the Assembly similar requests aiming at the improvement of the domestic machinery of administration and the problem of restoring to Eritrea its right in the Federation.

3. The term of the present Legislative Assembly is due to terminate in a few months, and if the unsolved problems are left to the second Legislative Assembly, we believe that it will create misgivings in the minds of the people and would be detrimental to both the states of the Federation.

4. According to what have been stated above, we beg Your Majesty to see that all the outstanding matters between the two Governments in the Federation are solved in an amicable way and brotherly deliberation and in the light of United Nations Resolution and the Eritrean Constitution so that every member in the Federation could know its just share, such as internal communications as provided for in Article 5(J) of the Eritrean Constitution, and the just and equitable share of Eritrea of the expenses of the Federal functions as provided for in Article 6(1) and also the revenue from Custom Duties on goods entering or leaving the Federation as provided for in Article 6(3) thereof. By effecting this, misunderstanding will disappear and in its stead cooperation and harmony will prevail.

5. Participation of the Eritreans in all the Federal functions whether Legislative, Executive, or Judicial organs conformably to Article 5 of the United Nations Resolution. The Moslem League also begs that Eritreans participate in the defence, foreign and diplomatic affairs, Currency, Finance, Commerce and Foreign Communications including the administration of the Eritrean Ports as provided in Article 3 of the United Nations Resolution. The persons who act in the said organs should be selected by the Eritrean Government according to Article 80 of the Eritrean constitution. We further beg that passports for travel in the foreign country be titled the Imperial Ethiopian-Eritrean Federation.

6. We believe that democratic principles necessitate that legislation is provided for by the people as shown in Article 18 of the Eritrean Constitution. Therefore the Moslem League begs that all the new drafts of proclamation, laws and Federal application, issued after 11 September, 1952, be referred to the concerned Eritreans so that they, as a second member in the Federation, could give an opinion thereon.

7. It happened that the Government of Eritrea has chosen ten persons to represent Eritrea

in the Imperial Federal Council and the Chamber of Federal Deputies, but up to now the people did not know what services have been rendered by them. Therefore the Moslem Conference begs that full reports of their activities, past and present, be issued. We have recently learnt that the five Eritrean members in the Imperial Federal Council have been removed from their office, but we do not know the reasons.

8. The situation of Eritrea as to the standard of living, employment, economic and commercial activities need be the concern of Your Majesty in that the different classes of people could secure the necessary means of living, find new projects to work on, thereby improvements in economics and commerce could be had.

9. The fundamental prerequisite in the pursuit of happiness and the progress of our country is the maintenance of the unity of the people and the extinction of the element of dissension among them. This can only be attained by effecting equality among the citizens of the country without allowing a certain group to have domination upon the other. Therefore, the Moslem League begs that observance for such equality among the citizens be had in the various governmental and public services.

10. We beg Your Majesty to pardon the paper "Voice of Eritrea", and its editor Elias Toclu.

11. The above are some of the important points that Moslem League begs to invite Your Attention to, hoping that our request would meet the approval of Your Majesty.

We have the honour to convey our highest esteem and respect and Loyalty to Your Majesty.

May Your Majesty accept our cordial regards and congratulations for Your gracious visit to Eritrea.

Copy to:

H.E. The Chief Executive of Eritrea.

H.E. The President of the Eritrean Assembly.

5. FO371/118744. Memorandum submitted by the Moslem League, Asmara, 11th Shawal, 1375; 21.5.56.

To: Eritrean Chief Executive
    President of the Eritrean Assembly and Members
    President of Supreme Court
    Secretary of Law and Justice
    Attorney General
To the Representative of H.I.M. the Emperor. For information only.

1. We have with much regret heard that some Hon. members of the Assembly have moved a motion intending to amend Article 89 of the Constitution to increase the number of judges of the Supreme Court. This motion we believe is violating the same article which purports that the number of the judges in the Supreme Court can not be increased unless on a proposal of the Court itself or by law, and such amendment is valid when approved by two successive legislature as Art. 93 (2) refers.

2. There is a very strong rumour among the people of Asmara which purports, that some members of the Assembly have decided to remove the President of the Assembly from Office for lack of confidence which action they have taken against the ex Vice-President Blatta Demsas on 24th September the last. If this rumour is true we should say that such removal is against the constitution and in no wise legal and such action is but a grave violation to Art.19 and Art.52 of the constitution.

Therefore, as we are the people who is the resource of power according to the provisions of Art. 18, 30, and 35 we hereby vehemently protest against the said action and we ask it should be stopped at once and if not, we shall transmit this news directly to H.I.M. the Emperor and demonstration shall be held everywhere in the country when necessity arises.

Delegates of the people

Ahmed Saleh Basaad
Haggi Imam Mussa
Adam Kusmalla
Shek Idris Hummed Saduy
Mohamed Yassi Mohamednur
Abdulaziz Ahmed Surar
Mohamed Ali Ahmed Abuhamid
Kalil Ali Lal
Ibrahim Mohamed Dirar
Osman Alhaj Mohamed
Said Daud
Ahmed Abdulkadir Bashir
Adbu Ahmed Hindi
Adbulmagid Mohamed Dankaly
Ahmed Saad Saleh
Alhaji Suleiman
Bashai Osman Mohamed
Alhaji Imam Mohamed
Abdi Hagos
Saleh Mohamed Aman

6. FO371/118744. H.E. The Chief Executive, Government of Eritrea Headquarters. (Memorandum submitted by the Moslem Mosques Committee Asmara, 11 Shawal, 1375; 21.5.1956)

We the undersigned the elected representatives of the people of Asmara in our capacity of Moslem Mosques' Committee and delegates to the Moslems of other provinces beg to pay, on behalf of them all our tribute to Your Excellency for your carrying out the duty of proclaiming officially the Holiday of Ed-Al-Fatr and also for receiving our mission who is submitting this memorandum. We very much regret your statement that you have learnt that the group who asked for and decided the cancelling of prayer on the first day of Ed-Al-Fatr were a minority. The fact is completely contrary to this, for the one who asked for the cancelling were all those who frequent the mosques of the capital.

As we are an elected committee by the Moslem people, we beg, in accordance with the provision of Art. 18, 30 and 35 of the Eritrean Constitution to draw your attention to the following items:

1. As a measure to avoid possible misunderstanding in connection with holidays in future, we beg your Excellency to submit to the Assembly an Act to replace proclamation no. 69 of 1949, to fix and limit the Eritrean National Holidays.

2. Conformably to article 38 of the constitution, we ask that the Arabic and Tigrinya languages be used officially in all the Eritrean Government Departments, offices and schools. Whoever violates this should be punished.

3. That in pursuance to Article 21 of the Constitution, the Eritrean flag be hoisted during public occasions in Eritrea, for the fact that it is the legal symbol of the autonomy resolved by the United Nations, accepted by the Eritrean people, and ratified by H.I.M. the Emperor.

4. That the educational curriculum in Eritrea be subject to article 31 (3). The Government should encourage the Moslem students to have instructions in Arabic language. This matter has attracted the attention of the Moslems and their comment thereon gave rise to doubts and misgivings. We beg to recommend the Government in this regard to import from abroad qualified teachers of Arabic in order to enable to Moslem students to have their high education in their own languages as it is the case in the other languages.

5. In view of the forthcoming general election, the non-existence of complementary law relating to it, the inconsistence of Proclamation No. 121 in some of its Articles to the Eritrean Constitution, we ask the Government in accordance with article 96 of the Constitution to take the necessary steps to see that consequences of illegal and unconstitutional elections are not suffered by the people.

6. The change of the irregular situation which has been and still adopted in depriving Muslim elements from occupying high posts in the Eritrean Government which fact is but an insult directed to the citizenship of the Muslims. We ask that all Eritreans should be equal in rights as well as it is in duties.

7. That strict orders are issued to all the officials, particularly the police to observe the law and the constitution and to respect the fundamental freedoms granted to the populations. Further, any official who violates article 19 of the constitution should be punished.

8. The execution of the people's various demands [were] submitted to the Government since its formation. These demands were completely or in part disregarded as if the Government was not the Government of the people. For instance the petitions submitted on 25.2.1956 about the tempering which took place in [regard] to Identity Cards Law application which made a large part of the people refrain from issuing the cards.

9. We vehemently request the Government to give consideration to all applications sub-

mitted by the Moslem educated youth who want to obtain employment. It is understood that such applications were all disregarded. Likewise the Government must consider all applications submitted by Moslem traders for business licenses, or free enterprise which fact seems to be religious and ethnical discrimination adopted against the Muslims who kept patient ever since the formation of the Eritrean Government in 1952.

10. We ask and recommend the Government to change the policy adopted in the Department of the Interior which is exclusively formed of Christians starting from the Secretary down to the messengers. It is understood that the Government deliberately excluded the Muslim elements from this vital department which has a direct connection with the population. Such action is very serious for it renders the Muslims in the position of foreigners not citizens. There is no advisor in their affairs in this Department. It is deeply believed that this thing did not happen inadvertently but was purposely done.

11. We urge the Government to take steps to restore the internal Eritrean Department which have been taken by the Ethiopian Imperial Government under the name of the Federal Government. These departments were: the internal communications as Eritrean Railways and Ropeways, Eritrean Posts and Telecommunications, Internal Roads and then the legal revenue of Customs on goods entering or leaving Eritrea. [Of] All these matters Eritrea was deprived in spite of the existence of a Government entrusted to maintain and ask for them in accordance with the Constitutional undertaking you have openly taken before the Assembly.

12. We ask that measures be taken to see that Eritrea exercises a real participation in a real Federal system applied legally according with the provisions of the U.N Resolution which recommended the establishment of a Federal Unity between two distinct units known as Eritrea from one part and Ethiopia from the other.

Your Excellency, as you are aware, the writing of memorandums and petitions are valueless if their contents are not appreciated or if there is no good will to study them and execute them in the light of law and justice. The Eritrean people whom we are part of, have submitted during the last few years several demands. We are full of hope that our demands will not meet the fate which have been met by the previous demands. In conclusion, please accept from us in the name of the Muslim people our kindest regards and respect.

Copy to H.E. the President of the Assembly and the Honourable Members of the Assembly.

7. FO371/118744. Confidential. British Consulate-General, Asmara to J.E.Killick Esq., British Embassy, Addis Ababa. Asmara, 19.6 1956

In my letter no. 501 of March 10, I reported that the campaign for the new elections in Eritrea in 1956 would probably commence at the end of June and that voting would take place towards the end of July or the beginning of August. Whilst the programme of parliamentary sessions also set out in my letter has, so far been fulfilled, a crisis in the procedure for the holding of the elections seems to be developing coupled with changes in the Assembly.

2. Under Article No. 45 of the Eritrean Constitution it is the duty of the Eritrean Supreme Court to appoint an Electoral High commission to supervise "all electoral proceedings (including the compiling of electoral rolls) and for preventing or putting a stop to irregularities". The implementation of this Article No. 45 is to be "prescribed by law". Shearer, the President of the Supreme Court tells me that legislation to give full effect to Article 45 was prepared by Bennet, the Legal Consultant to the British Administration and was submitted to the Assembly some time in 1953 but was thrown out by them. They also refused to discuss the matter when two members suggested doing so in March, 1956. Apart from that there seems to have been no attempt to give effect to this clause of Article 45, and in fact you will see from the attached copies of a petition addressed to the President of the Supreme Court that the Chief Executive—which, in effect, means the Palace—intends to proceed with the elections under the provisions of British Proclamation No. 121.

3. Hearing of this, Shearer wrote a very moderate and reasonable letter to the Chief Executive drawing his attention to the provisions of the Constitution and asking to see any legal advice he may have taken on the subject. Mr. F.F. Russell, the Legal Advisor of the Eritrean Government had advised the Chief Executive that since the relevant law had not been passed by the Assembly it would be in order to proceed with the elections under Proclamation No. 121. Shearer realises, of course, that there are various steps the Chief Executive—and the Palace—could take to stultify the actions of the Supreme Court if it decided to proceed with the appointment of an Electoral High Commission. There is, at present, no provision for the payment of such a Commission. Their efforts in the constituencies would, of course, be completely nullified if District Officers were instructed to withhold their support, and there is always the possibility of the members falling sick.

4. Nevertheless, in Shearer's view, Russell's advice is unsound. Under Article 76 (1) "the Chief Executive shall ensure that the Constitution and the Laws are enforced" and he took an oath to do so under Article 72. The members of the Assembly also took an oath to "defend the Constitution and its Laws" (article 53) and I understand that Shearer pointed this out to the Chief Executive in his letter.

5. Meanwhile Keshi Dimetros, the Vice-President of the Assembly, a fanatical Unionist, is reported to have proposed, as soon as he heard of the opposition of the supreme Court that Shearer should be given three months notice! It was later pointed out to him that this was impracticable, but Shearer was then approached by a former Secretary of Finance who said that the authorities were proposing to offer him a large sum of money if he would resign, but begged him no to do so since he was really needed here. So far, I gather the offer has not materialised.

6. Then as you will see from the second petition enclosed herein, that of May 21 from the Moslem Mosques Committee to the Chief Executive, there was a proposal to pack the Supreme Court by appointing further judges up to a total of 19, although the sponsors of this idea seemed to be unaware of Article 89 which stipulates that it is only "on the proposal of the (Supreme) Court" itself that the numbers of the judges can be increased.

7. This last scheme for making the Courts subservient to the wishes of the Executive was intimately connected with changes in the Assembly. Sir James Shearer also sent a copy of the letter he had addressed to the Chief Executive, to the President of the Assembly, Saiyid Idris Muhamed Adum, and the latter, as a Moslem, was doubtless pleased to find he had the backing of the Courts in thinking it would be unconstitutional to conduct the elections under Proclamation No. 121. In any case, he gave Shearer's letter a very wide circulation throughout the country, and thereby incurred the severe displeasure of the Palace.

8. Having decided that he must be replaced for his 'indiscipline', the Palace had to make some concession to those Moslem members of the Assembly whose votes they wanted against Saiyid Idris, and they gave way, therefore, on the subject of the packing of the Supreme Court. The Moslems were, in any case, nervous lest, having got rid of Saiyid Idris, the authorities, supported by a subservient Supreme Court, should then proceed to alter the Constitution as they wished. In the event, a Moslem member, Sheik Osman Abdurrahman, proposed, in the House on June 13 that "this Assembly, having lost confidence in Sheik Idris Muhamed Adum, decides that he shall today vacate the office of the President of the Eritrean Assembly" The motion was carried by 43 votes to nil with no abstentions, and Saiyid Idris left the Presidential chair. Both the officials of the Assembly and the Press were strictly enjoined by the Palace to give the matter no prominence and in fact it occupied less than fifteen lines of very small print in the papers of June 14. The following day, June 14, with the Vice-President, Keshi Dimetros in the chair, the Assembly elected Sheik Hamid Farag Hamid as its President. Sheik Hamid, a Moslem of about 50 years of age, from the Agordat district (as was Saiyid Idris), had the reputation of cooperating fully with the British Administration in Moslem-Coptic disputes and is said to be a man of strong personality. It is interesting to note, however, that he is a close confidant of Saiyid Ali Redai whom Saiyid Idris Muhamed Adum ousted from the Presidential chair on July 28, 1955.

9. The decision of the Supreme Court on the petition submitted to them has not yet been known. Somewhat surprisingly, since some of the Italian Judges take their instructions from the Palace, I gather that they were unanimous in opinion when they discussed the subject, but whether their reply will take the form of a verdict (that elections under Proclamation 121 would be unconstitutional) or will merely voice their opinion on the complaints in the petition is also unknown. But whatever their decision it seems unlikely that the Palace will now lose face to the extent of permitting the appointment of an Electoral High Commission.

10. I will keep you informed of developments. In the meantime I am sending a copy of this letter to African Department of the Foreign Office.

E.J. Howes

8. FO371/118744. BCA to FO, Asmara, 12.9.56. Report on the elections for the Second Assembly of Eritrea

Annex I
Eritrean Elections, 1956.

Nomination Day — August 15. Polling Day — September 5 and 6.

Number of seats 68	
Number of candidates	188
Christians elected	32
Moslems elected	32
Christians re-elected	17
Moslems re-elected	15
Christians unopposed	10
Moslems unopposed	20
Results challenged	4
Former members unopposed	22
New members	32
New members unopposed	8

[At the time of the writing of the report, four seats had yet to be filled.] Square bracket added.

Annex II
Election district

Asmara division	Political affiliation
1. Demsas Woldemikael	UP
2. Ibrahim Ali Bekit	AU
3. Solomon Hailemelekot	UP
4. Berhanu Ahmeddin	AU
5. Habtesghi Ogbasghi	UP
6. Fessha Woldemariam	AU
7. Keshi Meascio Bein	UP

Massawa Division	
8. Hajj Osman Mohamed Hindi	AU
9. Ato Misgun Bokru	UP

Akeleguzai division	
10. Ato Ghebrekidan Tessema	AU
11. Bashai Habte Tesfamikael	UP
12. Dejach Berhe Asberom	AU
13. Ato Tewolde Tedla	UP
14. Fit. Negash Bariaeghzi	UP
15. Dej. Ghebrezghi Guangul	AU
16. Fit. Saleh Omar	--
17. Sayid Ahmed Saleh Barole	--
18. Sayid Sunabara Damana	AU
19. Graz. Abdalla Omar	--
20. Lij. Alemseged Belai	UP
21. Azmatch Reda Guangul	UP

Serae Division

22. Bashai Berhane Tecle	UP
23. Azmatch Fasil Habtu	UP
24. Kegnaz Yihdego Ghebrerufael	UP
25. Keshi. Woldeyohannes Tzadu	UP
26. Ato Tesfai Zemikael	--
27. Dimetros Gebremariam	UP
28. Ato Nega Naizghi	UP
29. Ato Ogbe Haile	UP
30. Azmatch Woldemikael Beraki	UP
31. Graz. Asberom Woldeghiorghis	UP
32. Ato Ghebremikael Derzo	UP
33. Graz. Tesfamikael Werke	UP

Hamassien division

34. Bashai Tekeste Seleba	--
35. Bashai Ghebrehiwet Tesfai	UP
36. Azmatch Hagos Sereke	UP
37. Ato Berhe Ghebrehiwet	UP
38. Ato Belai Tekie	UP
39. Graz. Ghebremariam T.	UP

Keren division

40. Sayid Hussien Kafeel	--
41. Sayid Ismail Daud	--
42. Sayid Sefaf Hiyabu	UP
43. Cavalier Abbe Mohamed	--
44. Ato Abreha Wonderas	UP
45. Sheik Hamid Sayid Hamid	--
46. Sayid Yosuf Faki Ali	--
47. Sayid Mohamed Ali Abdalla	--
48. Sayid Omar Sheik Mohamed Amir	--
49. Sayid Mohamed Sayid M.Hassano	--
50. Hajj. Mohamed Mussa Mender	--
51. Sayid Abdu Sheik Ali	--
52. Sayid Osman Mohamed	--
53. Sayid Osman Abderahman Sheferai	--
54. Sayid Omar Adem Idris	--
55. Sayid El Hassan Mohamed Anokla	--
56. Sayid Hamid Ferej Hamid	--
57. Sayid Adem Saleiman Dighe	--
58. Sayid Mohamed Badume Kassu	--
59. Sayid fayid Tinga Longhi	--
60. Sayid Mohamed Arey Agaba	--

Massawa sub-division

61. Sayid Mohamed Ali Sheik el Amin	--
62. Sheik Kekkia Pasha	UP
63. Sayid Mohamed Ali Maliki	--

Assab division

64. Rashid Sirru	--

Key to abbreviations
UP = the Unionist Party
AU = Anti-Unionist
This includes all those who were active within the Moslem League as well as those who wanted to maintain the federal status of Eritrea.
-- stands for those who did not publicly express their political affiliation.

9. FO371/125539. Memorandum submitted by the Moslem League 27.3.1957

Asmara, 23 of Sciaban, 1376; 27.3.57.

To: H.I.M. the August Emperor of Ethiopia, Sovereign óf the Federation. From: The Moslem League.

We the Eritrean voters submit the following according to Article 7 (d) of the United Nations Resolution and Art. 18, 30, and 35 of the Eritrean Constitution.

1. Eritrea and Ethiopia are two states united federally under Your Imperial Crown. According to law neither of them is an integral part of the other.

2. The Central Government which presides over the said two states and function [manages] the affairs provided for in Art. 3 of the United Nations Resolution, is not as we believe legally constituted to this day.

3. On the end of December 1956 and at the outset of January 1957 where was published in the papers the names of the members in the Imperial federal Council—the number of them was ten of whom 9 were Eritreans and one Ethiopian and this is a violation of Art. 5 of the U.N. Resolution and Art. 7 of the Eritrean Constitution which provides that the Federal Council shall be composed of equal number of Ethiopians and Eritreans.

4. On the current month of March we perused in the papers a proclamation n.152 of 1956—Ethiopia Electoral Law. The Law mentioned in its preamble that in so far as Eritrea is a "part" of the Ethiopian Empire, the people of Eritrea will proceed to elect their representatives in the Ethiopian Chamber of Deputies. We believe that the said proclamation is a violation of the United Nations Resolution and the Eritrean Constitution. Because Eritrea is an autonomous government in its legislative, executive, and judicial affairs. Eritrea is by no means a part of Ethiopia to participate in an election for the Internal Chamber of Deputies belonging to the Ethiopian Government.

5. As we are voters we can participate in the Federal Legislative Council of the Central Government which presides the affairs of the two governments in the Federation if it is established according to Law. We will never participate in the Ethiopian legislative Council because we believe that such participation is a violation of the U.N.Resolution and the Eritrean Constitution as well as it is a suppression of the rights of Eritrea in its consideration as an integral part of Ethiopia, the first which indicates that Eritrea is not an autonomous govern-ment in the Federation. Therefore, we vehemently beg Your Majesty to reconsider para.3 and above. Your Majesty, accept our deepest respect and loyalty.

Signed by 500 voters.

[The original of this memo was signed by about 500 voters. Only a copy of the mimeo exists at the PRO.] Square bracket added.

10. FO371/125539. Visit of Her Majesty's Ambassador to Eritrea, between the 11th and 24th of November, 1957

Addis Ababa, December 7, 1957.

I have the honour to submit the following observations on the present situation in Eritrea, which I visited for the first time between the 11th and 24th of November.

2. The predominant impression left on any visitor to Asmara and Massawa, the two principal towns, must be one of depression and decay. This is not to say that these towns are altogether badly kept; on the contrary, their municipalities, now almost wholly Eritrean in composition, are exhibiting a praiseworthy sense of civic responsibility, although handicapped by the low standards of the indigenous population. But throughout their European quarters are signs of poverty and stagnation of trade, and of a total lack of confidence in the future of the territory. Beggars abound; many European shops are deserted or closed; "liquidazione" [sale] notices are on many business premises; and there is a complete absence of the bustle of activity which accompanies a thriving economy.

3. These visual impressions are enhanced in conversation with foreigners of all kinds. The Italian community since the end of the British Administration in 1952 has shrunk from 17,000 to 11,000, and the majority of those remaining would clearly leave tomorrow if they saw any chance of establishing themselves anywhere. Indian and Jewish merchants and the shopkeepers with whom I spoke were dispirited and listless. The few remaining British officials are working on their contracts but neither expect, nor for the most part want, to renew them.

4. This air of depression does not, however, give the whole picture. I am informed that the total volume of business in Eritrea, which since the end of the British Administration has remained at a more or less constant low level, is now, according to bank figures, beginning to show a slight increase. But the Eritrean economy is clearly in the final stage of a run-down from the purely artificial European level created by the Fascists, which their heavy subsidies alone could support, to a level more compatible with the meagre natural resources of the country. This painful process has been accelerated by the depressing effect of Ethiopian official control, which not only tends to stifle enterprise by obstruction, graft, and procrastination but, by the adoption of unwise measures (such as the raising of customs duties on certain essential products to exorbitant heights, which has encouraged smuggling over the long desert frontier with the Sudan at the expense of legitimate imports), has tended to frighten away even those Italians and other foreigners who were prepared to remain in the country and without whom the economy was bound to decline all the more rapidly. Once bottom has been reached, however, there seems no reason to suppose that Eritrea will not be able to rub along, but only on normal African standards.

5. The present decline could be arrested only if oil were found or other profitable enterprises established. These possibilities cannot be ruled out; but there is little sign that either will eventuate. The Italian AGIP Company have long been negotiating for an oil exploration concession, and even if their negotiations, at present apparently suspended by the Ethiopians for political reasons, prove abortive, the Shell Company and possibly other companies are prepared to try their luck; but the fate of oil exploration on both sides of the Red Sea does not encourage optimism that this source of wealth will accrue to Eritrea. Prospects of large scale mineral or agricultural development seem excluded by the country's lack of natural resources. The Emperor's Viceroy is in negotiation with an Italian group to establish a cement works; and I heard while in Asmara of a Belgian project for extracting iron ore from the Red Sea coast and of various small Italian projects; but even if the promoters can overcome the immense obstacles provided by Ethiopian

obstructionism and avidity, nothing so far would seem likely to have a decisive effect on the Eritrean economy.

6. In these circumstances it is difficult to resist the conviction that the present Eritrean set-up, and particularly an Assembly of sixty-eight members with little real power, constitutes an unjustifiable burden on this small and poor country.

7. I have dealt first with the economic aspect, because it appears to me fundamentally to affect the outlook and mentality of the population, both European and indigenous. Politically, virtually the only question of importance is whether Ethiopia will attempt to incorporate Eritrea completely, if so when. On this the position appears obscure. Advocates of union fill most key positions; and it is generally conceded that the Eritrean Assembly, as now constituted, could be made to vote for incorporation at any time. Moreover, my impression is that this development, if it came about, would be accepted with little demur by the majority of the Christian population, and that such objection as a section of the Moslems might make could probably be settled without much difficulty. Nevertheless, the risk of raising a hornets' nest for Ethiopia in the United Nations has hitherto deterred the Emperor from taking the final step which he undoubtedly regards as logical and necessary, and may continue to do so for the present; and Sir James Shearer, the dour Scottish President of the Supreme Court of Eritrea, who appears to regard himself as a constitutional watchdog, will remain an obstacle to any unconstitutional development in Eritrea until he retires two years hence.

8. On the other hand, the Imperial Federal Council, half Ethiopian and half Eritrean, which should have been set up under the terms of article 5 of the United Nations Resolution of 2nd December, 1950, to advise on Federal affairs, has never been constituted, and under the Ethiopian Electoral Law, based on the 1955 Constitution, Eritrea has secured only 14 seats out of 203 in the new Assembly. The Emperor's Speech from the Throne of the 2nd November last contained two references to "reintegration of Eritrea with the Motherland"; and while Eritreans remain a large majority in their Administration, there seems little doubt that the real power resides in the hands of the Emperor's Viceroy and the Ethiopian Federal officials. It looks, in fact, as though the Emperor's intention is to make Eritrean-Ethiopian union unobtrusively a fait accompli.

9. Meanwhile the Administration appears at least to function no worse than in the rest of Ethiopia. Security has evidently improved since the promulgation last summer of a new law against banditry which provides for far heavier penalties than could previously be imposed; and the number of shifta outrages on the main roads has markedly decreased. The Chief Executive, a shrewd and tough, if unscrupulous, Eritrean who now has almost complete control over the Administration in view of the prolonged absences of the emperor's Viceroy from Eritrea, dealt firmly with a recent attempt by agitators to promote a general strike, and is evidently prepared to deal equally firmly with any recrudescence of the trouble which occurred in the secondary schools last summer. The Administration hardly seems popular; but its unpopularity may well be due as much to economic causes as to its shortcomings.

10. British interests and influence in Eritrea have since 1952 declined in much the same manner as the economy. Within two years almost all the remaining British advisers will have left, and the British community will be reduced to a few hundred of Indian or Arab origin, a missionary or two, and the resident representatives of such local British firms as consider it worth while to maintain branches in Eritrea.

11. Left to itself, and provided that Ethiopia proper preserves its integrity, Eritrea seems destined gradually to sink to the status of an ordinary province, slightly better endowed than most with roads, buildings and (for the present) foreign artisans and business con-

cerns, and with a port over-large for its need, but with an economy and an administration neither better nor worse than that of the rest of the Empire. It is to be hoped that the recent abortive attempt by the sponsors of the Afro-Asian Solidarity Conference to secure separate Eritrean representation at it does not foreshadow a Moslem (or Communist) attempt to disturb the process by making Eritrea once again a political issue; for such an attempt would seem incapable of benefiting anyone, least of all the Eritreans.

G.W.Furlonge

Table 1. Recapitulatory statement of commercial licences held by firms in Asmara

Class of business	1953	1956	1959
Retail	1348	1315	1325
Wholesale	162	161	287
Export-import	334	334	327
agencies-			
Business on commission	62	60	
Industrial activities	395	456	627
Handicrafts	745	968	1009

Source: FO371/138059. BCA to BEAA, 1.4.59.

Table 2. Import permits utilized during 1956

Commodities	Value in pound sterling
Grey sheetings	75,967
Yarn	40,340
Drills Khaki	1,687
Drills white	---
Drills grey	---
Raw cotton	19,527
Shirtings	473
Rayons	28,350
Blankets	12,855
Woolen suitings	38,900
Other woolens	44,239
Haberdashery	79,936
Sundry textiles	106,547
Gunny bags	90,275
Boots and shoes	52,311
Salt and sugar	378,436
Other foodstuffs	425,374
Vehicles	289,295
Spare parts	119,198
Tires and Tubes	130,584
Fuel	5,148
Chemicals, industrial	110,631
Machinery	158,699
Medicines	132,098
Building materials	264,750
Corrugated iron sheets	43,131

Electrical materials	104,879
Stationery, periodicals	167,475
Household materials	121,509
Sundry goods	405,482
Total	3,448,166

Source: FO371/138059. BCA to BEAA, 1.4.59.

Total imports in Ethiopian dollars: 33,184,401. This import figure was derived from the State Bank of Ethiopia over its Asmara office which had jurisdiction — an area much larger than Eritrea since Tigrai and Gonder were included.

[The import figures were destined to meet the import demands of Tigrai and Begemidir (Gonder). Likewise, the total Eritrean export figure included, as it always did, products originating in northern Ethiopia.] Note in bracket added.

11. FO371/131245. Copy. Telegram. Asmara 5.3. 1958. (Memorandum submitted by the Moslem League and Federalist Youth Party of Eritrea)

His Imperial Majesty, Sovereign of Federation, Addis Ababa.

Most respectfully and in accordance of para. seven of the Federal Act and art. 22 (J) of the Eritrean Constitution, we forward the following petition.

1. Situation in Eritrea has become grave and requires Your Majesty's urgent attention.

2. Federal Court in Eritrea has kept Mohamed Omar Kadi upon his return from the United Nations under Your Majesty's patronage under investigation in order to proceed against him.

3. Eritrean government is using fearful means against population the result of which that at Agordat many persons were imprisoned and some tribal chiefs removed from their traditional public functions. At Keren, Police using firearms have wounded 12 people' and about a hundred persons imprisoned. As a consequence, western province is in general strike for protest.

4. We think these deeds of the police are acts of revenge for the complaints presented by us to Your Majesty during Your last visit to Eritrea. The same spirit of revenge is also taking place against Mohamed Omar Kadi because he delivered a complaint to the United Nations on behalf of the Eritrean people.

However these facts contradict federal and Eritrean Constitution and human rights.

It needs intervention of Your Majesty to put right the situation seriously grave as Your Majesty is the guarantor of human rights over all the areas of the Federation.

We humbly beg Your Gracious reply to our request and accept our sincere greetings and thanks.

Eritrean Moslem League and Partito Giovanile Federalisti Eritrea. [Federalist Youth Party of Eritrea. This was the first time that a federalist youth movement appeared in a common cause with the ML.]

Signed

Ibrahim Sultan	Teklehaimanot Bokru
Suleiman Ahmed	Tesfai Redda
Imam Mussa	Tesfazghi Haile
Idris Mohamed	Adum Tesfamikael Ogkbankiel
Yassin Jemel	Berhe Andemikael
Mohamed El Hassan	Abraha Hagos
Hamid Hamdan	Gebrezghier Weldeabzghi
Omar Akito	Abraha Futur
Saleh Mussa.	Tseggai Eyassu.

12. FO371/131245. BCA to BEAA, Asmara, 23.5.58. Enclosure. (Memorandum submitted by the Moslem League and Federalist Youth Party of Eritrea)

To His Imperial Majesty, Sovereign of Federation, Addis Ababa.

We leaders and members of:

i). Eritrean Muslim League which party had important role in the definition of Eritrean future with Federation based above all on faith in Your Majesty's Guarantee to all inhabitants various kind of tradition and freedom;

ii). Members of Eritrean Federalist Youth Association;

iii). Sympathizers of both parties who have on the fifth of March instant sent a telegram to Your Imperial Majesty protesting against provocative actions taken by local government and police against peaceful people and denial of fundamental liberties enjoyment in any manner so that situation instead of getting better became worst.

1. Elements of Eritrean Federalist Youth Association which sent that telegram are imprisoned since March 8 without judgement.

2. Very large number pertaining our party are under process in Agordat and Keren.

3. Mohamed Omar Kadi imprisoned since March 20 by Federal Court which refused any kind of guarantee.

4. Yesterday group of much respectable members of Moslem League including members of High Executive Committee were imprisoned with great astonishment of people. They are accused of having six months ago sent a telegram to the UNO asking for exact application and respect of Federal Act therefore we believe as it appears that all such actions and continuous seizure of persons due to reaction by government for having sent that complaint to Your Majesty. We fear of worst future being authorities in Eritrea continuing their provocative actions with obscure intentions. We therefore, dare once again telegraph to Your August Majesty to intervene and embank bad current in action comparable to undemocratic regimes. [We appeal to Your Majesty's urgent and careful interest.] We forward our heartfelt respect.

Signed: Ibrahim Sultan; Idris Mohamed Adum; Teklehaimanot Bokru; Saleh Mussa; Omar Akito; Yassin Jimel; Hamid Hamdan; Moh Elhussien; Solomon Mogos; Eyassu Russom; Mikael Goitom; Abraha Hagos; Tesfai Redda; Tssegai Eyassu; Gebrenegus Gebreyesus.

13. Report of the auditor general on the accounts of the government of Eritrea for the financial year, 1960-61 (from 11.9 1960 to 10.9.61)

Revenue in thousands of Ethiopian dollars

Customs	4,627
Excise	2,753
Other duties	1,514
Licences	723
Direct taxation	5,220
Fines	87
Penalties	103
Sale of property	40
Sale of produce	100
Concessions and cultivation tax	215
Letting, Lending & investments	270
Trading	550
Services	435
Municipal	140
Loans recovered	80
Total revenue	16,880

Expenditure in thousands of Ethiopian dollars

Assembly	409
Audit	30
Chief executive & secretaries	220
Secretariat administration	280
Public relations	195
Districts administration	1,100
Police and prisons	4,130
Accounts	370
Inland revenue	105
excise and commercial taxes	86
Finance Guards	235
Controller general of revenue	126
Industry and commerce	20
Agriculture and forestry	410
Veterinary	220
Courts of Law	435
Legal	115
Education	1,710
Medical	2,275
Labour	75
Public works	885
Transport	730
Printing and stationery	170
Total expenditure	15,000

The editor general noted that salaries consumed 70 per cent of all expenditure.
[1 USD was equivalent to 2.07 Eth. dollars.]
I am indebted to Grazmatch Gebre-Medhin Tessema for the document.